Build Your Own LAN and Save a Bundle

Build Your Own LAN and Save a Bundle

Aubrey Pilgrim

Windcrest®/McGraw-Hill

FIRST EDITION
FIRST PRINTING

Library of Congress Cataloging-in-Publication Data

Pilgrim, Aubrey.
    Build your own LAN and save a bundle / by Aubrey Pilgrim.
        p.   cm.
    ISBN 0-8306-4088-6   ISBN 0-8306-4089-4 (pbk.)
    1. Local area networks (Computer networks)—Amateurs' manuals.
I. Title.
TK9969.P566   1992
004.6′8—dc20   92-5692
                                                                CIP

TAB Books offers software for sale. For information and a catalog, please
contact TAB Software Department, Blue Ridge Summit, PA 17294-0850.

Acquisitions Editor: Ron Powers
Book Editor: Patti McCarty
Managing Editor: Sandra L. Johnson
Director of Production: Katherine G. Brown
Book Design: Jaclyn J. Boone
Cover: Sandra Blair Design and Brent Blair Photography, Harrisburg, PA

Contents

Noted

Noted

Noted

Acknowledgments

I am very grateful for the suggestions and help given me by Mr. Robert Rossito, Vice President of Syscon Resources Corp., 1953 Butler Ave., Los Angeles, CA 90025, (800) 540-9498, fax (213) 477-5999. Syscon Resources consults, designs, and installs all types of network systems. They also sell several software packages for networks and network management.

Introduction

If you are the owner of a small business, just getting started in computer networking, or are interested in learning more about how your computer and network operate, then this book is for you.

Why another book on networks

I subscribe to more than 50 computer and networking magazines to keep up with the industry. Most of the articles and ads in these magazines are aimed at large corporations and big businesses. (Of course, that is where they find the big money.) They seem to overlook small businesses and people who are just getting started in computers and networking.

Several networking books are on the market but most of them are also written for large corporations and big businesses. Windcrest/McGraw-Hill decided that it was time for a networking book for the many thousands of small businesses. And that is the reason for this book.

Why you need a network

Millions of small businesses and offices have two or more computers that they might not be utilizing fully. One of the best ways to get the most from your computers is to connect them together in a local area network (LAN). If your computer is tied into a network, then all of the computers on the network can be an extension of your computer. And the reverse is true—all of the computers in the network are available to you. This setup can vastly increase the functionality, power, and utility of your computer, as well as giving you more power, increased proficiency, and increased productivity.

You can build your own

You have a choice of several types of networks. Some of them are very complex and sophisticated and might also require very expensive hardware and software, as well as engineers, consultants, and other highly trained personnel to install and maintain. But many low-cost systems might involve nothing more than a simple cable between two computers and some inexpensive software.

Several companies have taken note of the many small businesses who can benefit from networks so they have begun to bundle easy-to-install "plug-and-play" systems. These systems come complete with software and hardware. All you need to do is take them out of the carton and plug them in. I will discuss these and other systems so that you can make an informed decision as to what you should buy. I will also compare the cost and advantages of buying a plug-and-play system as opposed to buying separate components and connecting them yourself.

I will discuss all types of systems, but will concentrate primarily on the low-cost simple systems. Installing and maintaining these systems will not require highly trained personnel. Anyone should be able to set them up and run them. I will discuss several of the systems in detail so that you can make an informed decision as to what to buy. With the help of this book, you can make a survey to determine what type of system you need and how much it might cost.

Most of the systems I will be discussing conform to the *Open Systems Interconnect* (OSI) model proposed by the *International Standards Organization* (ISO). This conformance means that hardware and software from different vendors will be compatible and interchangeable—a great help because thousands of products are on the market, with lots of competition. You can shop around to find the best bargain.

Build your own server and workstations

In addition to the LAN cables, hardware, and software, you need computer servers and stations. It is possible to connect the IBM *Micro Channel Architecture* (MCA) PS/2, Apple Macintosh, and other types of systems into a network. But the vast majority of computers on the market conform to the *Industry Standard Architecture* (ISA). The ISA computers used to be known as IBM compatibles. Because so many ISA computers are in existence, billions of dollars worth of components are available, many more than for any other system. These components are all standard and interchangeable.

Competition among the vendors who sell ISA products is stiff, so the prices are much less than for the IBM MCA or Macintosh products. If you want to buy a disk drive, a plug-in board, or almost any component for the MCA or Macintosh systems, it will cost from 10 to 50 percent more than an ISA component. A decently configured IBM PS/2 or Macintosh will cost at least $2,400. You can buy an equivalent ISA computer for about $1,200.

I will show how you can assemble your own workstations and servers. It is very easy to do. Once you have purchased the components, it takes less than an hour to assemble one. I will include easy-to-understand instructions and lots of photos that show the assembly process. Anyone can assemble a computer. This includes anything from the least expensive XT up to the fastest and most powerful 486. You will be able to build and configure your computers any way you want to and you can save a bundle doing it yourself.

Cost

Unless you are one of the corporations with an unlimited budget, cost is an important consideration. How much a network costs will depend a lot on you. What do you want? How much do you want to spend? Most of the hardware components are available from discount houses. The cost will depend a lot on how well you shop and the components you buy.

If you don't have a lot of money, you can start off with a small network, then add to it later. Your business will probably grow, so you will need to add to it anyway. It is very easy to add to a LAN.

Please keep in mind that all costs presented here are current at the time this book was written. Perform your cost analysis with this mind. It is possible that you can actually get better prices than the ones I mention in this book.

Acronyms

More acronyms and abbreviations seem to be associated with networks than any other technology. I will explain them the first time they are used. You can also refer to the comprehensive glossary at the back of this book.

Product names

I will name several products in this book. (The names are the copyright or registered trademark of the company that produces them). Doing so does not mean that I am endorsing any one product over another. Thousands of network components are available. I could not possibly evaluate all of them. I have installed and tried some of them. But I have relied on magazines like *LAN Times*, *Data Communications*, *Reseller News*, *LAN Computing*, *Networking Management*, *LAN Magazine*, *PC Magazine*, *PC Week*, *InfoWorld*, *Computer Shopper*, *PC World*, and several others that are listed in chapter 13.

Some of the magazines, such as *PC Magazine* and *Data Communications*, have laboratories devoted to testing and evaluating products. Their test reports have been very helpful, but quite often the products they test have very little difference. So they might give one company a higher rating for having a product that is a fraction of a millisecond faster than another. Or their tests might be done on products that are designed for large corporations and very large systems.

Quite often the products they test are very expensive brand-name products. This book is written primarily for small businesses and small systems. In most instances, these small businesses will have a very tight budget. So I have tried to find the least expensive products to discuss.

Many of the less expensive products are clones, or compatible copies of a brand-name product. Most of the clone products are reliable and dependable. Network products have been around long enough that most of the bugs have been worked out or eliminated.

Chapter contents

Here is a brief description of the chapter contents:

CHAPTER 1, An overview of networks, shows you how to choose the right LAN by assessing your needs and your objectives, and looking at the benefits versus cost. Basic LAN components and cost, software, hardware, cables, boards, servers, workstations, topologies, and systems are discussed in chapter 1.

CHAPTER 2, Zero-slot LANs, describes the simplest LAN that you can build. Descriptions of zero-slot LANS and some of the vendors are presented in this chapter.

CHAPTER 3, Entry-level systems, discusses how to choose the type of system you will use. Descriptions and reviews of some of the systems and some of the vendors are given. The pros and cons of client-server systems versus peer-to-peer systems are discussed, as well as bundled systems.

CHAPTER 4, Large systems, discusses client-server systems, topologies, and cables—Ethernet, token ring, and ARCnet.

CHAPTER 5, Cables, discusses cables, bridges, routers, and gateways and the connection of different types of systems. Different LAN configurations, or topologies—Bus, Star, and ring—are presented and the advantages and disadvantages of each system are discussed. Types of cables used by each system and the tools you will need to build your own LAN are discussed.

CHAPTER 6, Building your own server and workstations, presents detailed instructions for the assembly of a 386SX, 386DX, 486SX, or 486DX server and detailed instructions for the assembly of a low-cost 8088, 286, 386SX, or 386 workstation. Many photos are also included.

CHAPTER 7, Disk drives, discusses disk storage options for the server, as well as the types of floppy and hard disks, ESDI, SCSI, IDE, optical disks, worms, CD-ROM, and data compression.

CHAPTER 8, Backups, describes backup systems, software, tape, disk mirroring, and the importance of UPS.

CHAPTER 9, Monitors, discusses monitors and adapters.

CHAPTER 10, Communications, discusses E-mail, modems and fax servers, and connecting remote PCs with a modem.

CHAPTER 11, Printers, discusses printers and printer-sharing systems—laser, dot matrix, laser color.

CHAPTER 12, Essential software, discusses the software you will need such as, word processors, database, spreadsheets, accounting, E-mail, communications, desktop publishing, and utilities.

CHAPTER 13, Mail order and magazines, lists vendors, magazines, and books that should help you install, use, and maintain your network.

CHAPTER 14, LAN management and troubleshooting, discusses LAN-management software, troubleshooting, and preventive maintenance.

The appendix lists network user groups and the glossary lists the definitions of useful terms related to implementing and maintaining a LAN.

Chapter 1

Overview of networks

A local area network (LAN) can be an asset to any small business or company that has two or more computers. This chapter provides an overview of LANs to give you a basic understanding of what is available and how to begin assessing your situation.

Why install a network?

Installing a network is an economical way to increase productivity. If a business has several computers, it can be expensive to buy separate software packages for each one. But if the computers are tied together, the resources of each one can be made available to all of the others.

Data tracking and updating are easier using a network than some traditional methods. For instance, suppose your company has a large database of customers. This database could be installed on a hard disk on one computer and be available to all others. Each computer on the network could take orders and each one could update the database. All of the inventory and stock on hand could be in a database on one computer and be available to all networked PCs. The inventory or stock status could be updated by any one of the PCs.

Printer sharing is an excellent benefit of networks. Printers are often idle. With a network, several computers can be tied to one printer, eliminating much of the idle time and reducing the number of printers you have to buy. Figure 1-1 shows a printer-sharing system from Western Telematic, (800) 854-7226.

Almost every business can use a network to great advantage. Studies have shown that, typically, a network will pay for itself in savings within 6 to 12 months.

What is a network?

Typically, a computer *network* consists of two or more computers connected together so that they can share data, files, and information. Networks are usually composed of two major components besides the PCs: a *hardware* component, such as a plug-in board; and a *software* component that controls the flow of data between the PCs.

Several vendors make the hardware, such as plug-in boards, for Ethernet, ARCnet, or token ring. All of these systems will run under the control of Novell, IBM, Microsoft, or other proprietary software. (A *proprietary system* of software or hardware is designed by a particular manufacturer using their specifications. A proprietary system does not have to conform to the OSI or other standard protocols). Novell software controls about 70 percent of all the presently installed LANs, especially the large corporate systems. Novell also manufactures plug-in boards, but they sell much more software than hardware.

Many of the companies who make hardware systems have their own proprietary software, while others give you a choice of using Novell, Microsoft, or some other

1-1 A printer-sharing switch from Western Telematic. (Western Telematic)

software with their hardware. The proprietary system might be less expensive initially, but it might not give you all the utility need later or allow you to expand to a larger system.

A simple network, such as a zero-slot LAN, might be nothing more than a cable that plugs into the serial or parallel port of each computer. A *zero-slot* LAN does not require a board that plugs into one of the computer motherboard slots. This type of system is rather slow and limited to only two or three devices, thereby limiting what can be done with it.

Like a simple network, a complex network also needs a physical connection, but it uses complex electronics to tie several stations to a single pair of wires. A complex network might be compared to a long street with several houses on it. Each house has a driveway connecting it to the street. On this street, there might be cars going in the same direction or going in both directions at the same time. When each car reaches its destination, it goes up the driveway to a house.

A network lets several users access the same data on a server. Several people can be working on files, invoices, or filling orders all at once. Without the network, each task would have to be done separately.

Network examples

The network used by the airlines and their ticket agencies is an example of a very large network. Can you imagine the trouble if several travel agents or ticket agents sold the same seats on a particular flight? To avoid this problem, the computer used by travel agents or ticket agents is tied to a much larger mainframe computer. The mainframe locks out any seat on a flight that has already been sold.

The telephone system is another example of a very large network. You can pick up the telephone and connect to any person in the world who has a telephone. Using the same system, a computer can connect to other computers anywhere in the world if they both have the proper software and hardware. Computer connections are usually made over the same wires that connect the telephone. It is not nearly as easy to connect to another computer as it is to talk to someone on the phone. But the technology is advancing and someday it will be as easy.

LAN, MAN, and WAN

The major types of area networks are international, national, regional, metropolitan, and local. In this book, I concentrate on local area networks (LAN) and not too much on metropolitan area networks (MAN) or wide area networks (WAN).

Bridges, routers, and gateways can be used to connect two or more LANs, MANs, and WANs. Some of these devices allow different systems such as PCs and Macintoshes to be connected together. See chapter 4 for a detailed discussion of bridges, routers, and gateways.

A network does not have to be as large as the airline system. If there are two or more computers in an office or small business, the company can usually benefit from the use of a network.

Microcomputers vs. minicomputers

One good reason to use microcomputers rather than minicomputers or mainframes is that the hardware is much less expensive. Hardware for a minicomputer can cost from $10,000 to $100,000. Microcomputers can cost from about $300 for an XT to about $6,000 for a 486.

The software is also much less expensive. Software for minicomputers and mainframes is usually customized and can cost $5,000 up to $250,000. Thousands of off-the-shelf software for microcomputers cost from $50 to $1,000.

Software companies usually charge a nominal fee or license to use their programs on a network. The license fee is usually based on the number of users or nodes on the network.

Cost of a network

It is difficult to say what a network will cost because there are so many options and variables. Cost will depend on what type of software and hardware you buy, where you buy it, and the number of users on the network. All prices in this text are current at the time this book was written.

List price vs. discount price

You should shop around when buying any component, including software. For instance, here are some prices for Novell NetWare from Vitek, a distributor, (800) 366-6655, and Innovative Technology, a discount store, (800) 253-4001:

Novell v.2.2	Vitek	Innovative Technology
5 users	$895	$699
10 users	1,995	1,449
50 users	3,495	2,449
100 users	5,495	3,899

Novell v.3.11	Vitek	Innovative Technology
20 users	$3,495	$2,499
100 users	6,995	4,899
250 users	12,495	8,599

The Netlogic Company, (714) 581-7255, advertises Novell version 2.2 for five users for $489 and Novell version 3.11 for 20 users at $1,899. It pays to shop around.

Vitek also offers the Novell NE1000 8-bit interface card for $190. Innovative Technology offers a 100 percent NE1000-compatible card for $120. A NE2000 16-bit card from Vitek is $235; a NE2000-compatible card from Innovative Technology is $145. Adapter cards for IBM's *Micro Channel Architecture* (MCA) and the Macintosh will cost $100 to $200 more than an equivalent IBM compatible or *Industry Standard Architecture* (ISA) board.

Here is approximately what the various components might cost for a five-unit network assuming the server is a 386DX or equivalent with a 200-megabyte (Mb) hard disk:

Component	ISA Compatible	IBM MCA	Macintosh
Server	$1,000	$2,800	$2,800
Workstations × 4	2,400	6,000	6,000
Adapters × 5	750	1,250	1,250
Software	700	700	700
Total	$4,850	$10,750	$10,750

As you can see, there can be a large difference in cost for the same product from different vendors. I do not know why anyone would pay more than twice as much for a system just because it has a brand-name label. You should be able to assemble a good network that has a 386 server with a 200Mb hard disk and four 286 workstations for less than $5,000—including software, interface boards, and cables.

The Moses Company, (408) 358-1550, has developed several proprietary systems, including a three-system kit of their ChosenLAN for a list price of $578. This system operates at 3.58 megabits per second (mbps). The kit includes adapter boards, cables, and software and is one of the least expensive networks that you can buy. (The kit is pictured and discussed in chapter 3, Fig. 3-1.)

You don't have to do it all at once

You don't have to install a large network. Even two computers connected together will help. You can always add more computers later as your business and needs grow.

Use your existing PCs

You can reduce the cost of a network if you already have one or more PCs. If all the PCs you have are IBM compatible, it will be a snap to network them together. It will be even easier if they are all Macintosh. The Macintosh comes with a built-in network interface so you don't have to buy adapter boards. All you need is a cable to connect them together. But this system operates at only 230 kbps, which is rather slow compared to Ethernet at 10 mbps. Because the Macintosh system is also limited in what it can do, you can add Ethernet or other cards to the Macintosh to get full network utilities.

If you have a mixture of IBM compatible and Macintosh computers, you can still tie them together but it will be more difficult because you will need special software and hardware. In addition, you might not be able to utilize fully all of the Macintosh capabilities on the DOS machines or all of the DOS capabilities on the Macintoshes. If at all possible, try to use the same type of computer throughout your network and you will have a lot less problems.

If you have an Amiga or any of the other less popular types of computers, you might not be able to connect them. Hundreds of companies manufacture software and hardware for the IBM compatible, and to a lesser extent, for the Macintosh, but there are very few, if any, for the Amiga.

Build your own computers

If you don't yet have computers, or you want to add more, I will teach you how to assemble your own powerful server and workstations in chapter 6. You can buy the major components, such as the motherboard, disk drives, adapter boards, monitor, and keyboard, from several different vendors. You can shop around to get the best buy. Once you have the components, it takes less than an hour to plug them together into a working computer. It is very simple to do. Anyone can do it.

Analysts and consultants

At one time network systems were very complex. Highly trained engineers, consultants, and technicians were needed to install and maintain these systems. Some large systems are still like that, but several systems now available are easy to install and maintain.

One of the first things you should do is to analyze your needs. You can hire an analyst to come in and determine what you need or you can hire a consultant to study your company and then install the system.

Not everyone needs a consultant or analyst. For those who think they do need one, you should give it careful consideration. First, analysts and consultants are expensive. Second, you probably know better than anyone else what you need unless you have a very large and complex business. And third, there is no guarantee that they know any more than you do. There are no college degrees, no state license, and no formal requirements for these titles. Anyone can call themselves an analyst or consultant.

Novell has set up a series of classes to certify the people who handle and install their systems. A person who successfully completes its courses is graduated as a Certified Novell Engineer (CNE).

Novell also has self-assessment tests. If you would like one of the free tests, or to find out more about Novell's training programs, call (800) 233-3382.

The LANDA (Local Area Network Dealers Association) has instituted a training program that certifies engineers not only for Novell, but for all types of LANs. The cost for the Novell or LANDA training is about $3,000 to $4,000 depending on your need.

Many people hold two- or three-day seminars for network training and usually charge from $895 to $1,195 for these seminars. I have never taken one of these seminars because I cannot learn enough in two or three days to justify the cost. Again, these seminars are usually not recognized by colleges or higher learning institutions. Many good consultants and analysts, however, have learned from hard study and experience. If you have a large complex business, they can give you some good advice and save you money and time.

If you have the type of business that requires an analyst or consultant, this book can still help you. After reading this book, you will be able to determine if you need an analyst or consultant and if the analyst or consultant is qualified.

Types of networks

The two most popular types of network systems for small businesses are the client-server and the peer-to-peer. These two systems are popular because they manage the computing load effectively, which means a more efficient use of the whole network.

Client-server

In the *client-server* system, each PC on the network receives and sends files through a dedicated server. It is somewhat like the telephone system. You might have a telephone at a desk that is only a few feet away from another but if you call the person at the nearby desk, the call must go all the way to the main terminal and then back to the telephone on the nearby desk.

Peer-to-peer

In the *peer-to-peer* system, each PC is connected to the others directly. It can send or receive files to or from any of the PCs on the network. Peer-to-peer systems are sometimes called *distributed-server networking*. Some network operating system software will let a PC alternately act as a client-server or as a peer.

Topologies

Topology is the physical design or layout of the network. The three major types of topologies are: *star, bus,* and *token ring*.

Star

The *star* topology has a hub or dedicated client-server in the center. It is similar to the telephone system. Each PC is connected to the central hub and communicates through it with the other PCs. If a computer on one of the legs goes down, it does not affect the rest of the network. But if the hub goes down, the whole network goes down.

The star topology is used most often with ARCnet and Ethernet UTP (unshielded twisted pair).

Bus

The *bus* topology is just a long single line with several computers attached to it. It is somewhat like a street that has several houses on it. A car on this street could stop at any address. Like the car, however, data travels on the bus and will stop at the computer or workstation to which it is addressed.

A bus system might have a *dedicated server* so that most traffic would be between the server and the workstations. Or it is possible that any workstation could exchange data with any other one in a peer-to-peer system.

One of the problems with most network systems is that only one PC or workstation can use the bus at any one time. If two units try to send data at the same time over this single line, the data becomes mixed and corrupted. This event is called a *collision*.

A system called *carrier sense multiple access with collision detection* (CSMA/CD) was developed, which listens for any traffic on the bus before transmitting. If two stations try to transmit at the same time, it will shut the system down for a brief period. After a short, random length of time, one of the senders can try to retransmit.

A bus system is usually used with Ethernet cards and cabling and might use Novell or other proprietary software to control the cards and the network.

Token ring

The *token-ring* topology is similar to the bus topology, except that the ends of the bus are connected so that it forms a complete ring. This system uses software to create an "electronic token" to prevent collisions. The token is passed from PC to PC on the ring and only the PC with the token can transmit. Tokens can also be used with the bus topology.

The Token-Ring system, developed by IBM, has hardware, or plug-in boards, which is more complicated than Ethernet and more expensive. In this system, if one computer on the circuit goes down, the whole system goes down.

Protocols

Protocols are specifications that describe rules and procedures to follow to assure that products will work together, even though the products might be from several different vendors.

Networks, as mentioned earlier, are made up of two basic components, *hardware* and controlling *software*. Quite often the hardware is made by one company and the software by another. The hardware and software work together because the manufacturers adhere to certain standards when designing and manufacturing the products. The foremost standard for LANs is the set of rules and protocols adopted by the *International Standards Organization/Open Systems Interface* (ISO/OSI). All hardware and software that conforms to the ISO/OSI protocol recommendations are similar.

You should be able to buy and use systems from different vendors and be assured that they will work together. But every manufacturer wants to have an edge, to be a little different from the competition. A recent study found that only 10 percent of all network sites are using the OSI protocols. About one-third are using the *Simple Network Management Protocols* (SNMP).

The SNMP system was developed by the Department of Defense (DOD), industry, and the academic community. The SNMP is part of the *Transmission Control Protocol/Internet Protocol* (TCP/IP), a set of protocols developed by the DOD.

The *Institute of Electrical and Electronic Engineers* (IEEE) also has committees that set standards. IEEE 802.3 standard defines the Ethernet system and IEEE standard 802.5 defines the token ring system.

The standards recommended by the *Consultative Committee on International Telephone and Telegraph* (CCITT) cover all types of communications, such as telephones, networks, modems, and faxes.

Multiprotocol internetworks

From the simple zero-slot LAN, networks become more and more complex and sophisticated as more speed, utility, and functions are added. The large networks need cables, plug-in boards, and controlling software. Many types of plug-in boards are manufactured. Some are reasonably priced and others are very expensive. Software to control the boards can be more expensive than the boards.

It is possible to connect almost any type of computer or network to any other using various protocols. For example, it is possible to connect *Systems Network Architecture* (SNA) systems to NetBIOS, NetWare's *Internet Packet Exchange* (IPX), AppleTalk, and others. But these multiprotocols can cause some very complex problems that are difficult to diagnose and solve. If at all possible, start out with a single system and stay with it. Your work will be a lot less complicated.

Asynchronous transmission

Most networks use an asynchronous transmission system very much like that developed by the modem industry to transmit data. In this system, data is divided into blocks, with start and stop bits to separate each block.

Frequency

The *frequency*, or speed, of the transmission can be very important. A zero-slot system might operate at about 115 kilobits per second (kbps), which is much too slow for some large files and operations. Most systems operate from 1 megabits per second (mbps) to 10 mbps. The FDDI systems can operate up to 100 mbps. Of course, the higher the speed, the greater the cost.

Software

Software to a computer is much like gasoline to an automobile: without software, the computer won't operate. The most important software for your LAN is the network operating system (NOS), disk operating system (DOS), and application software. Other essential software is discussed in chapter 12.

Network operating system (NOS)

A computer, whether a mainframe, a mini, or a desktop PC, must have operating system software. Software is the brain that controls the hardware. (*Hardware* is any component in the computer, such as the plug-in boards, chips and electronic components on the boards, disk drives, the monitor, printers, modems, and other devices.) Several types of operating-system software are available—such as DOS, Unix, and Apple. I will primarily be discussing DOS for the PC Industry Standard Architecture (ISA). ISA used to be known as the IBM PC standard, but IBM more or less abandoned this standard when they introduced their PS/2 systems with Micro Channel Architecture (MCA).

In addition to DOS, network systems also need a network operating system (NOS). Just as MS-DOS is used on the vast majority of PC systems, Novell NetWare is used on over 70 percent of the large network systems. Novell has several different packages: the 286 version costs $899 for a five-user system; the top of the line, version 3.11, can cost over $12,000. Novell's newest version can be used to control up to 1,000 computers. Novell also has NetWare Lite, a peer-to-peer NOS, with a list price of $99 per node. I have seen it discounted to $59 per node.

Another company that provides NOS software is LAN Manager from Microsoft. LAN Manager 2.1 has a list price of $1,995 for a 10-user system and a list price of $5,495 for an unlimited number of nodes. The discount price might be half of the list price so, by all means, shop around.

IBM markets a version of LAN Manager that they call LAN Server. At one time the two systems, like MS-DOS and PC-DOS, were very similar, but the longtime romance between Microsoft and IBM seems to have soured a bit. Both companies are now adding features to differentiate their products from the other.

Microsoft and Novell provide both DOS and Macintosh versions of their software.

Banyan Systems provides a Unix-based system for large networks that sells for $7,495.

Note that the prices quoted are current list prices at the time this book was written. Some of the prices might be much lower from discount houses.

Application software

Application software means programs like word processors, spreadsheets, databases, and thousands of other programs. If you need one of these programs on a single computer, you buy a single copy. When you need one of these programs for a network, you buy a license.

Networks can have from two to several hundred people using the same software and software manufacturers understand. The company is not expected to buy two hundred copies of the software. Most software manufacturers will allow a company to buy a license so the software can be used on more than one computer in a LAN or multiuser system. The cost of a license is usually much less than the cost of several separate software packages.

Security

Security, at some level, is necessary for most networks. For this reason, each user on the network is usually given a password. This password allows him or her to access only certain files of the data stored on the disk. For instance, the payroll department might have all of the employee salaries on a large disk. They probably would not want everyone to be able to peek at the portion of the disk that had the boss's salary and other perks.

File locking

On a multiuser network, the users are all using the same source, so the files and data can be controlled. On some systems, only one user can download and work on a particular file. Other users might be able to read the file, but not change or alter it as long as one person was processing it. This feature is called *file locking*.

Record locking

On some systems, two or more users might update or change portions or separate records of a file without the other's knowledge. Two users would not be able to update or change a particular record at the same time. This feature is called *record locking*. It is similar to the system that prevents airline ticket agents from selling the same seat twice.

Backups

The data on a LAN is very important. It might have all of the sales orders, payroll information, other accounting information, customer database, and other data that might be impossible to duplicate. Depending on the business, this data might be priceless. Yet it can all disappear in a fraction of a second. The server disk might crash or fail in some other way, the power might fail at a crucial moment, or any one of a thousand other problems might occur.

These disasters can be avoided if a copy of the data is made daily and stored in a safe place. The data can then be easily restored from the backup. (More about backups in chapter 8.)

Network hardware

Much of the hardware used on a network is the same as that found on a standard PC, but the LAN might also have specialized plug-in adapters, cables, hubs, bridges, routers, and gateways.

Some of the brand-name LAN hardware is rather expensive. But just like the PC-compatible clones, there are clones of most of the major network interface boards, as well as clones of hubs, bridges, routers, and gateways, but to lesser extent. Therefore, these components are usually a bit expensive.

Servers and storage

A *server* can be any PC, but it is usually a fast and powerful computer such as a 386 or 486 system. It will probably have a hard disk that can store several hundred megabytes of software, files, and data. This system could be accessed by the other computers in the network, allowing the smaller systems to have all of the benefits of the larger hard disk. (More about hard disks in chapter 7.)

Workstations or nodes

A *workstation* can be any point in a LAN where a PC is installed, such as a an IBM or Macintosh. It can be anything from a simple keyboard and "dumb" terminal to a high-powered 486, or anything in between.

Diskless workstations

A workstation can also be low-cost XT or 286 systems without floppy or hard disks, hence the name *diskless workstation*. It depends entirely on the server to supply data and to do the processing.

Because diskless workstations have no floppy disk drives, they cannot copy any of the software that is downloaded from the server. This feature can contribute to security. A company might have very sensitive data or plans that could be compromised if a copy fell into the hands of a competitor. A bank would not want its clerks to be able to copy their customers' records.

Diskless workstations might not be the best approach in some types of businesses and offices. Because the diskless workstation depends on the server, if it goes down, (and they all go down from time to time), the whole network is down. But if the stations have a floppy disk and hard disk, then other productive work can be carried out until the server is restored.

Adapter plug-in boards

The type of adapter needed depends on what kind of system you set up. An Ethernet system will need Ethernet boards, a token ring system will need token ring boards, and an ARCnet system will need ARCnet boards.

Several companies manufacture the different boards that conform to IEEE and other industry standards. Most of the boards have jumpers and switches that must be set to configure them to the system. The boards usually come with floppy disks that have software drivers for whatever system they will be used with.

Some boards come with extra memory. There are both 8- and 16-bit ISA boards, boards for IBM MCA and Macintosh, and 32-bit boards for the EISA system.

The cost of boards varies from vendor to vendor. Compatible clones exist for most of the major boards and some sell for about half the price of a brand-name board. Shop around for the best price by looking through ads in LAN magazines and computer magazines such as *Computer Shopper*.

Bundled systems

Several companies, such as Dell, Northgate, and Packard-Bell, are offering *bundled systems*. In these bundled systems, the company configures a system to your needs, installs the boards and software on the computers, and sells it as a package. I will discuss these systems further in chapter 3.

Cables and linking systems

Depending on the type of system you choose, cables can represent a major portion of the system cost. You shouldn't skimp on the quality of the cables. Try to get the best you can. According to some studies, cables and connectors can be the cause of over 30 percent of all downtime. Look in chapter 4 and chapter 5 for a thorough discussion of cables.

Tools   Here are a few basic tools that you will need for installing your cables:

- *Drill with several bits.*
- *Hole saw* to use with the drill.
- *Wire cutters and strippers.*
- *Crimpers* for installing various types of connectors onto the cables.

You will need to add more tools to your toolbox, but this list should get you started. Look at the "Tools" section in chapter 5 for a complete list.

Bottom-line cost

So many different options, vendors, and types of LANs exist that it is almost like buying a car. You can buy anything from a no-frills compact all the way up to a fully loaded Rolls Royce. The cost will depend on what type of LAN you want, how well you shop, and how much you want to spend.

If money is an important factor, and it almost always is, then you will be happy to know that you can start off small and add to the LAN later. LANs can grow and expand very easily. Two or more LANs can be tied together. LANs can be tied into a metropolitan area network (MAN), or a wide area network (WAN), or even a global network such as the telephone system.

Many different systems and hundreds of different manufacturers of hardware and software exist. After you have read this book you should be able to do a survey and make an informed decision as to what type of LAN you need and how much it will cost. If you make an informed decision, you can build a good LAN and save a bundle.

Sources

To make the most informed decision about your LAN purchase, take advantage of all the sources available to you. You can go to computer shows, read LAN magazines, computer magazines, and catalogs, and contact your local dealers. The more knowledge you have about LANs, the easier it will be to create a system that really satisfies your networking needs.

Shows

Thousands of vendors manufacture network products. One of the best ways to see the products all in one spot is to attend a network show or COMDEX shows. The Interface Group, (617) 449-8938, puts on a COMDEX show each spring in the east and each fall in Las Vegas. These two are the largest computer shows in the country.

Several shows each year are devoted entirely to networking. The Bruno Blenheim Company, (800) 829-3976, puts on a couple of networking shows each year. The World Expo Corporation, (800) 545-3976, puts on a couple of ComNet shows each year devoted entirely to networking.

Other minor shows are held each year that are usually advertised or written about in several networking and computer magazines.

LAN and computer magazines

Chapter 13 contains a list of selected networking and computer magazines. Some of the magazines are free to qualified subscribers and I explain how you can qualify. If you want to keep up with what is going on in this industry, you definitely should be subscribing to the networking and computer magazines.

Catalogs

Several companies who specialize in network products publish informative catalogs. The catalogs have photos, prices, and specifications of their products.

Some of the catalogs have lengthy articles describing how Ethernet, token ring, and ARCnet systems operate. They have diagrams of how the systems are connected and laid out. Some of them even have glossaries that explain the many network acronyms and terms.

For anyone just getting started in the network field, these catalogs are an excellent tutorial. Most of them have more valuable information than you would find in a $40 textbook. And the best part is that they are free. Just give the companies a call and they will be glad to send you a copy.

AlteCon Data Communications	(800) 888-8511
AMP NetConnect	(800) 522-6752
Anco Corporation	(800) 545-2626

Andrew Corporation	(800) 733-0331
Black Box Corporation	(412) 746-5565
Data Set Cable Company	(800) 344-9684
Misco Data Communications	(800) 333-5640
Patton Electronics	(301) 975-1000
South Hills DataComm	(800) 245-6215
Telebyte Cook Book	(800) 835-3298

By all means contact the companies and request these catalogs. However, you should be aware that most of the products in these catalogs are sold at or near the list price. The list price of products might be twice as high as the discount price. Look through the catalogs to get an idea of what you need. Then you might do better if you look through the LAN and computer magazines for the same products from discount houses.

Local dealers

If you live near a large city, you'll have access to several dealers, systems integrators, and consultants. Most of them will be listed in the telephone book. The prices from the local dealers might be a bit higher than mail order, but you usually get convenient support if you have problems.

Chapter 2

Zero-slot LANs

The need for a network is basically the need to exchange data and information, or the need to communicate. A zero-slot LAN is a simple way to communicate and is, therefore, worth consideration when you are planning your LAN.

Techniques for simplifying data communication—such as data compression, data switches, printer sharing, and high-density floppy disks—are also worth consideration and are discussed in this chapter. More sophisticated and complex LANs are covered in later chapters.

The shape of data

Let's start with the basic concept of data. Data signals are made up of square waves. A square wave can be made by interrupting a *direct current* (dc) voltage. If the interruptions are done at a precise time, a short period when the voltage is at +5 volts dc, it can represent a 1. When the voltage is shut off for a period of time, it can represent a 0. Of course, if the periods of time are twice as long, it can represent two 1s or two 0s. This method is how data is transferred in a LAN.

Some systems have both plus and minus dc. The system might use the plus voltage for 1s and the minus voltage as 0s.

Alternating current (ac), or analog voltages, are sine waves. Noise and static are analog-type voltages. They can attach to a square wave, but can easily be filtered out from digital signals. It is very difficult to filter out static and noise from analog signals. For this reason, most data is in the digital form. See Fig. 2-1.

What is a zero-slot LAN?

The phrase *zero-slot LAN* was coined by Frank J. Derfler, Jr., a writer for *PC Magazine* and director of the PC LAN laboratories. He is also the author of the book *PC Magazine Guide to Connectivity*, an excellent book on networking.

A zero-slot LAN does not require you to open up your computer and plug an adapter board into one of the motherboard slots. The simplest form is just a cable that plugs into the serial or parallel port connectors on the back of each computer. Then with the proper software, data can be transferred from one machine to the other. Zero-slot LANs are very limited in what they can accomplish. If you only need to transfer data from one machine to another occasionally, they might be all you need. They are relatively inexpensive, ranging in price from $55 to $150.

What happens inside?

Communication is a lot easier in some cases than in others. For example, it is very easy to connect two Macintoshes. They have a built-in network system and all you need is the cable. And it is also easy to connect two similar PCs together in a zero-slot configuration. However, it is a bit more difficult to connect a PC and a Macintosh, or a PC to a mainframe.

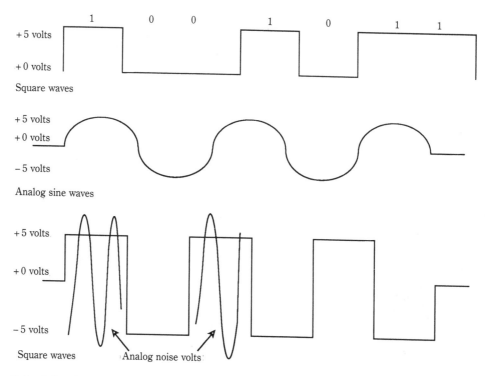

2-1 A drawing showing square waves, sine waves, and noise.

You might well ask why this is so. After all, you are only dealing with digital data, which simply consists of 0s and 1s. The PC, the Macintosh, and the mainframe all use these basic elements. However, they all use the 0s and 1s differently. It is almost like people from foreign countries trying to communicate. They need an interpreter to understand one another.

The main difference between the PC and the Macintosh is that the PC uses the Intel 80xxx central processing unit (CPU) and the Macintosh uses the Motorola 68xxx CPU. These CPUs, made up of transistors and microcircuits, are the brains of the computer. The Intel 386 CPU has 275,000 transistors on a piece of silicon that measures 0.275×0.275 inches. The 486 CPU has 1.2 million transistors etched on a small piece of silicon 0.4×0.65 inches. The CPUs in the minicomputers and mainframes are also quite different.

Each of the CPU systems turn its transistors on and off to route those little data bits around the innards of the computer in different ways. Special software and hardware is required to interpret the data from the various systems so that communication is possible.

Try to keep them all the same

It is possible to connect Macintoshes and PCs together on a network and to have Ethernet, token ring, and other types of networks tied together. But if at all possible, you will be much better off if you keep them all the same. You will have a lot less trouble and fewer problems if you install one type of network using all the same type of PCs. It is less expensive because you won't have to buy the special hardware and software.

Cost of PCs vs. Macintoshes vs. PS/2s

If you have a choice, install machines that conform to the Industry Standard Architecture (ISA). The ISA computers are what used to be known as IBM compatibles. Billions of dollars worth of basic components are available for these machines, so you can buy the components and assemble your own server or workstation. (More about this in chapter 6.)

At least 10 ISA computers are in existence for every Macintosh. Because of the competition, the cost of these machines are about half what a Macintosh costs. Also, about 10 times more software is available for the ISA computers than for the Macintosh. Again, because of the competition and the broad market base, the software might be less expensive.

The IBM PS/2 Micro Channel Architecture (MCA) machines use the same software as the ISA computers, but they do not use the same hardware and components. Most of it has to come from IBM. The PS/2s and MCA components can cost up to twice as much as an ISA component. For instance, the Ethernet adapter boards for a Macintosh or IBM MCA usually cost at least $100 more per board than for an ISA system.

One reason there are more ISA machines than Macintoshes is cost. A recent advertisement in the *Los Angeles Times* listed a Macintosh IIci with an 80Mb hard disk for $3,099. In small print below the ad it said, "keyboard and monitor not included." The cost of the monitor and keyboard would add another $600 to $900 to the cost for a total of about $4,000.

In the same issue of this paper, a 386DX, 33 MHz computer was advertised. It had a 120Mb hard disk, a 0.28 pixel Super VGA monitor, a mouse, keyboard, and a copy of Windows. The price was $1,645.

The Macintosh is easier for a novice to learn than an ISA machine and has good graphics capability. But, to me, there is no way that it can be worth $4,000 while an equivalent ISA machine costs only $1,645.

If you install an ISA system, you can repair and replace any defective components yourself. A Macintosh or PS/2 is difficult to repair and usually only licensed dealers and repair facilities work on these machines.

Determining the system you need

One of the first things that you should do is make an analysis and do a survey to determine what type of network you need. A large business or corporation that has lots of budgeted funds would call in a high-priced consultant and systems analyst to make a survey. But because you probably know better than anyone else what you want and what you can afford, you probably do not need a consultant or systems analyst.

If you have two or more computers in the office or work area, you would be better off connecting them together. What you use your computer for should help you determine the way you connect them and what hardware and software to use.

If you are using your computer for word processing, small databases, or small spreadsheets, then a zero-slot LAN could be all you need. These systems are a bit slow, so you might have to wait a few seconds for a file to transfer. A zero-slot connection can operate at a speed of 56 kilobits per second (kbps) and up to 115 kbps. The more sophisticated LANs might operate at 10 mbps or even up to 100 mbps, but of course they are much more expensive. If you can afford to wait a few seconds, and have only simple tasks, a zero-slot system might be the most cost-effective.

Printer sharing

It can be very expensive to have a separate printer for each computer in an office. Quite often a printer sits idle most of the time. The simplest way to connect two computers to a printer is by using a manual switch box, which allows you to switch from one to the other as needed.

You might need different types of printers at different times, so your office might have a laser and a dot matrix. Again, a simple switch can connect the different types of printers to the computer. Some more elegant, sophisticated, and expensive ways of printer sharing are explored in chapter 9.

Computer ports

Most of the ISA computers support four input/output (I/O) ports: two parallel and two serial ports. Some motherboards have built-in port interfaces with pins or a connector. All you need is a cable to connect to the peripheral. If the motherboard does not have the built-in I/O ports interface, then a plug-in board for serial and parallel ports must be used in one of the motherboard slots.

A computer usually has only eight slots, and they get filled up in a hurry. You might install various plug-in boards, such as LAN adapters, monitor adapters, disk controllers, modems, and fax cards. In order to save slots, some plug-in boards have several other functions on them. I have an Intel fax board that also has a modem on it. I also have a multifunction board that has two serial and two parallel ports, a VGA monitor driver, an IDE interface controller for two hard disks, and a controller for two floppy disks. This board saves about four slots that can be used for plugging in other goodies. A multifunction board can cost a bit more, but it is well worth the money.

The parallel ports are designated as LPT1 and LPT2. They are called "parallel" because data is fed to the ports over eight lines. It takes eight bits to make a character, so by placing one bit of a character on each of the eight lines, a whole character can be transmitted at one time. It is somewhat similar to having an eight-lane freeway with one car in each lane. A lot of traffic can move over the eight lanes.

The serial ports are designated COM1 and COM2. (Some systems are able to support COM3 and COM4, as well). The serial ports use only one line (and a ground line) for transmission. Only one bit at a time can be transmitted, so it takes longer to move eight bits over a serial system than over a parallel system.

The parallel ports can transmit data faster, but the distance of the signals is limited; a signal can only travel about 10 feet. Special signal amplifiers can be used to extend the distance. Most parallel ports are used for printers.

The signals from a serial port can be transmitted up to 50 feet. Special amplifiers can extend the distance to hundreds or thousands of feet. The serial ports might be used for printers, modems, a mouse, scanners, LAN adapters, and various other peripherals.

(If you would like to learn more about ports and communications, the U.S. Robotics Company, a modem manufacturer, publishes an excellent free booklet. It is titled "Communications Concepts." Call them at (708) 982-5001 for a free copy.)

The serial ports on computers are supposed to conform to the RS-232 specifications. You should be aware that the RS-232 is not an absolute standard. The original specification defined 25 different signals. In most cases today, only three lines are necessary: one to transmit data, one to receive data, and a common ground. Your computer might have a connector with either 9 or 25 pins or sockets. If the two computers don't have the same type of connectors, you might have to buy an adapter to change them to fit. The cables might have female sockets instead of male pins or vice versa. You might have to buy a *gender bender*, which is an adapter that changes the sockets to pins or vice versa.

Building your own cables vs. buying

If you are fairly knowledgeable about computers and really need to save a few dollars, you can build your own zero-slot LAN cables. If you know how to solder you can buy the cable and connectors and make your own cables. I have done it before, but I wouldn't do it again. It is time-consuming and frustrating.

If your time is worth anything at all, it is much cheaper to buy cables. A 6-foot cable can cost from $5 to $10, a 100-foot one might cost from $25 to $75. (Cables for other types of LANs are a different story; I talk about them in chapter 5.) Several companies sell almost any kind of cable that you would need. Here are just a few:

Accessory Connection	(214) 920-2536
AMP	(717) 561-6185
Altex Electronics	(800) 531-5369
Cables To Go	(800) 225-8646
Dalco	(800) 445-5342
National Computer Accessories	(916) 441-1568

Several other companies provide cables and components. Check the ads in computer magazines such as the *Computer Shopper*, *PC Sources*, *Computer Buying World*, and others.

Once you have the cables, all you need is a communications program, such as CrossTalk, Procomm, or Q-Modem. Again, I would not recommend building your own unless you have some technical knowledge and a lot of extra time.

All of the zero-slot vendors listed in the following section supply the cables and software as a unit and most of them include several very useful software utilities, which are well worth the cost.

Zero-slot LAN vendors

Here are just a few of the many zero-slot products:

- Amica Company's PC-Hooker Turbo, (800) 888-8455, transfers files between two PCs through serial or parallel ports. Has on-line help, DOS utilities, modem capabilities, and auto-install. List price is $129.95.
- Artisoft's LANtastic Z, (602) 293-6363, interconnects two PCs using existing serial or parallel ports. Operates in the background, shares programs, data, printers, and other resources. List price is $125.
- B.G. Micro Company Low Cost Lan, (214) 271-5546, connects two or three PCs using serial ports and a five-wire cable. Runs in the background at 115K. Shares devices, files, and resources. Uses 14K of RAM. Price is $55 to $75 depending on cables and lengths.
- Datastorm's Hot Wire, (314) 443-3282, from the makers of Procomm Plus, it comes with a 7-foot cable with four different connectors. Its software also allows it to be used with modems to transfer data. It has a macro facility, a menu bar with a point-and-shoot dual directory, simultaneous display of both source and target directory contents, file sorting by name, extension, date, or time, and several other good features. List price is $129.
- Fifth Generation System's Brooklyn Bridge, (800) 873-4384, comes with a cable that lets you connect laptops or desktops to each other or to a LAN. Has pull-down menus, mouse support, and split screens. You can transfer a file or a whole directory with the point-and-shoot process. Among its several other utilities are ones that let you view, sort, print, copy, or backup a file from a remote PC. See Fig. 2-2. The list price is $139.95.
- GetC's File Shuttle Express, (800) 663-8066 or (604) 684-3230, comes without cables. Instead, it has an adapter that lets you use your printer cables to transfer files. It can be used for laptops, PCs, or PS/2s and can even be used to transfer files from a laptop to a large server. It works through the parallel ports and will operate up to 100 feet. File Shuttle Express, which has both a DOS and a Windows version, has several good file-management utilities. You can tag and move an entire directory, make a directory, delete a directory or file, prune and graft, copy a file, change attributes, do backups, and other DOS functions. See Fig. 2-3. The list price is $139.
- Rupp Corporation's FastLynx, (800) 222-4229 or (212) 517-7775, comes with both serial and parallel cables that are each 8 feet long. The serial cables have both 9- and 25-pin connectors. These cables allow connection to any ISA or IBM PS/2. FastLynx can transfer files and directories between laptops and desktops or two desktops. It is easy to install and automatically selects the port. It has an error-checking system to protect files, a diagnostic program to

2-2 Brooklyn Bridge software and cables.

test ports and cables, and several other excellent disk-management utilities. See Fig. 2-4. The list price is $149.95.

- Traveling Software's LapLink, (800) 662-2652 or (206) 483-8088, comes with a cable that allows you to connect any two IBM-compatible computers or a laptop to a desktop. LapLink allows you to copy files, directories, or whole disks in either direction, has error checking for validity of transfer, and has several excellent disk-management utilities. The list price is $149.95.
- Moses Computers' SwiftLAN, (408) 358-1550, is an adapter that plugs into a standard parallel printer port. SwiftLAN can connect laptops and all types of desktops together and turn them into a fairly sophisticated LAN. It comes with Moses SwiftNOS operating software, which includes several utilities and drivers, and an easy-to-use menu system for installation and DOS operations. The kit comes with a 6-foot parallel printer cable and carrying case. See Fig. 2-5. The list price is $149.
- Alloy Computer's 386/MultiWare EZ, (508) 481-8500, takes advantage of the 386SX, 386DX, 486SX, or 486DX CPU protected-mode memory. 386/MultiWare EZ allows you to connect two other computers to the COM ports of a 386; one to COM1 and one to COM2. The CPU protected-memory mode of

2-3 GetC File Shuttle system.

a 386 or 486 allows multitasking and can set aside several areas of memory into 640K each. Each 640K area is treated just as if it were a separate computer. In effect, it gives you several "virtual 8086" computers.

With the 386/MultiWare EZ, the host and the attached computers can each operate up to eight different tasks simultaneously. Users can share peripherals such as printers or other resources of the host. The attached systems can be laptops, dumb terminals, PCs, or Macintoshes. Special software is required for Macintoshes at additional cost. RS-232 cables are required and the cables may be as long as 50 feet each. The 386/MultiWare EZ has a list price of $349.

This is only a partial listing of the products available. Look through any of the computer magazines for others. Note that the prices quoted here are list prices at the time this book was written. They should be lower at discount houses.

Disadvantages of zero-slot LANs

Zero-slot LANs are usually limited to two or three computers, so they do not allow for growth. They are also limited in the data sharing they can do and are rather slow, with a maximum of 115 kbps, compared to the average speed on an Ethernet system of 10 mbps.

2-4 FastLynx software and cables.

2-5 Moses SwiftLAN zero-slot system. (Moses Computers)

Data switches

A data switch can have from eight to 64 or more ports. Computers, printers, plotters, modems, fax machines, and other peripherals can be connected to these ports. The data switches have their own microprocessor. The microprocessor can electronically control the ports to allow the computers or other devices to be connected together. Data switches are a good way to share printers with several computers.

The data switches connect to the serial ports of the computers and devices. One disadvantage is that they usually operate at a rather slow frequency of only 19,200 bits per second (bps). Some systems double this frequency to 38,400 bps. The data-switch manufacturers usually provide software for the switches, but they can also be operated using software provided by programs such as Brooklyn Bridge or LapLink.

Here are some companies, and some with specific products listed, who provide data switches:

Fifth Generation's Logical Connection Plus	(800) 873-4384
Datacom's MetroLAN	(800) 243-2333
Ralin's Solectek	(800) 752-9512
Buffalo Products	(800) 345-2356
Cables To Go	(800) 225-8646
Dalco	(800) 445-5342
National Computer Accessories	(916) 441-1568
Computer Friends	(800) 829-9991
Technologic Systems	(513) 644-2230
Data Switches from Western Telematic	(800) 854-7226

Some of the switches, such as the N series Master Switch from Rose Electronics, (800) 333-9343, and NetCommander NC16 from Digital Products, (800) 243-2333, are true networking products. Call the companies for brochures and price lists.

Data compression

In the past, a good solution to compressing large data files has not been available. A 3½-inch floppy disk could only hold up to 1.44Mb and it seemed to take forever to copy a large file. But that has all changed now. Stac Electronics and several other companies have developed methods of data compression that let you double the amount of data stored on any floppy disk, hard disk, or even a tape.

The Stac system uses software only, or for a bit more speed, it uses an 8-bit or a 16-bit coprocessor board. See Fig. 2-6. If you are interested in this product call or write:

Stac Electronics
5993 Avenida Encinas
Carlsbad, CA 92008
(619) 431-7474

2-6   Stac compression software and hardware.

Prices: software only, $149; 8-bit coprocessor, $199; 16-bit coprocessor, $249; and a MCA coprocessor, $299.

Very high density floppy disks

The Brier Technology Company and the Insite Company have developed very high density (VHD) floppy disk drives that store 21Mb on a 3½-inch floppy disk. Using Stacker compression, you can store 42Mb on these floppy disks. The floppy disks look just like any other 3½-inch floppy disks, but they have special embedded *servo* (see glossary) tracks that control the heads.

With the Brier Technology's QuadFLEXTRA, instead of 80 tracks per side, the disks are formatted with 516 tracks per side. And instead of 18 sectors per track, these disks have 40 sectors per track of 512 bytes each. The disks cost $25 each, and the drive for them costs $495. Being able to store 42Mb on a $25 disk is fantastic. These drives have a typical access time of 35 milliseconds (ms), about ten times faster than an ordinary floppy disk. These drive systems are an excellent method of backing up your hard disks. Unlike a tape backup system, a 42Mb floppy disk allows you to read or write selective files.

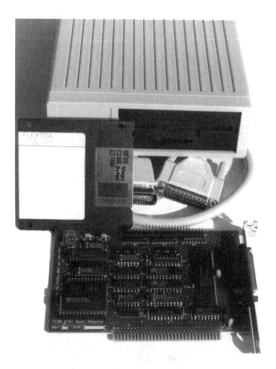

2-7 Brier Flextra 20Mb floppy disk.

The QuadFLEXTRA is distributed by the Quadram Corporation. See Fig. 2-7. If you are interested in this product call or write:

Quadram Corporation
One Quad Way
Norcross, GA 30093-2919
(404) 923-6666

The list price of the drive is $495 (includes SCSI (Small Computer System Interface) controller) and disks are $25 each.

The Insite Company has also developed a 20Mb 3½-inch floppy disk drive. The system uses a floppy disk that has laser-etched servo tracks. The system can read and write to the 720K or 1.44Mb floppy disks. It uses two different heads, one to read and write to the VHD floppy disks, and the standard head for the 720K and 1.44Mb floppy disks.

The Insite Company, (408) 946-8080, has its drive system on the market for a list price of $525.

Chapter 3

Entry-level systems

An entry-level system consists of the basic components you will use in the first phase of your LAN. Most small businesses stay with an entry-level system until their business grows and they are ready to expand. In this chapter, you will learn more about different components, system designs, and basic software you should evaluate before you begin to build.

This LAN is your LAN: The LAN manager

To assemble a viable network someone should be the LAN manager, LAN administrator, or LAN boss. It doesn't matter what he or she is called, someone should be in charge of the network. This person should:

- be aware of, or in charge of, each change, alteration, or addition to the network.
- have a computerized log or a book, with the complete records and documentation of the server and each workstation.
- know what components are inside the server and each workstation, as well as the configuration of each board.

Having this information and documentation will make it much easier to troubleshoot whenever the network goes down. I know "down" is a dirty word, but almost all networks go down from time to time. The more you know about your network, the easier it will be to get it back up.

If you happen to be the boss, and you don't have time for the day-to-day administration, pick a knowledgeable employee and give him or her the job. You might also give the person a fancy title such as *manager of information systems*, or *vice president in charge of LAN management*. If the title is fancy enough, you might not have to increase their salary. (Additional duties of a LAN manager are discussed in chapter 14.)

Several software programs, such as CheckIt LAN from Touchstone, (800) 531-0450, are suitable for the management of a small LAN.

The floor plan

One of the difficulties in setting up a network is the number of options from which you must choose. The type of system you install usually determines the physical layout of the system, the *topology*.

Before reading further in this chapter, one of the first things you should do is draw a map or physical plan of where each computer or workstation will be located. This map should determine what type of system and topology you will install. (Refer back to chapter 1 for detailed information on the three main topologies—bus, token ring, and star.)

Peer-to-peer vs. client-server

Several peer-to-peer entry-level systems are ideal for small businesses. *Peer* means equal, so a peer-to-peer network means that all computers in the network are equals. They can all contribute and share their resources with the other computers in the network.

In a *client-server* system, usually one computer with a large hard disk acts as the server for the workstations. If it is a *dedicated server*, all it does is provide and manage data for the client workstations.

In a *peer-to-peer* system, you might not have a single computer in the network that acts as a server, or, at times, each of the computers acts as a server and other times like a client.

Both types of systems work well for small network systems but large networks usually rely on the client-server systems.

I will primarily discuss peer-to-peer in this chapter and client-server systems in the next. However, it is difficult to separate the two completely, so you'll find a bit of both in each chapter.

What you need for a network

A network is made up of two components—software and hardware—and like the song says about love and marriage, you can't have one without the other.

NOS software & NIC hardware

Only a few network operating system (NOS) manufacturers exist, but hundreds of companies make network interface cards (NICs), or adapter boards. In the three major types of systems—Ethernet, token ring, and ARCnet—almost all of the adapters that come from different manufacturers have drivers to allow them to operate on Novell's NetWare or Microsoft's LAN Manager. They are the two major network operating system manufacturers. Novell's NetWare has about 70 percent of the NOS market; Microsoft's LAN Manager, and several other smaller companies, have the rest of the market.

Software drivers

The three major network systems have different configurations and require certain types of components. For example, Ethernet has three different cabling systems—thick, thin, or unshielded twisted pairs (UTP).

The three major networks systems also run at different speeds. Ethernet runs at 10 mbps. The token ring system usually operates at 4 megabits per second (mbps) or 16 mbps. ARCnet usually operates in a star or a bus topology at 2.5 mbps or at 20 mbps.

The adapter boards will have switches and jumpers to configure them to the various systems. But the adapter boards will need *software drivers* to tell the NOS what boards they are and how they are configured. When you buy an adapter board it will come with a floppy disk that has the software driver on it.

Some of the low-cost adapters might not have all of the necessary drivers for your system. When you buy a network interface card be sure to ask what drivers come with it.

Protocols & standards

It might seem amazing that software from a few companies works with almost all of the different NICs or adapter boards. The reason is that the adapter boards from the various manufacturers conform to certain protocols and standards. The U.S. Government is responsible to a large extent in establishing basic standards. The Department of Defense (DOD) developed a set of protocols for their networks and for the suppliers who sell to the government called Transmission Control Protocol/Internet Protocol (TCP/IP). So many companies have adopted this protocol that it has become a standard.

The Institute of Electrical and Electronic Engineers (IEEE) has also contributed to the standardization of communication protocols. The IEEE is an international society of professional engineers that has set up committees to study, formulate, and recommend many electrical and electronic standards. They are responsible for the IEEE 802.3 standard for Ethernet and IEEE standard 802.5 for token ring.

The Consultative Committee on International Telegraph and Telephone, or Comité Consultatif Internationale de Telegraphique et Telephonique (CCITT), is a committee set up under the United Nations. The CCITT has recommended standards for international telephone, telegraph, fax, modems, networks, and most other means of communications.

The OSI model

The International Standards Organization (ISO) is closely allied with the CCITT. They developed the Open Systems Interconnection (OSI) protocols, which go several steps beyond the TCP/IP protocols. The ISO/OSI model defines seven layers of specifications. These specifications cover all aspects of communications, both hardware and software. Some of the specifications are very complex and complicated.

You don't really need to know all of the details of the seven layers in order to build a network or to use one. Here are the seven layers and a very brief description of each:

1. *Physical.* Concerns the electrical and physical hardware connection and the transmitting of data over the physical wires. It includes connectors, signaling, and software.
2. *Data-Link.* Consists of protocols to control the stream of data from one machine or device to another. It strings messages together in blocks and packets.
3. *Network.* Provides a software interface between the physical and data-link layers.
4. *Transport.* Does many of the same things as the Network layer and

provides for the transparent transfer of packets and blocks of data between devices.

5. *Session.* Provides standards to move data between application programs.

6. *Presentation.* Formats data for viewing and for use on specific equipment. This layer is sometimes concerned with security, encryption, and codes. Microsoft Windows and IBM's Presentation Manager are two programs that operate in the Presentation layer environment.

7. *Application.* Defines the network operating systems and application programs. Its specification covers almost all application programs such as file sharing, electronic mail, database management, spreadsheets, word processors, and others.

The DOD has also adopted a version of the OSI model. They call it Government Open Systems Interface Protocol (GOSIP). Another protocol that works with TCP/IP is Simple Network Management Protocol (SNMP), which is used by the government and several large companies.

Private company protocols

There are many other protocols such as Systems Network Architecture (SNA) developed by IBM. Many other large companies such as AT&T, DEC, and Hewlett-Packard have developed similar protocols. Some of these protocols have been adopted by the industry as standards.

It is good to know that all of these specifications and protocols exist, but you might not need to study them in depth. It is not necessary to be a design or mechanical engineer in order to drive a car. Neither is it really necessary that you know all of the communications specifications and protocols to be able to set up an entry-level network. As long as you have some assurance that the products you buy conform to the recognized protocols, you should have few problems.

A good network should work in the background. You should not even be aware that it is a network and should operate as if the whole network is a single computer on your desktop.

The big three: Ethernet, token ring, and ARCnet

The three main types of systems in use today are Ethernet, token ring, and ARCnet. These three systems account for over 90 percent of all installed LANs. There is a lot of hardware and software available for these systems from many different sources. These systems can work in a small peer-to-peer system or in a large network system. I will discuss these systems in more detail in the next chapter.

Proprietary systems

Several companies have developed their own systems. Some of these systems are completely proprietary to that particular company's software and hardware, while others are compatible with one or more of the big three. Then there are those who are compatible with the major NOS software, such as NetWare or LAN Manager.

The proprietary systems might not offer the sophisticated complex functions and utilities found in the large systems. But they have almost everything you need for a small business and they are inexpensive and easy to set up. Almost anyone can set up one of these systems without having to call in an expert, analyst, or consultant.

Software

As stated earlier, two major components are needed in a network system—hardware and software. The software needed is a network operating system (NOS) and disk operating system (DOS). Choosing the NOS is more crucial than choosing the hardware. There are only a few NOS manufacturers but there are thousands of network hardware manufacturers.

Among the large corporation networks, Novell's NetWare is installed on about 70 percent of the systems. The other 30 percent belongs to Microsoft's LAN Manager, Banyan's VINES, IBM's NetBIOS, and several other small proprietary systems.

Novell has the majority of network software, but they would also like to have more of the DOS systems. Novell has recently merged with Digital Research, which developed DR DOS. This merger gives Novell DR DOS, which is completely compatible with MS-DOS. DR DOS even offers some commands and utilities not found in MS-DOS.

DOS alone is not a good network operating system because it is not designed for multiusers. OS/2 is well suited for multiusers and is part of Microsoft's LAN Manager. Ordinarily, on most of the large network systems, the network operating system replaces DOS. The peer-to-peer systems software usually runs on top of DOS. Many companies have written drivers and patches that lets DOS work with their proprietary systems.

Novell NetWare Lite

NetWare Lite comes on a single 720K floppy disk. It has a single 162-page manual. Most of these pages have only two or three sentences or a very simple line drawing of a train. The manual is written for first-time users and gives several examples and analogies. It should be very helpful for anyone just starting out in networks.

As you might expect, NetWare Lite is a real lightweight in what it can do compared to NetWare 2.2 or NetWare 3.11. But it will let you connect as many as 25 computers together, using any of the major adapter cards.

The software has a serial number on each disk. You must use the original disk to install it on a machine, so you must buy a separate copy for each computer. The software lists for $99, but several discount houses advertise it for as little as $59 per copy.

A low-cost starter system

Using NetWare Lite can be an inexpensive way to set up a network. Several discount houses advertise ARCnet cards for as little as $55 each, and Ethernet cards for as little as $95 each. A two-station network ARCnet, including software, adapters, cables, and a passive hub, should cost about $275. A two-station Ethernet system including software, adapters and cables should cost about the same. You could add two computers for about $800 each and have a fairly good starter system for less than $2,000.

Eagle Technology and the Tech Data Corporation, (800) 237-8931, have put together a NetWare Lite starter kit. It includes DR DOS 6.0, two copies of NetWare Lite, two 16-bit Ethernet adapter boards, a 20-foot cable, and BNC T connectors and terminators. The list price for this kit is $649. You should be able to find this package at a discount house for considerably less.

NetWare Lite might come bundled with the DR DOS 6.0 because Novell is pushing it as an operating system to replace MS-DOS.

NetWare Lite might be okay for a small business, but it does not have nearly all of the functions, utilities, power, and sophistication of a full-fledged NOS like NetWare 2.2 or 3.11. For one thing, NetWare Lite limits you to 25 nodes. If you expect your business to grow, or that you will need to take advantage of some of the more sophisticated aspects of networking, you might consider NetWare 2.2, NetWare 3.11, or LAN Manager.

LANtastic

The Artisoft Company, (602) 293-6363, has its own software that is compatible with NetWare and LAN Manager called LANtastic/AI (for Adapter Independent). The software for each node has a list price of $99 and some of the discount houses sell it for $75 or less. At $75 each, you could set up a five-user system for only $375 for the NOS software.

Like NetWare Lite, the LANtastic software has a different serial number on each disk. You must use the original disk to install it on a node or workstation, so you have to buy a separate copy for each node. The Artisoft LANtastic NOS software can support up to 300 users. A license for up to 300 users is $2,499.

Artisoft also manufactures its own 8- and 16-bit adapters. The 16-bit Ethernet adapters list for $225 each, but the LANtastic software will operate with most of the other network interface cards or adapters. So you can shop around for discount-priced adapters and use the LANtastic software for a very inexpensive system.

Artisoft offers a two-station LANtastic starter kit. The Edimax LAN Professional Company, (408) 496-1105, advertises a LANtastic kit with software and two ARCnet adapters for $249.95. A starter kit with two 16-bit Ethernet adapters is advertised for $395.

Moses Computers

Moses Computers, (408) 358-1550, has developed its own proprietary network systems. The PromiseLAN system operates at 1.79 mbps on unshielded twisted pair telephone cables. It is a peer-to-peer system that works with DOS. A kit with two adapters, a network operating system, and a 25-foot cable has a list price of $299. Additional adapters have a list price of $182.

The Moses ChosenLAN system operates at 3.58 mbps. A kit of three adapters, a network operating system, and cables has a list price of $578. One of the adapters is a *quad* (see glossary) with four ports. This feature allows for the connection of four single adapters in a star/bus arrangement. Other quad adapters can be added or daisy chained so that a total of 53 nodes can be installed on a network. See Fig. 3-1.

3-1 Moses ChosenLAN software and hardware. (Moses Computers)

The Moses systems are very good, low-cost, entry-level networks and can do almost anything that a small business might want to do.

Invisible Software

Invisible Software, (415) 570-5967, has developed a proprietary network operating system called Net/30. It is a high-performance DOS-based peer-to-peer system. The system is compatible with Novell.

Invisible Software has developed its own adapters for unshielded twisted pair or coaxial cables for 10 mbps Ethernet. The company includes its operating system for each adapter, which has a list price of $349 for Industry Standard Architecture (ISA) machines and $469 for IBM MCA computers.

Invisible Software also manufactures several other adapters, hubs, and network peripheral equipment.

Alloy Computer

Alloy Computer, (508) 481-8500, has a DOS-based proprietary entry-level system that its system uses and an intelligent multiport (IMP) plug-in adapter card. The IMP card has its own CPU and is then connected to an alloy terminal array panel (TAP) which provides connections for up to 21 users. Users can be laptops, dumb terminals, PCs, or Macintoshes. Alloy has IMP adapter cards for 8- and 16-bit ISA and for IBM's MCA. See Fig. 3-2.

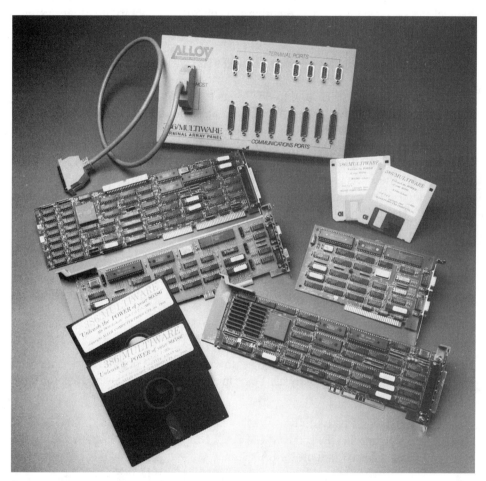

3-2 Alloy 386 MultiWare LAN system. (Alloy)

It is a multitasking, multiuser time-slicing system. Each task is given a standard time slice of 16 milliseconds. (A *time slice* is a designated interval of time that a job or task is allowed to use a resource without being preempted.)

This system uses all of the standard DOS commands along with a menu-driven user interface provided by 386/MultiWare. The 386/MultiWare system is compatible with ARCnet, Ethernet, and NetWare. A 386/MultiWare system and ARCnet can be run from the same host or server.

Alloy has a MW386E, entry-level system for two to five users for $595 and a 2- to 21-user system for $995. The company offers several other software and hardware items, so call them for a brochure and price list.

ISA-to-Macintosh connection

The Macintosh systems are quite different than the ISA-compatible systems. To connect the two you must have something to convert the data to the other system. The conversion can be done with software or a combination of software and special hardware.

If you are installing a large system, Novell's NetWare can allow the connection of Macintoshes and PCs.

The Sitka Company, (800) 445-8677, has two approaches for connecting PCs and Macintoshes. One is called DosTOPS and the other MacTOPS. Call for brochures and more information.

The Black Box Corporation, (412) 746-5530, has Dayna Talk plug-in boards that will allow the linking of the Macintosh to an IBM PS/2, IBM PC, or ISA compatible. The board for the PC is listed for $299 and the board for the Macintosh is $399. You will also need to buy NET PLUS connectors for the boards at $59.95 each. The system can use the PhoneNet UTP cables.

You will need to buy a copy of TOPS for the Macintosh and a copy for the PC. The system can communicate at speeds up to 1.7 mbps.

The Farallon Company, (510) 596-9100, manufactures several products that can link the Macintosh and ISA PCs together. Figure 3-3 shows the Farallon PhoneNet 380 board that plugs into an ISA PC. The PhoneNet cable then plugs into the Macintosh's built-in AppleTalk system.

Other entry-level systems

Here are just a few more companies that provide peer-to-peer network operating systems. I can't possibly list them all. You can call these companies and ask for their brochures.

Compex's ReadyLINK	(714) 630-7302
Grapevine LAN Products' GV LAN OS	(206) 869-2707
Hayes Microcomputer's LANStep	(404) 441-1617
Webcorp	(415) 331-1449
Zytec Systems Triac & pcNOS	(800) 798-3502

NOS for large systems

The list price of a network operating system for some of the large systems is much too expensive for many small businesses. But if you shop around you might find the software at a discount price that is less than half the list price. For instance, NetWare 2.2 has a list price of $895 for five users. The Netlogic Company, (714) 581-7255,

3-3 Farallon PC Board and PhoneNet connection to a Macintosh. (Farallon)

advertises it for $489. NetWare 3.11 lists for $3,495 for 20 users, but is offered by Netlogic for $1,899.

If you expect your business to grow, it might be worthwhile to invest in a full network operating system, such as NetWare 2.2, NetWare 3.11, or LAN Manager 2.1.

NetWare 2.2

NetWare 2.2 is a complete network system for 8- and 16-bit computers. It is designed to meet the needs of most small businesses, professional offices, and work groups. Novell combined the best of several of their earlier systems, such as Entry Level Systems (ELS) I & II, Advanced NetWare, and Systems Fault Tolerance (SFT) into NetWare 2.2. This provides a robust and powerful system that does just about everything one would want. At $489 for a five-user system, it would cost about $100 more than LANtastic, but would be much more powerful.

I mentioned earlier that you have to buy a separate copy of NetWare Lite for each station because the software is serialized and you cannot have two serial numbers on the same network. The control of the number of users on NetWare 2.x or 3.x software is a little different. This software is loaded on a server. When these systems are loaded on the server, it will let you configure it only for the number of users that you paid for. If you paid for 10, you will not be able to configure the LAN for 11 workstations.

NetWare 3.11

NetWare 3.11 can take advantage of 8-bit, 16-bit, or 32-bit systems. It can support DOS, Windows, OS/2, UNIX, and Macintosh and handle up to 1,000 users. It is the most powerful and sophisticated system that is available.

It seems that Novell would like to eliminate their NetWare 2.x systems. According to a news report, they have lowered the price of their NetWare 3.x and added several features to the newest releases. But they have done nothing to improve the NetWare 2.x. It is reported that they have asked their dealers to push the 3.x instead of the 2.x systems.

LAN Manager 2.1

Microsoft LAN Manager can also take advantage of 8-bit, 16-bit, or 32-bit systems and it also supports DOS, Windows, OS/2, and multiprocessors. It can handle peer-to-peer systems, client-server systems, or both, and can handle up to 992 users per server. It uses OS/2 on the servers. Client workstations can use OS/2, but most of them will probably use DOS because much more application software is available and most users are already familiar with DOS. Using OS/2 on the servers gives the whole network the benefit of this powerful system.

LAN Manager is a large system, it comes on 24 3½-inch 1.44Mb floppy disks, which includes the full OS/2 software, LAN Manager software, Sytos Plus, and network backup software.

Most users will appreciate OS/2's High-Performance File System (HPFS). This system works with the FAT to allow file names longer than the eight characters allowed under DOS. It is much easier to find a file if you can give it a good descriptive name. Eight characters, even with the three-character extension, is just not enough in many cases.

The LAN Manager package has 11 manuals. Among them are an *Administrator's Guide,* an *Administrator's Reference*, an *Installation and Configuration Guide*, a *User's Guide for MS-DOS*, a small *User's Guide for OS/2*, a large *OS/2 User's Guide*, and two manuals for Sytos Plus, the backup software. Figure 3-4 shows some of the manuals.

LAN Manager also comes with an instructional videotape. The videotape can be very helpful to a first-time user in setting up a system. It walks you through the various possible configurations, gives examples, and references each section of the manual that covers the same subject. Several other companies offer network training on videotape and charge up to $700 for a tape. The LAN Manager tape is free with the software.

LAN Manager is ideal for large or small systems but it has not been around as long as Novell NetWare, especially the newer 2.1 version. The LAN Manager's list price for 10 users is $1,995 and for an unlimited number of users is $5,495. You should be able to find it at discount houses for about half this amount.

Microsoft has added several networking features to its Windows New Technology (NT). These features add several new functions and utilities to Windows. Many programs are now much easier to run on a network.

3-4 LAN Manager software.

Cost of a five-user network

Again, many variables determine the cost of a build-your-own, five-user network, but here is a fairly good estimate:

Item	Cost
Computer, 386 server, 200Mb hard disk	$1,200
Computer, 286 workstation ($600 × 4)	2,400
Novell NetWare, 2.2. five users	489
Ethernet adapters ($100 × 5)	500
Cables, 500 feet UTP, connectors	100
Total	$4,689

Depending on how well you shop, you might be able to beat this price. Or you might want a system that is considerably different than the basic items shown here. Many choices and options will determine the cost.

Bundled systems

Several companies, such as Packard Bell, Northgate, Dell, and Innovative Technology are offering "plug and play" systems. Packard Bell, (800) 733-1616, offers a system that comes with a 486 server and three workstations for a price of $14,499, or $3,624.75 per station. This price includes LAN Manager and several other software packages. A 25-station LAN costs $61,699, or $2,467.96 per station.

Northgate, (612) 943-8181 or (800) 548-1993, offers customization for just about any type of system that you want. A typical 486 file server with a 300Mb hard disk would cost $6,763. A typical work station would cost $2,156. Four workstations would total $8,624 plus the $6,763 server for a total of $15,387.

Dell, (800) 545-3794, also offers network systems using NetWare Lite. The cost will vary with the products chosen.

Innovative Technology, (800) 253-4001, offers a five-user system for $4,795 that includes a server and four workstations. The server is a 40 MHz 386DX computer with 4Mb of RAM, a 120Mb hard disk, a 1.2Mb floppy disk drive, a monochrome monitor, and Ethernet card. Each diskless workstation has a 20 MHz 286 computer with 1Mb of RAM, a monochrome monitor, and an Ethernet card. Innovative Technology has a free 32-page networking guide that is very informative.

Again, you should shop around. A small company in the Los Angeles area called Binomial, (714) 595-8293, offers a 33 MHz 386DX server and four 286 workstations for $3,795 plus $515 for a five-user NetWare 2.2 system, for a total of $4,310. The server has a 130Mb hard disk and the workstations have a 1.2Mb floppy disk drive. A 40Mb hard disk can be added to each workstation for $175 each. A 130Mb server and four 40Mb workstations would cost $5,010.

This system was advertised in *Computer Currents*. Elsewhere in this magazine were ads for all of the components listed in the bundled system. If you bought the components and assembled the server and workstations yourself, you could save over $1,000 on this system. I will show you how easy it is to assemble your own LAN in chapter 6.

Chapter 4

Large systems

A large system will use one or more of the big three systems—Ethernet, token ring, or ARCnet—and possibly interconnect with a smaller Ethernet, token ring, or ARCnet system.

A large system might have several hundred computers and several different types of systems and workstations. For example, a college campus might have several Macintosh computers in the language department, several ISA systems in the science labs, and a Sun Unix system with several workstations in the student records department. All of these systems could then be tied together.

Of course, this type of system is very complex, expensive, and requires expert engineers and technicians to install and maintain. This is not the type of system that is focused on in this book. I discuss it in this chapter only to illustrate the vast benefits and capabilities of network systems and to show you that you can still take advantage of these benefits even if you only have four or five computers. If your business grows, your network can grow right along with it.

Ethernet

The most popular network system is Ethernet. The IEEE 802.3 specifications were developed for this system.

Bob Metcalf is given principal credit for inventing Ethernet while working at the Xerox Palo Alto Research Center (PARC) in 1973. The vast majority of all installed network systems are Ethernet. Metcalf says that there are now over one million Ethernet LANs installed with more than ten million computers on them. He says that within a few years there will be 25 million computers on Ethernet LANs.

The Ethernet shielded coaxial LANs use a bus topology. A *bus* is just a line with several terminals on it and a terminating connector on each end. The Ethernet unshielded twisted pair (UTP) systems use a star-type bus.

Only one message at a time can traverse an Ethernet system, but it operates at 10 mbps, so it doesn't take long to transmit a file. It uses *carrier sense multiple access with collision detection* (CSMA/CD). The electronics on the network interface card (NIC) listens to the line and if no transmission is occurring, it allows the user to proceed. If two users attempt to transmit at the same time, the NICs detect the signals and shut both users down. The NIC waits a random amount of time and then retries.

Much has been made of the fact that Ethernet pauses when it detects two systems trying to transmit at the same time. But these pauses are just a few milliseconds. IBM tried, but failed, to prove that its Token-Ring was faster at 4 mbps than the 10 mbps CSMA/CD Ethernet system. Bob Metcalf says that, at the present time, most networks sit idle most of the time. Someday faster systems might be needed, he says, but 10 mbps is more than sufficient at the present time.

I would respectfully disagree with him. More and more companies, especially the larger ones, are extensively using LANs for computer-aided design (CAD), computer-aided manufacturing (CAM), and for graphics. These and other complex application programs can be very large and require lots of time to transfer. Many companies are now considering the Fiber Distributed Data Interface (FDDI), which uses fiberoptics and can operate at 100 mbps.

Of course, if you do not have a need to run this type of software, or if you have more time than money, then 10 mbps is probably all you need.

The Ethernet CSMA/CD system might be compared to a panel of very polite speakers seated at a long table. Each speaker has a microphone. It is possible that two of them would try to speak at the same time, but it would be garbled. Because they are polite, they will listen before they start to speak. If another person starts to speak at the same time, they will both stop and wait a while for the other to speak.

The Ethernet system can use several types of cable: thick coaxial, thin coaxial, and unshielded twisted pair (UTP).

Thick coaxial cables

The original type of cable is a large, thick coaxial cable that is rather expensive, stiff, and difficult to work with. It is usually yellow and some have called it a "frozen yellow garden hose." It will allow up to 500 meters (1,640 feet) before the signal has to be regenerated. The price of this cable varies from $1 to $2 per foot. Connectors for this cable cost from $2.50 to $12 each. Each end of the bus must also have a 50-ohm terminating connector, which is a resistor to match the cable impedance. These connectors can cost from $2.50 to $15 each.

Connection to the thick cable is through transceivers. As many as 100 transceivers can be attached to the main trunk and each transceiver can have ports for as many as 16 workstations. Up to 1,024 workstations can be attached to the main trunk through the transceivers. If more stations are needed, a repeater can be installed to add another 500-meter segment. See Fig. 4-1.

Thin coaxial cables

The thin RG 58 coaxial cable, which is smaller in diameter than the thick coaxial cable, can also be used. It is less expensive than the thick—from 75 cents to $1.50 per foot—so it is sometimes jokingly referred to as "cheapernet." The thin coaxial cable is much more flexible and can be bent and routed more easily than the thick coaxial cable. It can be attached directly to the adapter through a BNC T connector without having to use a transceiver or hub. But it can only transmit the signal for 305 meters (about 1,000 feet) before it must be regenerated. It must have a 50-ohm terminator at each end of the bus. Figure 4-2 shows a thin Ethernet connection through a BNC with a terminator. Connectors and terminators will run about the same as for the thick coaxial cable listed above. See Fig. 4-3 for a representation of a thin Ethernet system.

Unshielded twisted pair (UTP) cables

The Ethernet system can also use unshielded twisted pair (UTP) cables. These are the same as the telephone wires and are the least expensive of all types of cable. They are also the easiest to handle and install. But the signal is only good for about 100

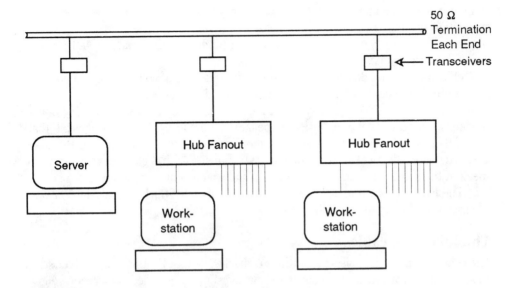

50 Ω
Termination
Each End
Transceivers

4-1 A thick Ethernet system.

meters, or about 325 feet, before it must be regenerated. UTP cable costs about ten cents a foot. Connectors can cost from 25 cents to $1 each. A terminator for UTP can cost from $2 to $6.

UTPs use the star topology, so you must install a hub for the connections. The hub can be *passive*, that is, nothing more than a box with connections for the UTP cables, and can cost from $50 to $150. Or it can be *active*, that is, it has five or more ports. The active hub can act as a repeater or have some sort of built-in intelligence and can cost from $500 to $2,000, depending on the number of ports and built-in functions.

Figure 4-4 is a representation of an Ethernet or ARCnet UTP system using the star topology. Figure 4-5 is a concentrator, or hub, for UTP wires from the AMP Corporation, (800) 522-6752. (More about cables in the next chapter.)

Ethernet NICs

The Ethernet network interface card (NIC) will have connectors for the type of cable that you decide to use—thick, thin, or UTP.

The adapters for the standard thick cable will have a DB 15 connector called an *attachment unit interface* (AUI) port. The thick cable acts as a main trunk line and does not attach directly to the adapter. Instead, the main trunk might have several transceivers. The transceiver is sometimes called a *medium attachment unit* (MAU). (This acronym (MAU) can also stand for multistation access unit, a component of a token ring system.)

A drop cable of shielded twisted pairs is used to connect the workstation adapter to a transceiver. The drop cables have a maximum length of 50 meters, or 165 feet.

4-2 An Ethernet NIC with a terminator.

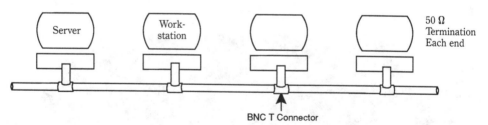

4-3 A thin Ethernet system.

The AUI port on the adapter can also be used to connect a hub or concentrator for unshielded twisted pair (UTP) cables. The maximum distance of a UTP cable between a hub and the adapter in a workstation is 100 meters, or 328 feet. The UTP system uses the star topology with the hub in the center. The hub can support several workstations and can cost from $500 to $1,500.

Most of the Ethernet adapter boards have both the AUI port and a BNC connector. The thin coaxial cable can be attached directly to the BNC connector on

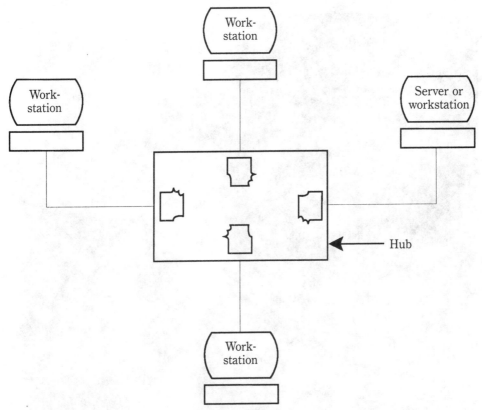

4-4 A star configuration for an ARCnet or Ethernet UTP system.

4-5 An AMP UTP hub, or concentrator. (AMP)

the adapter with a BNC T connector. With a T connector, if a message is addressed to a particular workstation, it goes down the cable and bypasses all the other workstations until it arrives at the proper address.

The thin Ethernet cable is a bit expensive compared to UTP. But for a small system, it might be the least expensive because it does not require a hub or transceiver.

Adapters

Several different types of Ethernet adapters or NICs can be used, such as the:

- Industry Standard Architecture (ISA) 8-bit and 16-bit cards
- 32-bit Micro Channel Architecture (MCA) cards for IBM PS/2s
- Extended Industry Standard Architecture (EISA) cards
- Ethernet cards for the Macintosh

Some of the 8-bit cards can cost from $75 to $200. The 16-bit cards can cost from $100 to $500. The MCA, EISA, and Macintosh cards can cost from $500 to $1,000 each. Some of the MCA and EISA cards cost more because they have a built-in intelligent configuration system.

Some of the MCA and EISA cards are also able to take advantage of *bus mastering,* which allows the card to temporarily take over the bus and quickly transfer data in and out of RAM without interrupting the processor.

Zenith Electronics Corporation, (708) 391-8000, manufactures several different Ethernet adapters. Figure 4-6 shows an MCA card on the right, two 8-bit ISA cards

4-6 Five different Ethernet boards from Zenith. (Zenith)

on the left, and two 16-bit ISA cards in the center. Note that the one 8-bit card and 16-bit card in the center and lower portion of the photo have all three types of connectors. They have a BNC for thin coaxial, a DB-15 AUI for thick coaxial, and a RJ45 for UTP.

Adapter card configuration   Computers use certain areas of memory for plug-in devices. The computers have a limited number of these addresses, or *interrupt request lines* (IRQ). If two devices are set for the same IRQ, it will cause a conflict and they will not operate properly. You must set switches or jumpers on the cards to configure them for the proper IRQ. Some of the more expensive and advanced MCA and EISA cards can automatically read the system configuration, then configure themselves for the proper IRQ. Here is a list of the IRQ lines and memory addresses:

IRQ line	Memory address	Device
3	2F8h	COM2
3	2E0h	COM4
4	3F8h	COM1
4	2E8h	COM3
5	280h	Tape Ctrlr
5	3F0h	PC/XT Hd Ctrlr
5	278h	LPT2
6	3F0h	Flpy Ctrlr
7	378h	LPT1

You should receive some sort of documentation with your boards that shows which jumpers or switches to set. If you have trouble, you might need diagnostic software such as TouchStone's CheckIt LAN, (714) 969-7746. This software can check your system and tell you which devices are located at which IRQ. It also has several other excellent software diagnostic tools and can save you a lot of time and trouble.

Figure 4-7 shows some DIP switches and jumper-shorting blocks that are used to configure the adapter.

Station documentation   It is important that you make up a detailed record of how each board is configured when you install it. Write down how each switch and jumper is set. It can save a lot of time later if you have problems.

Laptop adapters   Several companies such as Invisible Software, (415) 570-5697, Xircom, (818) 878-7600, and Kodiak, (408) 441-6900, manufacture small external adapters that can be used with a laptop to tie into a network. The adapters plug into the parallel ports of PCs.

Built-in network adapters   The Chips and Technology (C&T) Company, Texas Instruments, and National Semiconductor are developing network adapter chips that can be installed on the motherboard. It will be just like another built-in port and there will be no need for network interface cards (NIC).

C&T chips will work with both Ethernet and token ring. (They have been referred to as "eithernet.") By installing them on the motherboard, it will save a slot and be much less expensive than buying NICs.

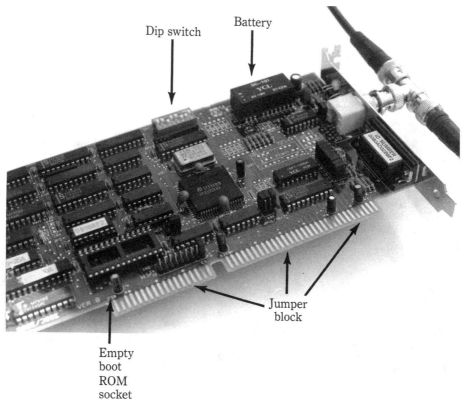

Dip switch

Battery

Jumper
block

Empty
boot
ROM
socket

4-7 Various jumpers and switches that must be set.

One problem faced when installing an adapter board is determining how to configure it so that it does not conflict with other devices. The boards must be set for the proper memory address and IRQ. If the chips are built in, then the factory will set it to the proper address.

A disadvantage is that the adapters need software drivers to work with the type of cables and network operating system software chosen. The motherboard vendors would have to supply the drivers.

Another slight disadvantage might be that if the chip becomes outdated, the whole motherboard will have to be scrapped. But that should not happen very often. Chances are that the motherboard will become obsolete before the network chip does. Apple builds in AppleTalk on the Macintosh but it is rather slow at 230 kbps and does not offer many of the advantages of the NICs.

A multifunction Ethernet adapter AMT Computers, (714) 598-7716, has a multifunction board called Sigma Six. See Fig. 4-8. It has a 16-bit Ethernet adapter, a 2400-baud modem, a 9600-baud fax, a Super VGA monitor adapter, two serial ports, one parallel port, IDE and floppy disk controller, Flash Eprom for storing DOS in ROM, and can be configured for IRQ interrupt lines using software. AMT calls this card Sigma Six because it can take the place of about six other boards.

Six different boards that would perform each of these functions would cost much

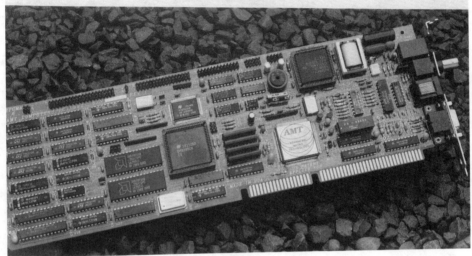

4-8 An Ethernet multifunction board from Sigma Six.

more than the Sigma Six price of $695. The standard motherboard has only eight slots and they can be filled very quickly. A good multifunction board that can save six slots is well worth $695. This card could be installed in a server so that all of the workstations could use the fax and modem.

The best buy

Ethernet is the most popular of all the network systems with more installed than any other kind (so it must be doing something right). Because of its popularity there are many vendors, which helps keep the prices down. Ethernet is the best system you can buy for the least amount of money.

Some adapters might cost more than others. One reason for the difference in the cost is that some cards might have more memory, remote boot ROM, and other goodies. The biggest reason for the cost difference is where you buy them and whether they are brand-name adapters. It will pay you to shop around and look through computer and LAN magazines to compare prices.

Token ring

The Token-Ring system, developed by IBM, conforms to the IEEE 802.5 specification. It uses a cable system that makes a complete ring. See Fig. 4-9.

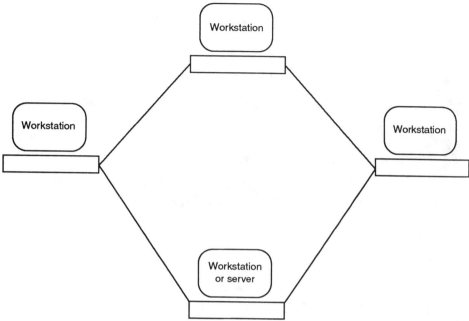

4-9 A token ring system.

Several computers may be attached to the ring. An electronic token is passed around the circle to each computer in turn and only that computer that has the token can transmit. With this system "collisions" do not occur because only one computer can ever be on the bus at any one time. The token ring system may also be compared to a panel of speakers seated around a circular table. But in this system, they have only one microphone. The microphone is on a small track and passes around the circle to each panelist. If a panelist has something to say, the microphone is taken, and when finished, it is passed on to the next panelist.

The token ring system can operate at 4 mbps or 16 mbps and use coaxial or UTP cables. The cables will cost about the same as the thin coaxial for Ethernet. The token ring can use a hub or concentrator, such as that pictured in Fig. 4-10 from the AMP Corporation. Note that it has connectors for both coaxial and UTP.

Token ring NICs

Like almost everything that is IBM or IBM related, the cost of the token ring network interface cards (NICs), or adapters, is two to three times greater than for some of the Ethernet adapters. The 4 mbps cards can cost from $400 to $500, the ones that operate at 4 mbps or 16 mbps can cost from $800 to $1,100 each. You won't often see them for sale by the discount houses. Most of the token ring systems are installed in large corporations that have IBM PCs and mainframes installed. These businesses usually don't worry about their budgets as much as small businesses.

4-10   A hub, or concentrator, for token ring shielded and unshielded twisted pairs (UTPs). (AMP)

ARCnet

ARCnet stands for *Attached Resource Computer network*. One of the early networks, developed by the Datapoint Company, it operates at 2.5 mbps, which is considerably slower than Ethernet or token ring.

The IEEE has not established a specification for the ARCnet technology, but it is a very solid and reliable system. Thousands of ARCnet systems have been installed and have operated flawlessly for many years. Several vendors manufacture ARCnet adapter boards and components, which are the least expensive of the major three.

ARCnet uses a star topology with a computer in the center. This computer attaches to an active hub that has several ports. Each one of these ports is a connection for the computer on that line. If more computers are needed, a passive hub can be inserted in one of these lines with two to four more ports. If the distance from the active hub is more than 2,000 feet, then another active hub with four or more ports can be inserted to regenerate the signal.

ARCnet uses a type of token passing that is different than IBM's system. Each card comes with a set of switches that can be set for anywhere from 1 to 255. The token is passed from computer to computer sequentially, depending on the numerical number assigned to the NIC.

ARCnet may also be used in a bus topology. ARCnet has recently announced a 20 mbps system, but at this time, not many units are available.

Cables: Coaxial or UTP

ARCnet may use RG 62 coaxial, which is very similar to the RG 58 cables used for thin Ethernet. ARCnet may also use UTP cables.

ARCnet NICs

The ARCnet network interface cards (NICs), or adapters, are the least expensive of all the systems. IEEE has no specification for ARCnet adapters but vendors conform very closely to its original specifications. It is expected that eventually the IEEE will adopt a set of standards for it.

Both 8- and 16-bit cards are available for ARCnet. Several companies are working to develop ARCnet adapters that operate at a speed of 20 mbps.

Repeaters, bridges, routers, and gateways

You might never need to know much about repeaters, bridges, routers, and gateways if you only have a small system. But just in case, I will discuss each of them briefly. Most of the hardware devices listed here also require special software. As is usually the case, the software might cost more than the hardware.

Repeaters

A *repeater* regenerates and amplifies a signal so it can travel the length of an additional segment of cable.

Here is why a repeater is necessary. First, depending on the type of cable, a signal will travel a finite distance before it starts to fade, decay, and become unintelligible. A signal on a thick Ethernet system can travel up to 500 meters, or 1,640 feet, before it begins to fade. On a thin Ethernet, it begins to fade after only 185 meters, or 606 feet. The same signal on UTP will last for only 100 meters, or 328 feet. These lengths of cable are called *segments*.

When the signal begins to fade, a repeater can regenerate and amplify the signal so that it can travel the length of an additional segment.

The signal might also pick up a lot of static, noise, and other unwanted analog voltages, especially those on a UTP system. A repeater can strip away the analog voltages, re-shape the square waves, and send out a good clean digital signal. A repeater can cost from $500 to $1,500.

Bridges

Bridges can be used to link two or more similar networks, act as repeaters, and have an intelligence. They can learn the addresses of the workstations on each side of the networks and only allow those that are addressed to the other side to cross over. A bridge can cost from $1,000 to $6,000 or more.

Routers

A *router* allows communication between two networks using different protocols. The router checks and converts packets of data between the different protocols and sends them to the proper address. A router can cost from $1,500 to $6,000 or more.

A *brouter* combines the functions of a bridge and a router.

Gateways

Gateways can be used to link very different types of networks together. The gateway checks each packet and converts it to the proper protocol to which it is addressed. It is often used to link PC networks to mainframes.

The bottom line

If you can afford to wait a few microseconds, ARCnet is the least expensive system to set up and is very trustworthy and reliable as it plods along at 2.5 mbps.

The Ethernet thin coaxial system is the next choice if you only have a few computers. It will cost just a bit more than ARCnet, but it will zip along at 10 mbps. If you must connect several computers over a long distance, you might consider going with Ethernet over UTP.

Sources

Several catalogs are listed in chapter 1. If you overlooked them and did not subscribe, I suggest that you do so now. The catalogs are free, but they have invaluable information for any person who is just getting started in networking. You should also be subscribing to several magazines, such as those listed in chapter 13.

Chapter 5

Cables

Cables are a vital part of the network. I talked briefly about cables in the previous chapter but because they are so important, you should learn more about them.

Depending on the type of system you choose, cables can represent a major portion of the system cost. In a large company, a network might cost from $300 to $1,000 per node. You shouldn't skimp on the quality of the cables. Try to get the best you can. According to some studies, cables and connectors can be the cause of over 30 percent of all downtime.

Your LAN plan

You should plan well for the cabling. Draw a diagram and calculate the distances between each station. This plan should include the distances around corners, up the walls, and all other necessary lengths. You should allow an extra 5 to 10 feet at each workstation in case you want to move the computer.

The plan should try to place the cable so that it will not be exposed to traffic or rough handling. It should be run along baseboards in a plastic or metal conduit. There might be times when it will have to be installed beneath a carpet to reach a station. *Flat cables* can be used for this type of installation.

You might have to drill holes in walls, put in false floors, or pull the cable through drop-down ceiling panels. If there is a possibility of a future expansion, install extra cables. It is fairly easy to pull several cables through at once, but can be very difficult to go back later and pull more through.

It appears that most systems will eventually use unshielded twisted pair (UTP) cables, the same type of cabling used by telephone companies. Even if you are installing coaxial cable now, it might be a good idea to install a bundle of twisted pair. You might even consider laying in a fiberoptic cable for future use.

Types of cables

The main type of cables used in a LAN are shielded twisted pair, unshielded twisted pair, and thick and thin Ethernet.

Shielded

You can choose from several different types of shielded cable. The cable will have a central copper wire encased in a fairly large *dielectric* insulation (see glossary). There is usually a braided wire shield over this and a plastic insulation overall. The shield is usually grounded on both ends, so that any stray noise or radiation from the transmitted signal is shunted to ground.

Impedance   The type of insulation around the central core of the wire and between the shield will determine the impedance of the cable. *Impedance* is a combination of the resistance of the center wire to the passage of electrons, the capacitance between the center wire and the shield, and the inductance between the center wire and the shield.

The frequency of the transmitted signal will also affect the impedance. The cables will need an *impedance-matching resistor termination*, which is a small cap that comes with the cable and must be on the first and last node of the network. For example, if you have 10 workstations, you will only need two impedance-matching resistors.

Ethernet thick and thin cables

Both thick and thin coaxial cables are used on Ethernet. There is no official RG designation for thick cables, but it is similar to RG-213 and is defined by IEEE 802.3. The thick cable, which has a distinctive yellow color, is large and difficult to bend, so it can be difficult to install in cramped places.

The thin Ethernet cable is fairly flexible and is similar to the cable used by cable TV systems.

Here are some Ethernet cable IEEE 802.3 specifications:

10Base5 Specifications for thick cable with a 50-ohm impedance. The *10* indicates a frequency of 10 mbps. The *base* means *baseband*, a transmission system where the entire bandwidth of the cable system is used for the single signal. This system is simple when compared to broadband where several channels might be used on the single cable for transmission such as in cable TV. The *5* means that the maximum cable length between repeaters is 500 meters, or 1640 feet.

10Base2 Specifications for thin cable with a 50-ohm impedance. *10Base* means the same as above. The *2* means that maximum cable length is almost 200 meters. (It is actually limited to 185 meters, or 607 feet).

AMP Corporation, (800) 522-6752, has an ingenious Thinnet Tap system shown in Fig. 5-1. This system allows you to easily connect to a thin coaxial cable.

10BaseT The *T* means twisted pair. These unshielded cables have a limit of about 100 meters, or about 325 feet. Figure 5-2 shows a thin shielded coaxial cable and some unshielded twisted pair cables.

Unshielded twisted pairs (UTPs)

Until recent times, unshielded twisted pair (UTP) cable was used only for low-frequency transmissions. UTP cable picks up static, line noise, and might emit illegal radiated emissions. This is especially so at higher frequencies. But several advances in filtering and repeater technologies have been developed. IBM's Token-Ring can operate reliably at 16 mbps over UTPs. ARCnet has a new 20 mbps system that will operate on UTPs.

The UTP cable uses the RJ45 plugs and jacks, which are similar to the RJ11 jacks used on the standard telephone, except that they are a bit larger and have six contacts, instead of the four on the telephone jack.

Figure 5-3 shows a couple of UTP RJ45 plugs and jacks from the AMP Corporation.

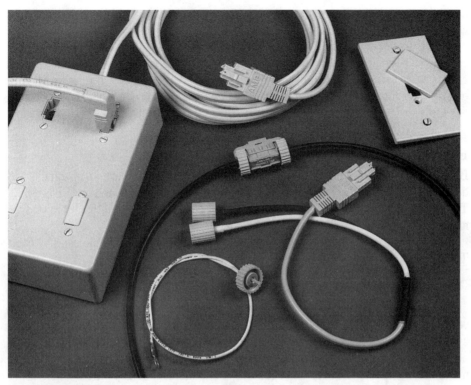

5-1 AMP Thinnet Tap system for making connections to a thin Ethernet line. (AMP)

5-2
Unshielded twisted pairs, or UTPs, (top) and thin coaxial wires (bottom).

Several large companies are experimenting with 100 mbps over UTP. An IEEE committee is studying a proposal to create a standard for it and eventually 100 mbps over UTP will be commonplace.

There can be a significant amount of signal loss in UTPs, so the high-frequency UTPs are limited to about 100 meters in distance between stations or repeaters. The repeaters strip all of the noise and analog voltages from the data signals. They then amplify the signal back up to its original value. The cost of UTP cable is very reasonable at 5 to 10 cents per foot.

Why they are twisted When two parallel wires carry electrical voltages, capacitive and inductive forces build up between the two wires. These factors can

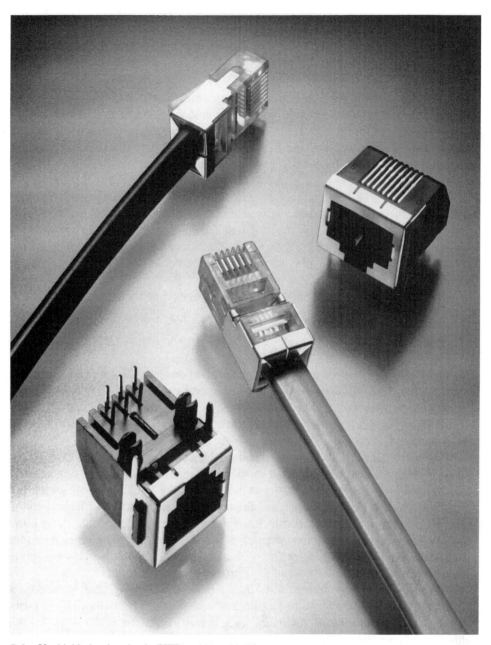

5-3 Unshielded twisted pair (UTP) cables with RJ45 connectors. (AMP)

cause deterioration and possible corruption of the data. The higher the frequency, the more pronounced these effects. Twisting the two wires helps to cancel out the capacitive and inductive effects.

Shielded vs. unshielded twisted pairs

As with most things in life, there are advantages and disadvantages in choosing the type of cable and system to install. The thick-shielded cable will let you install up to 1,024 workstations. To attach this many workstations, you attach up to 100 transceivers. Each transceiver can have as many as eight ports for the attachment of workstations. A transceiver can cost $300 to $1,000 or more, depending on the number of ports.

The thin Ethernet cable will allow you to attach up to 30 devices on each 600-foot segment. Additional workstations can be added by installing a single or multiport repeater. UTP systems require a wiring hub and are installed in a star topology. A wiring hub for UTP can cost from $500 up to $2,000 depending on the number of ports and whether the hub has goodies such as intelligent configuration and switching. A hub might also be called a *concentrator*.

Repeaters can cost from $600 to $3,000, depending on the number of ports and brand.

Cable costs

Shielded cable offers the best insulation and protection from noise and interference. It can support transmissions up to several megabits per second and allows greater distances between repeaters. But shielded cable can be expensive. It might cost one to two dollars or more per foot. If you have a 10Base5 network of 1,640 feet, the cable alone could cost over $3,000.

One cable company advertises a standard thick cable, 76.8 feet long for $102, or $186 for a high-temperature type that can be installed in a *plenum* (some type of duct, such air duct or heater duct). A 230-foot cable is $210 or $462 for the plenum type. They list several other lengths that are already made up. If you want custom lengths other than their preassembled lengths, they will cut them to your specified length and install the connectors. This company charges $58 plus 70 cents a foot for each custom thick cable and $58 plus $1.80 for the thick plenum custom lengths. This amount is about $10 per cable over the cost of their preassembled cables.

This same company charges $14.75 for a 6-foot thin RG-58 cable, $16.50 for a 15-foot one, and $19.50 for a 30-foot preassembled cable. A custom length costs $13.25 plus 25 cents per foot. A plenum grade thin RG-58 custom cable costs $13.25 plus 52 cents per foot.

They advertise bulk thin cable for 25 cents per foot, or 52 cents per foot for the plenum type. If your network requires several cables, it might be worthwhile to order a bulk roll of cable and connectors and make your own. It is really not that difficult to attach the connectors. You will be able to make them to the optimum lengths. You might have to buy some tools. But if you have a lot of cables to make up, you will save quite a lot of money.

Cost considerations

There are so many variables and choices you can see why it is so difficult to even estimate what a large network system would cost. The standard thick Ethernet cable is expensive, and you need transceivers, but you can attach up to 1,024 devices to a single 500-meter or 1,640-foot trunk.

Thin Ethernet is easier to handle and is less expensive, but you are limited to 30 devices for every 185 meters, or 607 feet, in length. If you are only going to have 5 to 30 workstations, the thin Ethernet is probably the best for you because you don't need a hub.

The UTP cable is the least expensive, but you must use a hub with UTP. The hub can have 10 to 30 ports that branch out in a star topology, but these systems are limited to 100 meters, or about 325 feet, in length. For medium-to-large systems, UTP seems to be the most popular type of system today.

Figure 5-4 from AMP Corporation shows a shielded token ring cable and connector on the left, a UTP with an RJ45 connector in the center, and a thin coaxial with a BNC connector on the right.

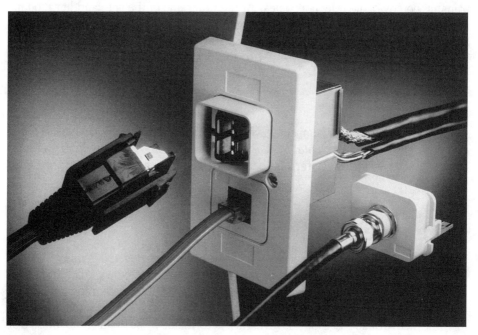

5-4   Three different types of cables: token ring shielded, unshielded twisted pair (UTP), and thin Ethernet. (AMP)

Digital vs. analog

High-frequency transmissions would not be possible with analog data. *Analog voltages* go up and down and can vary continuously. Voltage due to noise and interference is difficult to filter out because it is in the form of analog voltages.

Digital data is usually in the form of square waves. The data may go from the baseline zero up to about 5 volts, remain there for a certain length of time then return to 0. Remember that the signals depend on the precise timing of the computer clock. When the wave goes up, it can represent a 1, if it stays at the baseline for a certain period of time, it can represent a 0. If it goes up and stays up twice as long as normal, it can represent two 1s. Of course, if it stays at the baseline for twice as long, it can represent two 0s. Because the digital data is in the form of square waves, any analog voltage can be filtered out and removed.

Modems

One reason it is difficult to send data over telephone lines is that the telephone was designed for analog voice signals. This means that it has a very low frequency bandwidth, up to about 20 kbps. The only way you can send digital data over phone lines at the present time is with modems.

Modem is a contraction of the words *modulate* and *demodulate*. The modem takes the digital signal and modulates, or transforms, it into an analog signal for transmission over the telephone lines. At the other end of the line, another modem demodulates the analog signal back to a digital form. While traveling over the lines in an analog form, the data is subjected to static, noise, and other spurious analog voltages. These foreign voltages add to the analog data voltage. It is difficult to separate them.

ISDN

Eventually the telephone companies will install digital network phone lines. This is called *Integrated Services Digital Network* (ISDN). Some areas of the country already have it. ISDN will allow faster and better communications without the noise and static.

Wire types

Wire and cable manufacturers have developed several grades and levels of UTPs. Level 1 is the regular telephone type for voice. Level 2 can support data transmissions up to 4 megabits per second (mbps). Level 3 can support data transmissions up to 4 mbps. Level 4 is the type of cable recommended for the 16 mbps token ring and for Ethernet 10BaseT LANs. The levels are determined by such things as the size of the wire, the number of twists per foot, and the insulation.

IBM has developed standards for several types of cables. Like most things IBM, they are of high quality and expensive. The following are IBM's type descriptions:

- *Type 1*. Cable shielded with two twisted pairs of solid wire. The solid wire is easy to strip, but is not as flexible as stranded wire.
- *Type 2*. Four unshielded pairs of solid wire for voice telephone and two pairs of shielded wires.

- *Type 3*. Four unshielded twisted pairs for voice or data. This is the type often used for UTPs up to 4 mbps.
- *Type 4*. Used for 16 mbps UTP.
- *Type 5*. Two fiberoptic strands.
- *Type 6*. Shielded cable with two twisted pairs of stranded wire.
- *Type 8*. A special flat twisted pair that is designed to be laid under carpets.
- *Type 9*. Two shielded twisted pairs covered with a special flame-retardant coating for use in plenums.

American Wire Gauge (AWG)

Most wire and cables conform to the American Wire Gauge (AWG). The smaller the number of the AWG, the larger the diameter of the wire, the less the resistance to the signal. Most of the UTPs will be 22, 24, or 26 AWG. The 22 AWG is larger than the other ones and would, therefore, have less resistance than the 26. You should use 22 or 24 if possible.

The wires might be solid or made up of very fine strands. The stranded wire is much more flexible, but it might be difficult to use it with some connectors, especially the *punch down block* connectors used by the telephone company. The punch down block connector has a flat piece of copper with a slit. The wires are pressed into the slit, which cuts through the plastic insulation and makes a good pressure contact. This type of connection is fast and reliable.

You might be able to use the standard telephone lines that are already installed in your building. Quite often a cable with four wires is used when the telephone lines are installed. Most telephones only use two of the four lines. The 10BaseT specification uses the standard telephone RJ11 connectors, just like the ones on your telephone and on telephone extension lines. You can buy a telephone extension line for a very nominal sum at any hardware or department store. You might be tempted to use these lines, but it could cause trouble because they are not twisted.

The type 3 UTP cable has two pairs of wires and is advertised for 5 cents per foot. You can also buy type 3 cable with three or four pairs of wires.

Fiber Distributed Data Interface (FDDI)

The *Fiber Distributed Data Interface* (FDDI) usually refers to glass fiberoptic cables. A beam of light can be introduced into a glass fiberoptic cable and it will stay inside the fiber, go around bends and turns and come out the other end.

Light can be turned on and off just like a voltage. If a light is turned on for a period of time, it can represent a 1. If it is turned off for a period of time it can represent a 0. Lasers can produce light that can be turned on and off hundreds of millions of times per second.

It is fairly simple to use digital data to turn a laser on and off to produce a laser light beam that is an exact replica of the digital data. So the digital voltage can be converted to light beams between stations, then back to digital voltage when it reaches its assigned address. The FDDI system uses a token system that is similar to the token ring system. Figure 5-5, from the AMP Corporation, shows an FDDI fiberoptic cable and connectors.

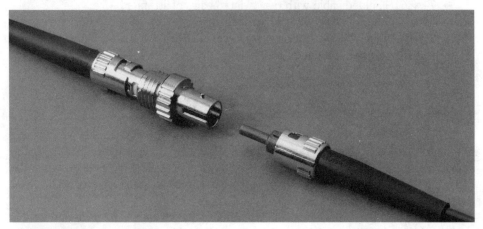

5-5 A fiberoptic cable. (AMP)

Fiberoptic cables are being used by several telephone companies in some areas, but they are expensive and difficult, so don't expect to see them nationwide for some time.

Some large networks are using FDDI for the backbone connections between bridges because it can carry a lot of data for long distances.

The fiberoptic cables are immune to noise and interference and do not radiate any emissions. They can operate at a very high frequency so a lot of data can be transmitted in a very short time. They offer good security because they are difficult to tap.

Some of the disadvantages of FDDI are that the fiberoptic cable is very expensive and it is very difficult to install connectors and hardware on fiberoptics. The connections are very critical and demand very close tolerances in the installation of the connectors.

The FDDI standard for transmission is 100 megabits per second (mbps). Some companies are experimenting with sending data that meet the FDDI standard over UTPs. It appears that with the newer technologies, data can be reliably transmitted over copper wire at 100 mbps. The distances over copper between repeaters will probably be limited to 100 meters or less.

Unless you have a very large system, you probably will not need FDDI at this time. But considering how fast the technology changes, you might need it tomorrow.

Wireless LANs

There are several reasons why you might want to install a wireless LAN. You might be in a building where it is difficult to lay cables or you might not be able to cut holes in the walls. You might have an asbestos ceiling, in which case you must be very careful and follow prescribed safety measures. You might have a situation where you have to move frequently, so any cables would have to be pulled out and reinstalled. There might be any number of other reasons why you might not be able to install cables.

Infrared and *radio frequency* are the two main types of wireless LANs.

Infrared

The remote control that you use with your TV uses an infrared light signal to change the channels. The remote control has transistor circuits that turn the infrared light on and off to create digital signals. The TV set has an eye that receives these signals and the signals are fed to a transistor circuit that causes the TV to respond.

Infrared can also be used to transmit digital data from a LAN. Such a system can be set up in a large open area office without expensive and unsightly cables. Each station would have a receiver and transmitter on an elevated pole or other object that would provide unimpeded direct line of sight to each station.

One of the disadvantages of the infrared systems is that there can be nothing between the stations that would block the light so you couldn't connect stations in different rooms or on different floors of a building and they are limited in the distance that they can travel.

BICC Communications, (800) 447-6526, manufactures InfraLAN, an infrared wireless system that works with LAN Manager, NetBIOS, VINES, and NetWare. It works with token ring and transmits data at 16 mbps for 80 meters, or about 263 feet, in a clear line of sight. Each device can support up to six users, for a total of 72. Each connection costs $400.

Photonics, (408) 370-3033, manufactures Photolink, an infrared wireless system for Macintoshes. It works with AppleTalk and transmits data at 238 kbps for 600 feet and can support up to four devices, for a total of up to 32 users. Each board lists for $1,195.

Radio frequency

Several companies are now manufacturing systems that use high-frequency radio waves. The FCC has been petitioned to assign a band of frequencies specifically for wireless networks.

The Black Box Corporation, (412) 746-5565, advertises a wireless radio system that can transmit up to 800 feet. It can penetrate most walls, even some metal ones. The system works with Ethernet, token ring, or ARCnet. The adapter cards are rather expensive at $1,390 each.

The NCR Company, (513) 445-1847, manufactures WaveLAN for PC and PS/2 workstations, with a list price of $1,390.

The Proxim Company, (415) 960-1630, manufactures RangeLAN, which costs $495 for each card.

Good news/bad news

A big advantage of wireless systems is that they are easy to install. The disadvantages are that some of these systems are limited to about 2 mbps and are still rather expensive. It is expected, however, that the prices will come down as more of them are installed.

Tools

You will probably need a few basic tools for installing your cables. Some were already mentioned in chapter 1. Here they are again plus a few more:

- *Drill with several bits.*
- *Hole saw* to use with the drill.
- *Wall plates* so that the cable just plugs into a connector.
- *Hammer.*
- *Screwdrivers.*
- *Pliers.*
- *Cables.* If you are installing a small system, you might be able to get by with preassembled cables. Many of the cable companies offer several lengths. But if you have a fairly complex system that will involve several lengths, you will probably be better off buying a bulk roll of wire and installing the connectors yourself. It is fairly easy to do.
- *Wire cutters and strippers.*
- *Soldering iron.*
- *Crimpers* for installing various types of connectors onto the cables. Figure 5-6, from AMP Corporation, shows a crimper for installing BNC connectors. Figure 5-7, from AMP Corporation, shows BNC connectors that have been crimped.
- *Ohmmeter.* One of the most important tools you will need. It is used to measure the continuity of your cables. You can check each cable to make sure that it is okay. You might even buy two ohmmeters so that you can check the system after it is installed, with an ohmmeter at each end of the system. This check can tell you immediately if there is a break in any of the cables or if any are not connected properly. You can buy a low-cost general purpose ohmmeter at any Radio Shack or other electronic parts store.

Catalogs

Several companies offer special tools for cables, electronics, computers, plant maintenance, and many other needs. The AMP Corporation, (800) 522-6752, supplied the photos for this chapter. Call for AMP's large catalog. The company has wire, cables, hubs, tools, and other network supplies. Another company is the Jensen Company, (602) 968-6231. Call for its comprehensive catalog.

The catalogs mentioned at the end of chapter 1 also have cables and tools.

5-6 A hand crimper needed to attach BNC connectors. (AMP)

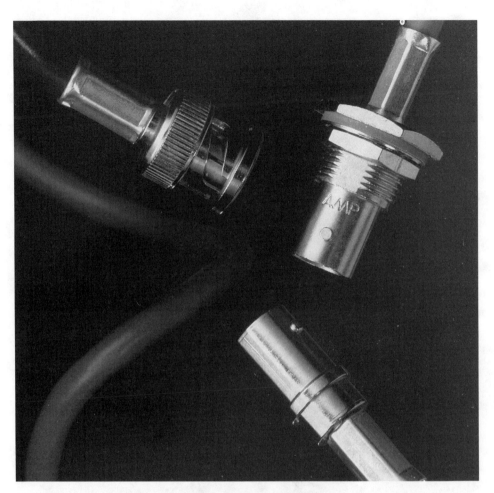

5-7 BNC connectors that have been crimped onto a cable. (AMP)

Chapter 6

Building your own server and workstations

You can save an estimated $1,000 or more on a server and four workstations if you buy the components and assemble them yourself. In this chapter, you will learn how to do this cost-saving assembly. You should find that it is easy to do.

Anyone can do it

If you are not too familiar with the innards of a computer, you might have some doubts about being able to build your own server and workstations. But believe me, anyone can do it. It takes no special skills or expertise.

Once you have bought all of the components, it will take you less than an hour to plug them together. No soldering, wiring, or electronic testing is required.

Literally thousands of different options are available to you when you build a LAN yourself. Of course, this variety might cause a problem if you have trouble making up your mind as to what you want. To help you decide, I'll explain several options in this chapter.

Cost

As I've said before, determining how much a system will cost is difficult to determine exactly. It will depend on how well you shop, the brands of the components, and what you want your computer to do.

The cost will also depend on the market. The market is so volatile the prices change almost hourly. I list some approximate costs. You can get an idea of the current prices by checking the ads in computer magazines. I have included a list of magazines in chapter 13 that will help keep you current with this ever-changing technology.

The all-important motherboard

All of the systems, whether PCs, XTs, 286s, 386s, or 486s, use basic components that are all similar. The primary difference among the systems is the motherboard. This most-important board determines the type of computer. The standard motherboard has eight slots for plug-in boards, such as network adapters, monitor adapters, disk controllers, and other devices. All of the slots have 62-pin connectors for the standard 8-bit PC bus. For 16-bit systems there are additional 36-pin connectors in front of some of the 62-pin connectors.

XT motherboards

XT motherboards use the Intel 8088 central processing unit (CPU). The XT (for eXtended Technology) is a second-generation PC introduced by IBM in 1983. Its CPU has 29,000 transistors, an amazing number at that time, and supports up to

640K of RAM. It can address only one megabyte of RAM, 640K of low RAM and 384K of high RAM that DOS reserves for video, BIOS, and other functions.

At the time it was first introduced, the XT operated at 4.77 MHz. Most of the XT systems today operate at from 8 to 12 MHz, but because they are 8-bit systems, they are still slow for many operations. However, it is fine for applications such as word processing or as a printer server. It is the least expensive system that you can buy or put together. An XT motherboard can cost as little as $45 but the XT is obsolete. There is such a small cost difference between the XT and the 286 that I would recommend you build the 286 or 386SX for workstations.

If you have an old XT, you could pull the motherboard out and replace it with a 286, 386SX, 386DX, 486SX, or 486DX. Any of these boards would give you a much more powerful and more useful computer. Figure 6-1 shows an XT motherboard. There might be a slight size difference between the XT and 286, 386, and 486 motherboards, but the mounting holes and slot positions are standard. So any motherboard can be exchanged with any other one.

AT or 286 motherboards

IBM introduced the AT (for Advanced Technology) in 1984. It uses the Intel 80286 CPU, which has 125,000 transistors and is a 16-bit system that can address up to 16Mb.

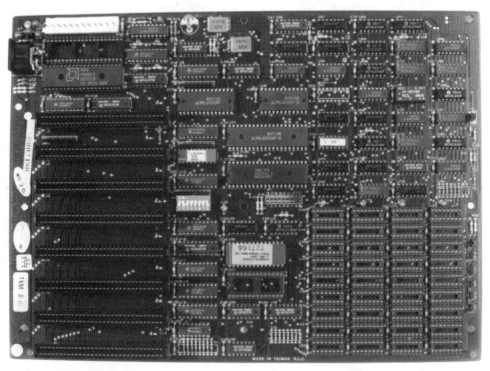

6-1 An XT motherboard.

When you run a program, it is loaded into RAM where it is manipulated, changed, or altered. Ordinarily, only one program at a time can be loaded into memory. If two programs were loaded, the data from each one would become mixed with the other and both programs would be hopelessly corrupted. But with the proper software, the 286 can operate in a protected mode. The protected mode allows the CPU to set up several separate 640K areas in RAM. A program can then be run in each of the 640K areas simultaneously.

The original 286 operated at 6 MHz. It now operates at 12 MHz, 16 MHz, 20 MHz, and 25 MHz. The 12 MHz motherboards can cost as little as $70, so this is the best choice for an inexpensive workstation.

If you have an older 286, you can upgrade it by replacing the motherboard with a 386SX, 386DX, 486SX, or 486DX. Figure 6-2 shows a 286 motherboard alongside a 386 motherboard. The original 286 AT board was about twice the size of this one. But using VLSI (very large scale integration) chips allowed them to reduce it.

The 286, 386, and 486 are all called AT systems.

The 386DX and 386SX

The original 286 and 386 standard motherboard and case was larger than the XT. But with advances in (VLSI), today most motherboards have been shrunk to a size as small as, or smaller than, the original XT motherboard.

6-2   A 286 motherboard (on the left) alongside a 386 motherboard.

Many, many options are available for both the 386SX and 386DX motherboards. The primary difference in the SX motherboard is that the 386SX has a 16-bit memory bus, while the 386DX has a 32-bit memory bus. The 386SX operates at a frequency of 16 MHz, 20 MHz, or 25 MHz; the 386DX at 25 MHz, 33 MHz, or 40 MHz.

With the Intel doubler, the 386DX will operate as high as 66 MHz. Both systems might offer options for built-in features and functions, such as on-board cache, IDE (Integrated Disk Electronics) hard disk interface, on-board cache, parallel and serial ports, game and mouse ports, VGA monitor driver, and other features. At the present time, the SX motherboards cost from $125 to $400.

Figure 6-3 shows a 386SX motherboard designed for the low-profile case. It has a single slot in the middle. A daughterboard, which provides additional work capacity, plugs into this slot. The daughterboard has three slots on one side and two on the other so that boards can be plugged in horizontally. It might be difficult to plug in five full-size boards in the daughterboard. This allows the overall height of the case to be about 1½ inches lower than standard cases.

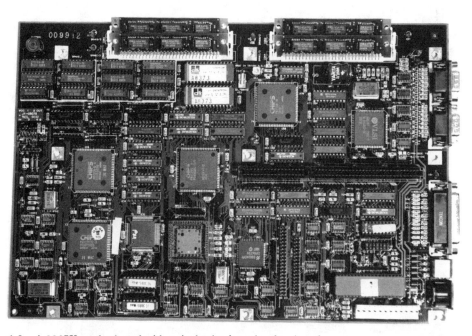

6-3 A 386SX motherboard with a single slot for a daughterboard.

I don't like these systems. I have lots of height over my desk so I don't mind the case being a little higher. On the plus side, this motherboard has a built-in IDE interface for controlling two hard disks, a built-in floppy disk controller, and built-in parallel and serial ports.

Figure 6-4 shows my first 386 motherboard. It was full size and cost $1,825 in 1987. Figure 6-5 shows a newer, "baby-size" (smaller than standard) 386DX

6-4 My first 386 motherboard.

6-5 A baby size 386 motherboard.

motherboard. Depending on speed, cache, and manufacturer, the 386DX mother-board might now cost from $300 to $700.

Cache

When running a program the CPU often loops in and out of memory many times, often using the same memory over and over. If a small *cache* (memory storage area) of high-speed memory is set up for the most-often-used memory, it can speed up the system considerably. Cache systems are usually found only on the 386 and 486 motherboards. The motherboard must be designed for a cache system, so not all of them have it. They usually cost a bit more, but they might be well worth it, especially for a server system.

Coprocessors

A *coprocessor* is a special-purpose processor chip that works in conjunction with the primary CPU to speed up time-consuming tasks. A coprocessor reduces the processing time of certain applications by as much as 500 percent. The software must be designed to take advantage of a coprocessor. Most of the spreadsheet, graphics, CAD, database, and hundreds of other programs will make use of a coprocessor if it is present. At this time, the cost of a 387SX-16 is about $100 and a 387SX-20 is about $120. A 387DX-25 and 387DX-33 are about $200.

486SX And 486DX

The 486DX CPU chip has 1,200,000 transistors on it. It is much more powerful than the 386. It has an 8K cache built into it. It processes data more efficiently than the 386 so that a 25-MHz 486 can outperform a 33-MHz 386. The 486DX has a built-in coprocessor that is not in the 486SX, which is the primary difference between them.

There is only a small price difference in the 486DX and the 486SX. The 486SX motherboard costs from $400 to $700. The 486DX is selling at a price of $600 to $900. If you can afford the price difference, I would recommend the 486DX. Figure 6-6 shows my first 486 motherboard. It was the standard AT size and had no built-in goodies at all, not even a printer port. I paid $4,450 for it in 1988. How times have changed. The newer 486 motherboards are the same small size as the original XT.

The 486DX can outperform some minicomputers. It is ideal for servers, or any application where you need speed and power. The 486 motherboards can be either Industry Standard Architecture (ISA) or Extended Industry Standard Architecture (EISA).

Industry Standard Architecture (ISA)

Industry Standard Architecture (ISA) is what used to be known as the IBM-AT standard. One of the greatest advantages of ISA systems is the extraordinary versatility and flexibility that it offers. At least $10 billion dollars worth of IBM-compatible, or ISA, computer components are in existence.

Most of the ISA components are interchangeable. You can take any board or peripheral from a genuine IBM XT or AT and plug it into any of the clones and it will

6-6 My first 486 motherboard.

work. You can also plug any of the components found in a clone into a genuine IBM or another clone and it will work. Because there are so many clone products and vendors, they are readily available almost anywhere. Because there is so much competition, they are relatively inexpensive.

ISA, EISA, and MCA

The original 8-bit PC and XT boards and motherboard slot connectors had 31 contacts on each side for a total of 62. This bus was more than sufficient for the power, grounds, refresh cycles, RAM, ROM, and all of the other I/O functions. When IBM introduced the 16-bit AT, several other new bus functions were added. IBM needed the 62 pins already in use on the bus, plus several more for the new functions. It needed a larger connector but a new connector could obsolete all of the hardware that was available at that time. IBM came up with a brilliant design. It simply added a second 36-pin connector in front of the standard 62-pin, providing a dual-purpose socket for 8-bit boards with 62 contacts, or for 16-bit boards with 98 contacts.

When the 32-bit 386 was introduced, IBM still used the 16-bit AT standard bus. But again, more contacts were needed. IBM added a second 62-pin slot connector in front of another one to provide 124 contacts for special 32-bit memory boards. Most manufacturers have abandoned this design. Most boards today have SIMM (single memory modules) or SIP (single inline package) (sockets with 32-bit bus lines for on-board memory. Except for the 32-bit memory bus, all of the 286, 386, and 486 ISA systems still use a 16-bit bus for ordinary data input/output (I/O).

In 1987, IBM introduced its PS/2 line with Micro Channel Architecture (MCA). This system added many new functions to the computer and required more connector contacts. But this time IBM designed a new bus and connector system that was completely incompatible with the billions of dollars worth of available hardware. Users were in about the same situation as the Apple users—they had only one vendor and the prices were very high.

It was readily admitted that the MCA offered some real advantages over the original IBM standard. One of the excellent features of the MCA system is the Programmed Option Select (POS). The MCA plug-in boards have a unique identification (ID) and when a board is plugged in, the bus recognizes it by its ID and automatically configures the board for use with the system interrupts, ports, and other system configurations. Or if there are any switches on the board, it will tell you how they should be set. One of the most difficult problems faced when installing a network adapter is configuring it to work in the system. The auto ID eliminates this problem.

MCA offers several other very good features such as *bus arbitration*, a system that evaluates bus requests and allocates time on a priority level. This feature relieves the CPU of some of its burdens. The MCA bus is also much faster than the original AT bus.

Although there are a few clones and a few third-party MCA boards, IBM is still the main source.

EISA manufacturers

IBM's MCA was a system that was no longer compatible with a large number of clone manufacturers. Many large corporate users abandoned the clones and adopted the IBM PS/2 systems because of the added functionality. It was clear that the manufacturers of clones were being hurt.

A group of IBM-compatible computer manufacturers got together and developed the Extended Industry Standard Architecture (EISA). This group included Advanced Logic Research (ALR), AST Research, Compaq Computer, Epson America, Everex Systems, Hewlett-Packard, Olivetti, Micronics, NEC, Tandy, Wyse Technology, and Zenith. This new standard includes the bus speed, arbitration, bus mastering, programmed option select, and most of the other functions found on the MCA. But unlike the MCA, the EISA bus is downward compatible. The new

EISA standard is designed so that the older-style XT and AT boards can still be used. It doesn't matter whether your boards are 8 bit, 16 bit, or 32 bit, the EISA bus will accept them.

In some areas, the EISA system will outperform the MCA system. But one of the biggest advantages of EISA over the MCA is that it is compatible with the billions of dollars worth of hardware produced earlier.

The EISA connector

I noted earlier that IBM designed the 16-bit AT bus by simply adding an extra 36-pin connector to the 8-bit, 62-pin connector. This idea was excellent because all of the earlier 8-bit boards could still be used.

The AT bus or ISA has 49 contacts per side, or 98 total. Each contact is 0.06 inches wide with 0.04 inches space between them. The total connector contact area of a board is 5.3 inches long.

The IBM MCA system needed 116 contacts, but IBM designed the MCA board by miniaturizing the contacts. Each of the MCA board contacts is 0.03 inches wide with 0.02 inches space between them. This is just half the space that is between contacts on the ISA boards. IBM put 116 contacts in a board only 2.8 inches long, which is about half the size of the ISA 16-bit connector area. All of the older ISA boards are completely unusable in the MCA system.

The EISA system also needed more contacts, so it added 100 more, for a total of 198 contacts. Now there are 82 more contacts in EISA than in the IBM MCA, which gives EISA an opportunity to add more functions than is possible with the MCA system. EISA simply added an extra row of contacts on the plug-in EISA boards by extending the contact area below the standard 98 ISA contacts. It connected the lower EISA contacts with etched lines in the 0.04-inch spaces between the 98 ISA contacts.

Unlike the MCA system, the EISA connector is designed so that it is compatible with all of the previous 8- and 16-bit boards, as well as the new 32-bit EISA board. The company achieved this result by designing a socket that was twice as deep as the original ISA slot or connector socket. This new socket has two sets of contacts, one set at the bottom of the socket for the added contacts and a set at the top portion for the original 98 contacts. At certain locations across the bottom of the socket, narrow tab projections act as keys. These tabs prevent an 8- or 16-bit board from being inserted to the full depth of the socket. The contacts of the 8- and 16-bit boards, therefore, mate with only the upper contacts.

The EISA boards have notches cut in them to coincide with the keys on the floor of the EISA socket. This way, the EISA boards can be inserted to the full depth so that both sets of contacts mate in the connector.

Do you need an EISA motherboard? The EISA motherboard provides much more speed, power, and functionality than the ISA, but it is more expensive. An EISA system is still much less expensive than an equivalent IBM PS/2 system.

Motherboard costs

Here are the approximate costs of the various motherboards:

Item	Cost (in dollars)
XT	50–60
286	70–90
386SX	120–300
386DX	300–700
486SX	400–700
486DX	600–900
486EISA	1,200–1,600

Common components

The common components of the computer are components such as the case, power supply, RAM memory sockets, monitor, multifunction boards, floppy disk drives, disk controllers, keyboard, and optional components.

Cost of common components

Here are the approximate costs of components other than the motherboards that are common to all systems:

Item	Cost (in dollars)
Case	30–105
Power supply	40–70
Monitor	65–900
Monitor adapter	40–200
Multifunction board	40–200
Floppy disk drive, 1.4Mb	50–75
Floppy disk drive, 1.2Mb	50–75
Hard disk 40Mb–300Mb	150–995
Disk controller	20–150
Keyboard	30–150
Total	515–2,920

To find the approximate cost of a system, add the cost of whatever motherboard you choose to the cost of the common components.

As you can see, the cost can vary widely, depending on the particular components. There is also a large variation in cost from dealer to dealer. Some of the high-volume dealers charge much less than the smaller ones, so it will pay you to shop around a bit and compare prices. These figures are only rough approximations. The market is so volatile that the prices can change overnight. If you are buying through the mail you might even call or check out the advertised prices before ordering. Often the advertisements have to be made one or two months before the magazine is published, so the prices can change considerably.

Case

The *case* usually comes with a chassis and cover, a bag of hardware, a speaker, plastic standoffs, and guides. The case will usually have a switch panel that might or might not be assembled and mounted. The switch panel will usually have a set of keys and a lock that locks out the keyboard without shutting off the power. The panel might have several switches and light-emitting diode (LED) indicators with wires that plug into the motherboard and other boards. There will probably be a switch for the turbo mode, a reset switch, a power LED indicator, and an LED for the hard disk activity.

Case-switch panel wires   You might have trouble connecting the various wires from the switch panel to the motherboard. The case is not usually made by the same manufacturer who made the motherboard. The wires from the switch panel are not often marked. You will have to follow the connector back to the LED or switch to determine which is the correct one. The motherboard will have pins near the front of the board for these connections. The connection for the hard-disk activity LED will usually plug into the hard disk controller board, or on the motherboard if it has a built-in IDE interface. You should receive some documentation or a diagram with the case that shows where the wires should connect. The motherboard will also have markings near each pin connector.

Types of cases   Several different types and sizes of cases are available, including the original, large, standard AT desktop; the smaller XT size desktop type; and the low-profile desktop type. Several standing tower cases are also available—the mini tower, the medium-size tower, and the full-size tower.

You will only be able to use the low-profile desktop with a motherboard that is designed for them. These motherboards have a single slot that accepts a vertical plug-in daughterboard. This daughterboard has three slots on one side and two on the other side to plug boards in horizontally.

Number of bays   No matter what type of case you buy, you should make sure that it has at least four bays for mounting disk drives. You will need two bays that are accessible when the cover is installed for the floppy disk drives. You should have at least two for hard disks.

For a server you might want to mount an extra hard disk, a tape backup drive, or a CD-ROM (compact disc, read-only memory) drive. For this you will need more bays. Of course, the more bays, the larger the case. The large tower cases can have seven or more bays.

Some of the bays might have provisions for mounting the drives on their edges or vertically. The hard disks can be mounted almost any way except upside down.

Power supply

Many vendors sell the case and power supply as a single unit. Most units sold today have a capacity of at least 200 watts, which should be sufficient for most ordinary systems.

RAM memory sockets

Most of the AT motherboards have provisions for 8Mb to 32Mb of memory on the board and have sockets for one or more of the three types of memory: dual inline package (DIP), single inline package (SIP), or single memory modules (SIMM).

Most of the motherboards are sold without memory, or 0K. Make sure that you buy the type of memory that fits your motherboard. You should also make sure to get the right speed memory. The fast 386 or 486 will require a 70 to 80 nanosecond (ns) rating.

You probably should have a minimum of 2Mb on the workstations and 4Mb or more on a server. Memory is rather inexpensive at this time, about $35 per megabyte.

Monitor

You can buy a monochrome monitor for $65. It's okay for some uses, but I prefer color, even for word processing. I also prefer high resolution. If necessary, I would use the rent money and maybe skip a few meals in order to have a good high-resolution color monitor.

If your server is also going to be used as a workstation, it should definitely have a good color monitor. Even the workstations will give you better production if they are color. Almost all application programs, especially programs like Windows, are easier to use and run with color.

You can get a fairly good VGA monitor for about $250. Look for one with the smallest *dot pitch*, which is the size of the smallest dot that a monitor can display. Some low-cost monitors might have a 0.52 millimeter (mm) dot pitch, which has a very poor resolution. A 0.28 mm or 0.31 mm dot pitch is much better. The good brand-name monitors will cost from $500 to several thousand dollars, depending on size and resolution. Monitors are discussed in more detail in chapter 9.

Monitor adapter   The monitor must have a plug-in board to drive it. Several monitor adaptors on the market cost from $40 to over $400. For more details, see chapter 9.

Multifunction boards

If your motherboard does not have built-in functions, you will need a board to drive your printer. You will also need ports for a modem, an extra printer, or a mouse. Several different kinds of multifunction boards exist. Most of them have functions such as serial and parallel ports. Some have an IDE interface, floppy disk controller, VGA, and several other features. Depending on the functions and utilities that are on the boards, they will cost from $40 to $700.

I mentioned the AMT Computer, (714) 598-6120, Sigma Six multifunction board in chapter 3. This board has an Ethernet adapter, Super VGA monitor adapter, modem, fax, serial and parallel ports, and several other functions on it.

Floppy disk drives

Many vendors are still selling 360K and 720K floppy disk drives. These drives are obsolete. The 1.2Mb will read and write to the 360K, as well as 1.2Mb. The 1.44Mb will read and write to the 720K, as well as the 1.44Mb. If you only buy one drive, make sure it is a 1.2Mb.

Hard disks

Several companies manufacture hard disks and they produce many types and grades of quality. The hard disk is such an important part of the computer system that I have devoted all of chapter 7 to it and floppy disk drives.

Basically, you should select a well-known brand, with an access speed as fast as possible, and most important, with the largest capacity that you can afford.

Disk controllers

The disks drives, both hard and floppy, must have a *controller*. The best controllers have both hard and floppy disk controllers on a single plug-in card. The IDE and SCSI drives have most of the controller electronics built into the hard drives, but they still need an interface to connect to the motherboard.

Keyboards

Data can be input to a computer in several different ways, such as by modem, scanners, a mouse, and by voice. But the keyboard is, by far, the most often used and most important input device. It is your most intimate contact with your computer.

Several different types of keyboards are available. Some can cost as little as $50 or as much as $250. Some of the low-priced ones that I have seen seem to do as well as the high-priced ones.

Optional components

You should buy a *mouse* for each station. It is almost impossible to run Windows and many other software packages without a mouse. A mouse can cost from $30 to $75.

A *scanner* is almost as essential as a mouse. Scanners can scan images and drawings and some allow you to scan in text so that you don't have to type it. The scanner can save hours of work.

A *CD-ROM* drive can be a great reference tool. One can be installed on a server so the whole network can take advantage of it. Hundreds of new CD-ROM discs are available with things like encyclopedias, dictionaries, thesauruses, and writing guides. Plus discs on law, medicine, biology, and other sciences.

Depending on the type of business you might want a *plotter*. You can use this for designs and drawings. A plotter is usually essential for anyone doing CAD/CAM or architectural work.

You might also want a fax and modem system. These components are discussed in chapter 10.

Where to find the parts

Most large cities have computer stores. Check the advertisements in the newspapers and in the telephone directory. Keep in mind that most retail computer stores usually sell items at or near the suggested list price. The list price of some items might be almost twice as much as the "street" price. You must shop wisely.

If you live near a large city such as San Francisco, New York, or Dallas, you probably know that there is a computer swap going on almost every weekend. These swaps are among the better places to shop. You can compare prices, look the parts over, and even try them out in some cases. It is even possible to haggle a bit with the dealers, especially near closing time. Some will even sell the items at or near cost rather than pack them up and cart them back to the main store.

Another alternative is to look through mail-order advertisements in computer magazines. In the past, you would hear some horror stories about a few unethical mail-order companies. But mail-order and computer advertisements are the lifeblood of computer magazines. A few phony advertisements can ruin a magazine. The magazines today are very careful about the advertisements they accept. The vast majority of the advertisers are honest and will deliver as promised. Mail order and computer magazines are discussed in detail in chapter 13.

Before assembling the components

Once you have bought all of the components, it will take less than an hour to plug them together. Figure 6-4 shows my first 386 motherboard. Even with a good discount, the motherboard still cost me $1,825. It was one of the better-designed motherboards at that time, with several built-in features and one megabyte of RAM. It had a standard 16 MHz 386DX CPU, but it had been selected to run at 20 MHz.

I recently bought a 386DX motherboard that operates at 40 MHz for $385. Today I can buy a 386SX that runs at 16 MHz for $120. I paid $4,450 for my first 486DX motherboard shown in Fig. 6-6. It operated at 25 MHz and had no built-in goodies. Today I can buy a better 486DX motherboard with several built-in functions that runs at 40 MHz for only $700. Or I can buy a 25 MHz 486SX for $450, which is $4,000 less than I paid for my first 486 motherboard in 1989. That is tremendous drop in prices in a period of about three years.

The prices will probably drop even more because Intel now has some competition. At one time Intel was the only manufacturer of 386 CPU chips. The 386 CPU chip has 275,000 transistors, so it is not an easy task to clone one. But American Micro Devices (AMD) has succeeded and is now producing 386 clones. Chips and Technology (C&T) and several other companies are also producing 386 CPU clones.

The 486 CPU is even more difficult to clone than the 386. It has 1.2 million transistors on a small chip. But AMD and some of the other companies have succeeded in cloning the 486 and are starting up production.

This added competition is very good news for us, the consumers. Not only does the competition force the prices down, it forces the vendors to improve the products. Intel has recently announced a new chip that will double the frequency of the 486 so that it will operate at 50 to 66 MHz. At the time of this writing, Intel is scheduled to release its 586 CPU chip.

Assembling the components

The components that you buy might not look like those in the photos, but basically they are the same. No matter whether you are assembling a 286 or 486, they all go together basically the same way. You should get some documentation when you buy your components. By all means follow any special instructions.

When I first assemble a computer, I connect everything together on a bench top, or the kitchen table, before installing it in the case. You should do the same by performing the following tasks:

1. Connect the power supply to the motherboard and the disk drives.
2. Connect the drives to the controller and then connect the monitor.
3. Turn the computer on and make sure that everything works.

When the computer is on, it is fairly easy to find any problems. Everything usually works okay, so I then install it in the case. (How to install it in the case is discussed towards the end of the chapter.)

After you have followed the previous steps, it is time to begin assembling the computer. Assembly is primarily connecting different components to each other. In the next few sections are instructions for putting the components together.

Connecting power supply to motherboard

Be very careful in connecting cables. Some of them can be plugged in backwards. If you do, you could severely damage the components. Figure 6-7 shows the main power to the board being plugged in. Be careful here because it is possible to plug these two connectors in backwards. The connector marked P8 goes toward the back of the board, with the four black wires in the center.

Connecting the hard disk

The MFM and RLL hard disks have a 34-wire flat controller cable and a 20-wire data cable. Figure 6-8 shows some controller cables. The cable on the bottom is for floppy disk drives. Note that it has a twist in some of the wires. This connector goes to the A: drive. The connector in the middle of this cable goes to the B: drive. The cable in the middle is for hard disk drives and has a connector in the middle that can be used for a second hard disk.

The two cables at the upper part of the photo are data cables for the hard disk drives. The IDE and SCSI drives have only one 40- or 50-wire flat controller cable.

Figure 6-9 shows a controller cable being connected to the edge connector of a MFM 40Mb hard disk. Note the slot cut between contacts two and three in the edge connector. The flat 34-wire gray cable will have a different color wire—blue, black, or red—on one side. This different color wire goes to contact number one on the hard disk edge connector.

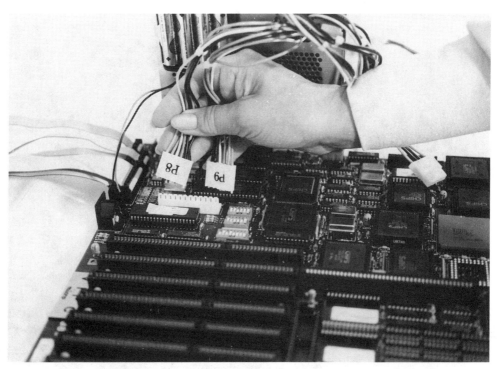

6-7 Plugging in the power to the motherboard.

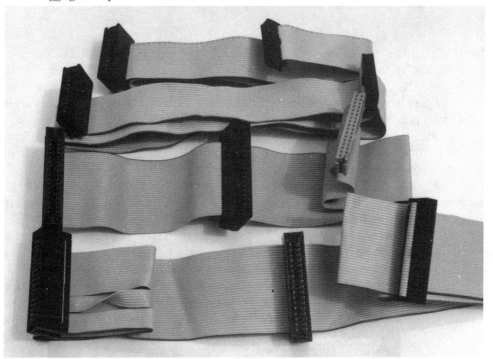

6-8 Some disk-drive cables.

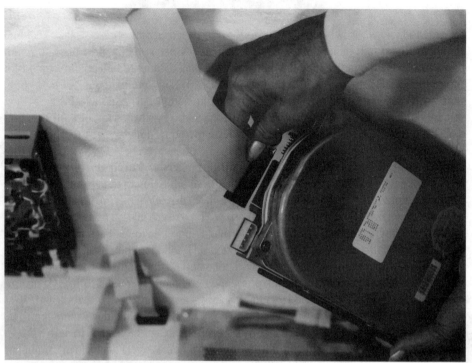

6-9 Attaching the controller cable to a hard drive.

The other end of the cable plugs into the hard disk controller board. See Fig. 6-10. The board should have some sort of marking to indicate pin one. Be very careful because this connector can possibly be plugged in backwards. This controller cable might have a connector in the middle of it. If so, it will be for a second hard disk drive if one is present.

Figure 6-11 shows the 20-wire data cable being connected to the hard disk edge connector. Note that it also can be plugged in backwards. This cable has a colored wire on one edge that indicates pin one.

Figure 6-12 shows the data cable being connected to the controller board. The controller board will have two sets of pins. If only one hard disk is used, the row of pins nearest the 34-wire connector is used. If a second hard disk is installed, then you'll have a second 20-wire data cable to connect to the row of pins near the front of the controller board.

Figure 6-13 shows the four-wire power cable being connected to the hard disk. It can only be plugged in one way. The power supply will have four of these identical cables for other hard drives and floppy disk drives. Your controller board might be different. You should have received some sort of documentation with your board. Check it and follow the instructions. If you bought an IDE-type hard disk, it will have only one cable and the controller or IDE interface might be built into the motherboard.

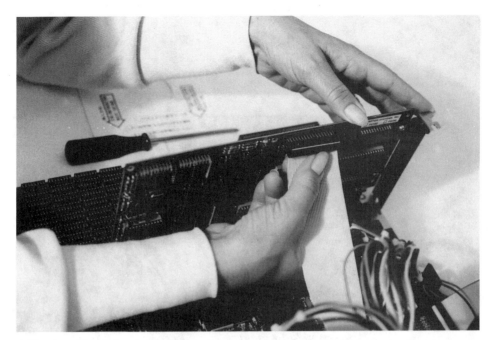

6-10   Attaching the controller cable to the controller card.

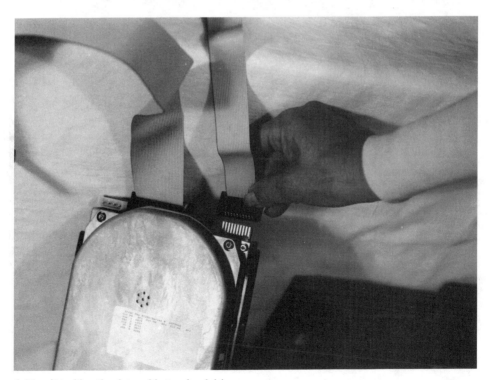

6-11   Attaching the data cable to a hard drive.

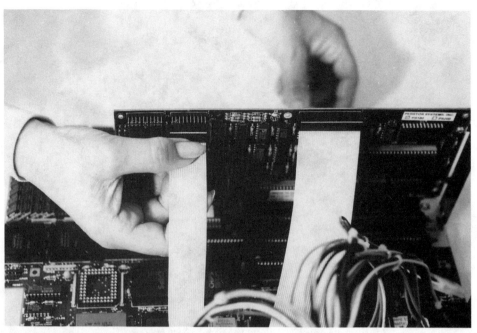

6-12 Connecting the data cable to the controller card.

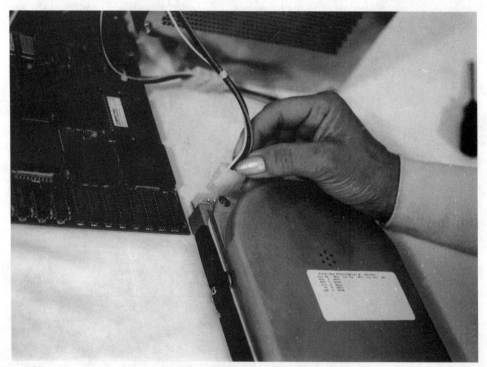

6-13 Connecting the power cable to a hard drive.

92 *Building your own server and workstations*

Connecting the floppy disk drives

Figure 6-14 shows the 34-wire controller cable being connected to drive A:. You can tell it is for drive A: because of the twist in the cable. This connector can be plugged in backwards. The cable will have a different colored wire on one edge to indicate pin one. The edge connector on the floppy disk will have a slot between contacts two and three. If you have a second floppy drive, the connector in the middle attaches to it.

6-14 Connecting the controller cable to the A: floppy drive.

Again, be careful that it is plugged in properly. I would recommend that your A: drive be a 1.2Mb 5¼-inch floppy disk drive and the B: drive a 1.44Mb 3½-inch floppy disk drive.

Figure 6-15 shows a 34-wire ribbon cable being connected to the floppy disk controller board. Again, you must be careful because it also can be plugged in backwards. There should be some indication on the board for pin one.

Figure 6-16 shows the power cable being connected to the floppy disk drive.

Connecting the keyboard and monitor

Figure 6-17 shows the keyboard connection at the rear of the motherboard. Figure 6-18 shows the connection for the monitor.

Ready to apply power

Figure 6-19 shows the assembled system, ready to apply power. If you don't already have DOS, you will need to buy a copy. You can use either DR DOS or MS-DOS. To

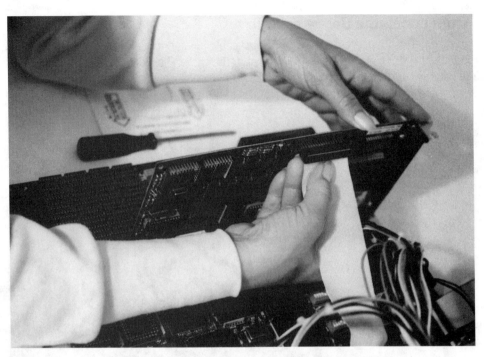

6-15 Connecting the floppy controller cable to the controller card.

6-16 Connecting the power to the floppy drive.

94 *Building your own server and workstations*

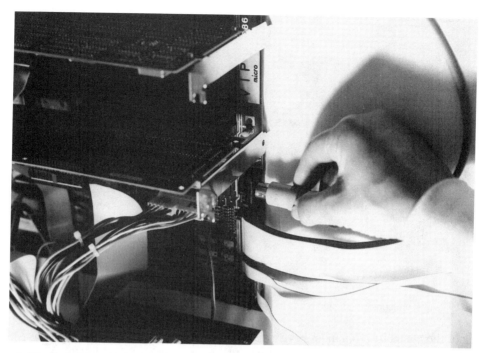

6-17   Connecting the keyboard to the back of the motherboard.

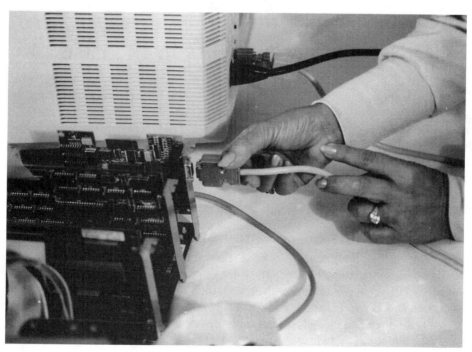

6-18   Connecting the monitor to the monitor-adapter board.

6-19 All connections made and ready to apply power.

boot the computer, you must have a bootable copy of DOS on a diskette for the A: drive. You can make either the 5¼-inch or the 3½-inch floppy disk drive the A: drive by attaching the end connector with the twist to that drive. If you have both drives, it is usually best to make the 5¼-drive the A: drive. Once the system is up and running, you can format your hard drives.

Installing the components in the case

After running the system on the bench with no problems, you can install it in the case. Figure 6-20 shows the installation of the power supply. Note the two raised tongues in the floor of the case. On the bottom of the power supply are two matching cutouts. Place the power supply over the raised tongues and slide it towards the back of the case.

Four screws are in the back of the case for the power supply. Figure 6-21 shows the back side of the motherboard. The four white objects are plastic standoffs that slide into grooves in the raised channels on the floor of the case. Two screws are used to hold the motherboard in place, one in the back center and one in the front.

Switch-panel wires

You will notice that there are a lot of loose wires at the front of the case. These wires are from the switches and LEDs on the front panel that came with the case. In some instances you might see 15 or 20 wires from the switches and LED indicators. You will probably have to trace the individual wires back to the switch or LED that it comes from, then find the pins on the motherboard for that connection.

Your motherboard and system might not use all of these wires and switches. You should get a manual with your motherboard that indicates where each of the wires

6-20 Installing the power supply.

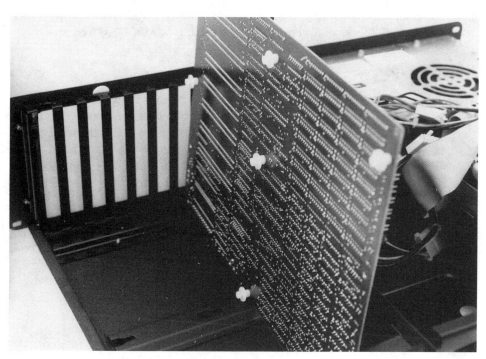

6-21 The back side of the motherboard showing the plastic standoffs.

6-22 All of the components installed in the case, ready for the cover.

should be connected. Most hard-disk controllers have a connection for the hard-disk activity. Figure 6-22 shows all components installed, ready for the cover.

Slot covers

You might not use all of the available slots, but the openings at the back of the case should be covered. Usually the only noise you hear from your computer is the fan in the power supply. It is supposed to draw air in from the open grill in the front of the case, pull this cool air over all the boards and components, then exhaust it out of the opening at the back of the power supply. If there are several other openings at the front of the computer, air will be drawn from them and might not accomplish the cooling necessary.

Heat is an enemy of semiconductors. Don't put anything in front of the computer that would cut off the intake of air or put anything in back of it that would prevent the outflow of air. Your computer will last a lot longer if you keep it from losing its cool!

Chapter 7

Disk drives

When building your own LAN, floppy disk drives and hard disks are an essential part of the server and workstations. This chapter looks at how the drives work and the purchases you will need to make to put them together.

Floppy disk basics

A floppy disk, which can be 3½ inches or 5¼ inches, is made from a plastic material called *polyethylene terephthalate*. It is coated on each side with a thin layer of magnetic material made primarily from iron oxide, or powdered rust. Bits of cobalt and other materials are added to give it special magnetic characteristics. The finished product is similar to the tape used in an audio cassette and videotape recorder. The next few sections discuss terms associated with floppy disks and floppy disk drives.

Tracks

A disk is similar in some respects to a phonograph record. A record has only one *track* that starts at the outer edge and winds toward the center. A 360K floppy disk has 40 single concentric tracks on each side. The first track is track 0 and the last is 39. The 1.2Mb and the 3½-inch disks have 80 concentric tracks on each side, numbered from 0 to 79.

Formatting

When you buy a floppy disk you must format it before it can be used. When it comes from the factory it is blank. *Formatting* records data on the disk to mark and number each track and sector.

Sectors

Each of the 40 tracks per side of the 360K and the 80 tracks per side of the 720K are formatted so that each track is divided into nine sectors. Each of the 80 tracks per side of the 1.2Mb high-density floppy disk is divided into 15 sectors. Each of the 80 tracks per side of the 1.44Mb is divided into 18 sectors. Each *sector* holds 512 bytes.

Allocation units

The older terminology was *cluster*, but *allocation unit* is a better term. On the 360K and 720K disks, DOS arranges for two sectors to be a single allocation unit, or cluster. But on 1.2Mb and 1.44Mb, a single 512-byte sector is an allocation unit. (On a hard disk, an allocation unit might be made up of from 4 sectors to as many as 16).

   Parts of two different files cannot be written, or placed, in a single allocation unit because the data from the two files would become mixed. The FAT (*file allocation table*) would become very confused if it had to try to separate data from two different files in the same allocation unit. On a 360K or 720K disk an allocation unit is two sectors or 1024 bytes. If a file is only two bytes, it will require a whole allocation unit.

FAT

The file allocation table (FAT) might be compared to a table of contents in a book. The location of each track and sector number is stored on track 0 in the FAT. Whenever a file is written on the disk, it is broken up into 512-byte chunks. Each of those chunks are written to the first empty sector, or allocation unit, that is found.

If it is a long file, several allocation units will be required. The system will search for empty units and fill them, so parts of the file may be scattered all over the disk. For instance, some might be on track 5, sectors 8 and 9, and on track 20, sectors 5 and 6. It doesn't matter where the data is because the FAT keeps track of each part's location. It can then electronically send the head to those tracks and sectors to read all of the file. If you add or erase any part of the file, the FAT will be updated accordingly. Because the tracks and sectors are numbered, the FAT can direct the heads to find data anywhere on the disk.

Directory limitations

DOS sets aside a limited amount of space for the number of files that can be held in the root directory of a floppy disk. For a 360K floppy disk it is 112. For any of the 80-track floppy disks, the maximum number is 224.

It is possible to put many more files on a floppy disk by creating directories. Multiple directories can be created on a floppy disk in the same manner as on a hard disk. Use the command MD directoryname. The MD is the command for "make directory." The directoryname is the name that you assign to the directory.

Cylinders

The tracks on each side of the floppy disk are directly opposite of each other; that is track 0 on side 0, or the top side, is exactly opposite track 0 on side 1, or the bottom side. If you could strip away all of the other tracks, the 0 track on the top and the 0 track on the bottom might look somewhat like a cylinder, even though it would be rather flat.

Heads

Two heads read and write on the floppy disk: head 0 on the top and head 1 on the bottom. When head 0 is over track 1, sector 1, on the top of the disk, head 1 is addressing track 1, sector 1 on the bottom side of the disk. The heads move from track to track as a single unit. Data is written to track 1 on the top side, then the heads are electronically switched to the bottom side and writing is continued to track 1 on the bottom side. It is much faster to switch between the heads electronically than to move them to a different track.

Tracks per inch (TPI)

The 40 tracks of a 360K floppy disk are laid down at a rate of 48 tracks per inch (TPI) so each of the 40 tracks is $\frac{1}{48}$ of an inch wide. The 80 tracks of the high-density 1.2Mb are laid down at a rate of 96 TPI, so each track is $\frac{1}{96}$ of an inch. The 80 tracks of the 3½-inch disks are laid down at a density of 135 TPI, or $\frac{1}{135}$ of an inch per track.

Read accuracy

The 5¼-inch floppy disks have a 1⅛-inch center hole. The floppy disk drive has a conical spindle that comes up through the hole when the drive latch is closed. This spindle centers the disk so that the heads will be able to find each track. The plastic material that the disk is made from is subject to environmental changes and wear and tear. The conical spindle might not center each disk exactly so head-to-track accuracy is difficult with more than 80 tracks. Most of the 360K floppy disks use a reinforcement hub ring, but it probably doesn't help much. The 1.2Mb floppy disks do not use a hub ring. Except for the hub ring, the 360K and 1.2Mb floppy disk look exactly the same.

The tracks of the 3½-inch floppy disks are narrower and greater in density per inch. But because of the metal hub, the head-tracking accuracy is much better than that of the 5¼-inch disks.

Hard disks have very accurate head-tracking systems. Some have a density of well over 1,000 tracks per inch, so a lot more data can be stored on a hard disk.

Rotation speed

The floppy disks have a very a smooth, lubricated surface. They rotate at a fairly slow 300 rpm. Magnetic lines of force deteriorate very fast with distance. So the closer the heads, the better they can read and write. The heads directly contact the floppy disks.

The hard disk rotates at 3,600 to 6,000 rpm. The heads and surface would be severely damaged if they came in contact at this speed, so the heads "fly" over the surface at a few millionths of an inch above it.

Floppy disk differences

The 360K and 1.2Mb floppy disks look exactly alike except for the hub ring on the 360K. But there is a large difference in the magnetic materials that determine the oersted (Oe) of each one. The *oersted* is a measure of the resistance of a material to being magnetized. The lower the Oe, the easier it is to be magnetized. The 360K has an Oe of 300, the 1.2Mb has an Oe of 600. The 360K disks are fairly easy to write to, so require a fairly low head current. The 1.2Mb is more difficult to magnetize, so a much higher head current is required. This current is switched to match whatever type of disk you tell the system you are using.

It is possible to format a 360K as a 1.2Mb. But it will have several bad sectors, especially near the center where the sectors are shorter. These sectors will be marked and locked out. The system might report that you have over a megabyte of space on a 360K disk. But I would not recommend that you use such a disk for any data that is important. You might use a 360K formatted disk as a 1.2Mb in an emergency, or for short-term use, but the data might eventually deteriorate and become unusable.

The 3½-inch floppy disk drives have several good features. The 720K disk can store twice as much data as a 360K disk, and the 1.44Mb four times as much in a smaller space. They have a hard plastic protective shell, so they are not easily damaged. They also have a spring-loaded shutter that automatically covers and protects the head opening when they are not in use.

The 720K and the 1.44Mb disks look alike except that the 1.44Mb has an extra square hole at the right rear corner. Most 3½-inch floppy disk drives have a switch that checks for the hole when you insert it. The Oe's of the 720K and the 1.44Mb are very close. Some people have punched holes in the right rear corner of the 720K disks and used them as 1.44Mb.

Another feature is the write-protect system. A plastic slide can be moved to open or close the small square hole in the left rear corner of the 3½-inch floppy disk. When the slide covers the opening, the disk is write-enabled. When the slide is moved to open the square hole, it is write-protected. This system of write protection is exactly opposite of that used in the 5¼-inch floppy disk.

If the square notch on the 5¼-inch floppy disk is left uncovered, light can shine through, allowing the disk to be written to or erased. If the notch is covered with opaque tape, it can only be read. Do not use clear tape. The system depends on a light shining through the notch. If clear tape is used, the disk can be written on or erased. Write-protection is important and is discussed in more detail in chapter 8.

Choosing a floppy disk drive

When choosing a floppy disk drive you should consider what you need to do with your system now and in the near future. Some drives can handle larger amounts of data than others, so if you foresee a lot of data manipulation, then these systems might be for you. The next few sections discuss costs and types of drives available to help you make a decision on the purchase of your floppy disk drive.

Cost of disks

The cost of all floppy disks is now quite reasonable. The 360K double-sided, double-density (DSDD) disks are selling for as low as 19 cents each, and the 720K DSDD disks are going for as little as 35 cents each.

The 1.2Mb high-density disks are selling at discount houses for as little as 39 cents apiece, and the 1.44Mb high-density disks are selling for as little as 55 cents each. You will find several ads in computer magazines.

Cost of drives

Many vendors are still advertising and selling 360K and 720K floppy disk drives. I don't know why anyone should buy one—they are obsolete. The 1.2Mb and 1.44Mb drives sell for about the same price, about $50 each.

Extended-density drives

Several companies are now offering a 3½-inch extended density (ED) 2.8Mb floppy disk drive. The 2.8Mb disks have a barium-ferrite media and use perpendicular recording to achieve the extended density. In standard recording, the particles are magnetized so that they lay horizontally in the media. In perpendicular recording, the particles are stood vertically on end for greater density.

The ED drives are downward-compatible and can read and write to the 720K and 1.44Mb disks. At the present time, the ED drives are rather expensive. IBM has announced that they will use them on one of their PS/2 units, which will no doubt cause them to become the new standard. By the time you read this, they should be fairly reasonable in price.

Very high density drives

Brier Technology, (408) 435-8463, and Insite, (408) 946-8080, have developed very high density (VHD) 3½-inch floppy disk drives that can store over 20Mb on a disk. There is no standard among the competing systems, so they use different methods to achieve the very high density.

One of the problems that was overcome in very high density drives was that of tracking. The drives have little trouble reading and writing to the 135 tracks per inch (TPI) of the standard 3½-inch floppy disk, but 20Mb requires many more tracks that are much closer. Brier Technology's Flextra uses special floppy disks that have special magnetic servo tracks embedded beneath the data tracks.

The Insite floppy disks have optical servo tracks that have been etched into the surface with a laser beam. A head then locks onto the servo tracks for accurate reading and writing to the data tracks. The Insite drive has a head with two different gaps, which makes it capable of reading and writing to the 20Mb format, as well as the 720K and 1.44Mb formats. The Insite drive is $555. Special disks for these systems cost about $20 each.

Briar Technology's Flextra drive is being distributed by the Q'COR Company, (800) 548-3420, and is priced at $495. Figure 7-1 shows an external Flextra 20Mb drive with a 3½-inch floppy disk and its SCSI controller and cable. Flextra also has internally mounted drives.

Bernoulli drives

The IOMEGA Corporation has a high-capacity Bernoulli floppy disk drive that allows the recording of up to 90Mb on a special floppy disk. The Bernoulli floppy disks spin much faster than a standard floppy disk, which forces the flexible disk to bend around the heads without actually touching them. This method is in accordance with the principle discovered by the Swiss scientist, Jakob Bernoulli (1654–1705).

The average access time for the Bernoulli and VHD disk drives is about 35 milliseconds (ms). The access time for a standard floppy disk drive is about 350 ms.

These drives are ideal for areas where the data is confidential. Each person in an office can have their own 90Mb floppy disk, which can be removed and locked up. This system is also great for backing up a hard disk.

The data compression system from Stac Electronics, (619) 431-7474, will allow you to double the storage capacity of these disks as well as standard floppy disks and

7-1 Brier Flextra 20Mb floppy drive.

your hard disk. Figure 2-6 (in chapter 2) shows the Stac software and its 8- and 16-bit coprocessor boards. The system can run on software only, or can be just a bit faster with the coprocessors.

IOMEGA has had the field to itself for several years, so the Bernoulli box has always been a bit expensive at about $1,500 for a drive and about $70 for each disk. But the Brier Technology and Insite companies are now giving them some competition with their very high density systems. The new 90Mb IOMEGA drive costs about $800 for a drive to $150 for each floppy disk.

Hard disk basics

The hard disk drive is similar to the floppy disk drive. It spins a disk that is coated, or plated, with a magnetic media. Hard disks are also formatted similarly to the floppy disks. But the 360K floppy disks have only 40 TPI; the hard disks might have from 300 to 2,400 TPI. The 360K floppy disk has 9 sectors per track; the hard disk might have 17 and up to 54 sectors per track. Both floppy and hard disks store 512 bytes per sector. Another major difference is the speed of rotation. A floppy disk rotates at about 300 rpm. A hard disk rotates at 3,600 rpm or more.

Leaving it turned on

Incidentally, another difference in the hard disk and the floppy disk drive is that the floppy disk drive comes on only when it is needed. Because of its mass, the hard disk takes quite a while to get up to speed and to stabilize. So, it comes on whenever the computer is turned on and spins as long as the computer is on.

If you are going to use your computer several times during the day, many experts have suggested that you leave it on all day. Every time an electronic circuit is turned on, a rush of current goes through it. Some people never turn their computer off.

Mean time before failure (MTBF)

The *mean time before failure* (MTBF) is a figure that represents how long the average drive should last before it fails. It is a figure that the manufacturer applies to the drive and is supposed to give you an idea of the reliability and quality of the drive. The higher the MTBF, the longer it should last. Most manufacturers claim 40,000 to 50,000 hours.

I have seen some advertised with a MTBF of 150,000 hours. If the computer was turned on 8 hours a day, 7 days a week, this means it should last for 18,750 days, or over 51 years. I don't know how the manufacturer could have determined this figure. Somehow I just don't quite believe it. I even find it difficult to believe the 50,000-hour figure, which would be 17 years at 8 hours a day.

The MTBF is just an average, somewhat like the average life of a man, which is about 73 years at this time. Some males die in infancy, a few others live to be 100, but with a little care most of us can beat the average and live longer. Maybe even as long as your hard disk.

Reading and writing

Everything that a computer does depends on precise timing. Crystals and oscillators are set up so that certain circuits perform a task at a specific time. The oscillator circuits are usually called *clock circuits*.

You have probably seen representations of magnetic lines of force around a magnet. To write data to the hard disk, electrical on and off pulses are sent to the head. These pulses magnetize small sections of the track to represent 0s and 1s. The magnetized spot on a disk track has similar lines of force. To read the data on the disk, the head is positioned over the track and the lines of force from each magnetized area cause a pulse of voltage to be induced in the head. During a precise block of time, an induced pulse of voltage can represent a 1, and the lack of a pulse a 0. The amount of magnetism that is induced on a disk when it is recorded is very small. It must be small so that it will not affect other tracks on each side of it or affect the tracks on the other side of the disk. Magnetic lines of force decrease as you move away from a magnet by the square of the distance. So the heads must be as close to the disk as possible.

The floppy disk heads actually contact the floppy disk. This causes some wear, but not very much because the rotation is fairly slow. The plastic floppy disks also have a special lubricant and are fairly slippery. But heads on the hard disk never touch the disk. The fragile heads and the disk would be severely damaged if they make contact at the fast speed of 3,600 rpm. The heads hover over the spinning disk, just millionths of an inch above it. The air must be filtered and pure because the smallest speck of dust or dirt can cause the head to crash.

Platters

A hard disk might have only one *platter* or as many as 10 or more. All of the platters, or disks, are stacked on a single shaft with just enough spacing between each one for the heads.

The surface of the hard disk platters must be very smooth. Because the heads are only a few millionths of an inch away from the surface, any unevenness could cause a head crash. The hard disk platters are usually made from aluminum, which is nonmagnetic, and lapped to a mirror finish. Some companies are now using a glass substrate. Once they have the smooth mirror finish, the disks are coated or plated with a magnetic material. Figure 7-2 shows a hard disk with the cover removed.

7-2   A hard disk with the cover removed showing the platters.

The platters also must be very rigid so that the close distance between the head and the platter surface is maintained. You should avoid any sudden movement of the computer or any jarring while the disk is spinning because it could cause the head to crash onto the disk and damage it. Most of the newer hard disks automatically move the heads to the center, away from the read/write surface, when the power is turned off.

Hard disk systems

The drive systems that are available today are Modified Frequency Modulation (MFM), Run Length Limited (RLL), Integrated Drive Electronics (IDE), Small Computer Systems Interface (SCSI), and Enhanced Small Device Interface (ESDI).

Modified Frequency Modulation (MFM) Most of the early hard disks used the *Modified Frequency Modulation* (MFM) drive. This system formats each track into 17 sectors per track. Just like the floppy disk system, 512 bytes can be stored in each sector. So if you multiply 512 bytes by 17 sectors you can see that 8704 bytes can be stored on each track.

Most of the MFM systems are reliable, but are slow, limited in capacity, bulky in size, and are practically obsolete. If you have more time than money, they are relatively inexpensive. They might be okay in a workstation.

Run Length Limited (RLL) The *Run Length Limited* (RLL) drive was developed by IBM some time ago for use on large mainframe hard disks. Adaptec Corporation, of Milpitas, first adapted the technology so that it could be used on PC hard disk controllers. This system divides each track into 26 sectors with 512 bytes in each sector or $26 \times 512 = 13,312$ bytes per track. This is over 50 percent more than the 8,704 per track allowed by the MFM system.

The RLL system also has a transfer rate 50 percent higher than MFM: 7.5 megabits per second (mbps).

Integrated Drive Electronics (IDE) The *Integrated Drive Electronics* (IDE) drive has the controller electronics built into the drive, allowing the manufacturer to optimize the drive's capabilities. It does not need an interface to the computer bus. Many motherboards now have this interface built-in. If it does not, you will need an interface to plug into one of your slots. This interface, with a floppy disk controller, can cost as little as $20. The IDE interface is also built into some multifunction boards. The IDE drives are usually small, fast, and have a fairly large capacity.

Small Computer Systems Interface (SCSI) The *Small Computer Systems Interface* (SCSI), pronounced "scuzzy," drive also has its controller built into the drive. It needs an interface, but up to seven other SCSI devices can be connected in a daisy chain to the one interface.

The SCSI drives are usually fast and have a high capacity. They can format from 26 to 54 sectors per track. The transfer time is usually from 10 mbps to 15 mbps. Most SCSI drives are used on large, high-end systems. Figure 7-3 shows the rear of a SCSI drive, which has a 50-wire ribbon cable.

Enhanced Small Device Interface (ESDI) The *Enhanced Small Device Interface* (ESDI), pronounced "ezdy," is a drive that operates at 10 or more mbps. It

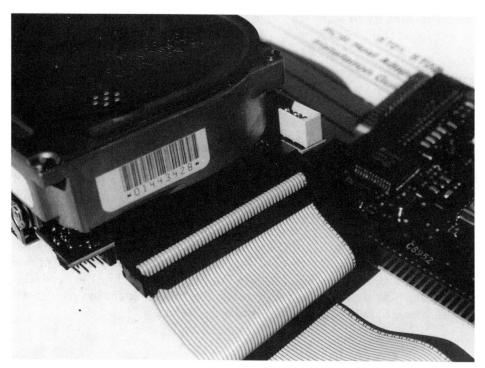

7-3 A SCSI drive with a 50-wire cable.

might format from 32 up to 54 sectors per track, is usually very fast, has a high capacity, and a high cost. EDSI drives are usually found on high-end systems.

Controllers

A hard disk needs a *controller* to handle the data going back and forth to the disk. In the early days, electronic boards were expensive and not very sophisticated. Most were so slow that the interleave would often have to be as much as 6 to 1. This means that it would read one sector, then let six more sectors pass beneath the head while it digested the input data. It would then be ready for the next sector, read the sector, and then wait for six more sectors to pass by. To be perfectly fair, it wasn't entirely the controller's fault. The early computers and disk drives were very slow compared to what we have today.

Controllers today are inexpensive, fast and sophisticated. Most controllers will now handle 1 to 1 interleave, or direct transfer, with no difficulty. In the early days you had to buy a separate controller board for the floppy disk drives and hard disks. Now almost all of the hard disk controllers have the controller for the floppy disk drive integrated on the board.

You need a controller that matches the type of hard disk you buy. An MFM drive will require an MFM controller. The same goes for RLL, IDE, SCSI, or ESDI. The controllers can vary greatly in price from about \$20 for an IDE up to several hundred for a high-end SCSI.

Formatting

A hard disk requires two levels of formatting, a low level and high level. In most cases, the low-level formatting is now done at the factory. This is especially so for IDE, ESDI, and SCSI hard disks, so you should not try to low-level format them. The documentation that comes with your hard disk should tell you whether it needs to be low-level formatted and how to do it.

You will probably have to do the high-level formatting. Use the DOS FDISK command to partition the disk, then high-level format each partition. DOS allows you to have up to 23 logical hard disks, representing all of the letters of the alphabet except A, B, and C. Letters A and B are reserved for floppy disk drives and C is reserved for the first active hard disk. I would recommend that you partition large disks into two or more logical drives. The reason is that if you have a crash or disk failure on one logical drive, the data in the other sections may still be recoverable. If it is one large disk and it fails, you might not be able to recover any of your data. Of course, you should always have your hard disk backed up.

Setting up CMOS ROM

CMOS (pronounced "see-moss") ROM (*complementary metal-oxide semiconductor, read-only memory*) must be set up to recognize the type of hard disk that you have installed. The system must know how many heads, how many cylinders, capacity, landing zone for the heads, and several other things. The documentation that came with your hard disk should give you this information.

Different model drives and drives from different manufacturers might all be different in some respect. The original IBM system grouped and recognized 15 different types, at the time, in 1984. Most of today's systems recognize 46 different types and will list a 47th type, where they let you type in the various characteristics if your drive does not fit any of the listed types.

Adding one or more hard disks

Most hard disk controllers and interfaces have provisions for adding a second hard disk. Some systems might require that the second hard disk be the same type, size, and from the same manufacturer. Other systems might not care as long as the second hard disk is the same general type. For instance, if your controller and first hard disk is an MFM, then the second hard disk must be MFM. Most hard disks have some sort of jumper or shorting bar that must be installed to operate the second hard disk.

It is possible to add two SCSI hard disks to a system that already has two MFM, RLL, or IDE drives. So you could have two SCSI drives and two of the other types. But you cannot mix MFM, RLL, or IDE hard disks. This would cause a conflict in the I/O interrupt system. Most of the SCSI drives use a special driver to avoid conflicts.

Hard cards

Several companies make plug-in hard cards that are small, fast, and can have a capacity of 40Mb to 200Mb. Hard cards are very easy to install. Just plug them into an empty slot on the motherboard. There are no cables or controllers to worry about and they usually come with a software driver that avoids I/O conflicts. They are usually a bit more expensive than an equivalent standard hard disk.

Choosing a hard disk

When you buy a hard disk you should consider several factors. Of course, the primary consideration will depend on what you need to do with your computer and how much you want to spend.

Other factors that should influence your buying decision are capacity, speed (or access time), and the type of drive. These factors are discussed briefly in the next few sections.

Capacity

Buy the biggest hard disk you can afford. No matter how big it is, it will soon be filled up. Don't even think of buying anything less than 100Mb for a server. A workstation should have at least 40Mb. New software programs have become more and more friendly, offer more and more options, and require more and more disk space.

Speed, or access time

Speed, or access time, is the time it takes a hard disk to locate and retrieve a sector of data. This includes the time that it takes to move the head to the track, settle down and read the data. For a high end, very fast disk, this might be as little as 9 milliseconds (ms). Some of the early hard disks required as much as 100 ms. I would recommend the fastest you can afford.

Type of hard disk: stepper or voice coil

Most of the less-expensive hard disks use a *stepper motor*. It moves the heads in discrete steps, or increments, across the disk until they are over the track to be read or written. You can usually hear the heads as they move from track to track.

The voice coil hard disks are quieter, a bit faster, and more reliable than the stepper motor hard disks. And, of course, more expensive. There might not be any marking on the hard disk to indicate whether it is a voice coil or not. But their spec sheets will show that they have an odd number of heads.

Actually they have an even number of heads, one on the top and bottom of each platter. But one head and platter surface is used as a servo control for the other heads. The servo head follows a tracking system recorded by the factory. When a program calls for data to be read from a specific track, the servo head moves to that track very quickly and accurately. Because all of the heads move as one, the head that is supposed to read the data is also moved to the proper track.

A voice coil system is very quiet. Unless there is a light-emitting diode (LED) indicator on the front panel, you might not realize that it is operating.

Compression

Compression allows you to reduce the size of a file, in some cases, by half or more. It has been around for several years. Most bulletin boards use one form or another so that they can save cost in storing the data and in telephone and modem costs.

Most large software companies are now shipping their products in a compressed form. Many of them use the PKzip format. They are unzipped, or expanded, when you load them on your hard disk.

In the past, one of the problems with compression was that it took a long time to compress the files and expand them. But several companies today offer both software and hardware compression systems that are almost as fast as the fastest hard disk. One that I have been using for some time is Stacker, from Stac Electronics, (619) 431-7474. For some types of data it can more than double the amount of space on a hard disk or floppy disk.

Stac Electronics has both a software and plug-in board, or a software-only version. The software-alone version costs $99. If you have a 100Mb hard disk, this system will let you store 200Mb. You cannot buy a hard disk for $99. Using the board version makes it just a bit faster. The 8-bit board lists for $199, the 16-bit board is $249. (See chapter 2, Fig. 2-6 for a photo from Stac Electronics.)

CD-ROM

The *compact disc, read-only memory* (CD-ROM) industry is one of the fastest growing of all the computer peripherals. Sony, Hitachi, Phillips, JVC, Amdek, Panasonic, and several other companies are manufacturing the drives. These drives are all compatible and can be interfaced to a 386 with a plug-in board.

Thousands of CD-ROM discs are available today. The off-the-shelf discs cover a wide variety of subjects—such as library and bookstore reference materials, general reference, literature, art, business, biology, medicine, physics, and most other branches of science and technology. Not to mention the CD-ROM discs on law, finances, geology, geography, government, and many others. In time, discs will be available on almost any subject that is found in a large library.

Several companies are advertising CD-ROM drives in computer magazines for about $350. Some are bundling the drive with several CD-ROM discs. Depending on the type of your business, a CD-ROM on your server might be well worth the money.

Chapter 8

Backups

As sure as more earthquakes will hit California, if you use a computer long enough, you will have at least one unfortunate disaster. There are thousands of ways to make mistakes and no way that you can prevent all of them. But if your data is backed up, it doesn't have to be a catastrophe. It is a lot better to be backed up than sorry.

Write-protect your software

When you buy a software program, the very first thing you should do is write-protect the floppy disks. It is very easy to become distracted and write on a program disk in error, which would probably ruin the program. The vendor might give you a new copy, but it would probably entail weeks of waiting and a lot of paperwork.

If you are using 5¼-inch floppy disks, you should cover the square write-protect notch with a piece of opaque tape. Don't use Scotch or clear tape. The drive focuses a light through the square notch. If the light detector can sense the light, it will allow the disk to be written on, read, or erased. If the notch is covered with opaque tape, the disk can be read, but cannot be written on or erased. Some vendors now distribute their programs on disks without the square notch.

If you are using 3½-inch floppy disks, you should move the small slide on the left rear side so that the square hole is open. The 3½-inch write-protect system is just the opposite of the 5¼-inch system. The 3½-inch drive uses a small microswitch to check the square hole. If it is open, the switch will allow the disk to be read, but not written on or erased. If the slide is moved to cover the square hole, the disk can be written on, read or erased.

It takes less than a minute to write-protect a disk and can save a lot of valuable time in the long run. If a program disk is ruined because it was not write-protected, it might take weeks to get a replacement for the original, or you might even have to buy a complete new program.

After you have made sure that the disks are write-protected, the second thing you should do is to use DISKCOPY to make exact copies of your original disks. The originals should then be stored away. Only the copies should be used. If you damage one of them, you can always make another copy from the original.

Unerase software

Anyone who works with computers for any length of time is bound to make a few errors. One of the best protections against errors is to have a backup. The second best protection is to have a good utility program such as Norton Utilities or PC Tools. These programs can unerase a file or even unformat a disk. When a file is erased, DOS goes to the FAT table and deletes the first letter of each file name. All of the data remains on the disk unless a new file is written over it. If you have erased a file in error, or formatted a disk in error, do not do anything to it until you have tried using a recover utility! This step is very important. Don't use the DOS Recover utility except as a last resort.

Use Norton Utilities, (213) 319-2000, or, if you are using Windows, use the Norton Desktop for Windows, (408) 253-9600; Mace Utilities, (504) 291-7221; PC Tools, (503) 690-8090; DOSUTILS, (612) 937-1107; or any of several other recovery utilities. These utilities let you restore the files by replacing the missing first letter of the file name.

Many people, including me, have erased files in error in the past. We are only human, so we will do it again. If you do not have backups and unerase software, you might wipe out data that is possibly worth thousands of dollars. You might have taken hundreds of hours to accumulate the data and it might be impossible to duplicate, but it can be completely gone in a fraction of second.

Even with the knowledge of what can happen, many people do not back up their precious data. Most of these people are those who have been fortunate enough not to have had a major catastrophe.

Some causes of data loss

Data loss can occur for many reasons, such as jumbled FAT or a head crash.

Jumbled FAT

I talked about the all-important file allocation table (FAT) in chapter 7. The FAT keeps a record of the location of all the files on the disk. Even if parts of a file are located in several sectors, FAT knows exactly where they are. If for some reason track 0, where the FAT is located, is damaged, erased or becomes defective, then you will not be able to read or write to any of the files on the disk.

Because the FAT is so important, programs such as PC Tools and Mace Utilities can make a copy of the FAT and store it in another location on the disk. Every time you add a file or edit one, the FAT changes. So these programs make a new copy every time the FAT is altered. If the original FAT is damaged, you can still get your data by using the alternate FAT.

Head crash

The heads of a hard disk "fly" over the disk just a few millionths of an inch from the surface. They have to be close in order to detect the small magnetic changes in the tracks. The disk spins at 3,600 rpm. If the heads contact the surface of the fast-spinning disk it can scratch it and ruin the disk. A sudden jar or bump to the computer while the hard disk is spinning can cause the heads to crash. Of course a mechanical failure or some other factor could also cause a crash. You should never move or bump your computer while the hard disk is running.

Most of the newer disks have a built-in park utility. When the power is removed and the hard disk is parked, the head is automatically moved to the center of the disk where there are no tracks. But some of the older disks do not have this utility. It is also possible for the head to crash if the power is suddenly removed such as in a power failure.

The technology of hard disks has improved tremendously over the last couple of years, but they are still mechanical devices. And as such, you can be sure that eventually they will wear out, fail, or crash.

Most hard disks are now relatively bugfree. Manufacturers quote figures of several thousand hours mean time before failure (MTBF). But these figures are only an average. There is no guarantee that a disk won't fail in the next few minutes. A hard disk is made up of several mechanical parts. If it is used long enough it will wear out or fail. Many vendors list MTBF figures of 40,000 to 150,000 hours, which makes you think that the hard disk should last for several years. But there are several businesses who do nothing but repair hard disks that have crashed or failed.

Crash recovery   A failure can be frustrating, time-consuming, and make you feel utterly helpless. In the unhappy event of a crash, depending on its severity, it is possible that some of your data can be recovered, one way or another.

Some companies specialize in recovering data and rebuilding hard disks. Many of them have sophisticated tools and software that can recover some data if the disk is not completely ruined. If it is possible to recover any of the data, Ontrack Computer Systems, (612) 937-1107, can probably do it. Several other companies also exist. Look in the computer magazine ads. A couple of companies that I have used to recover data are California Disk Drive Repair, (408) 727-2475, and Rotating Memory Service, (916) 939-7500.

The cost for recovery services can be rather expensive. But if you have data that is crucial, then it is usually worth it. Of course, having a backup is a lot cheaper.

Some excuses not to back up

There is really no good reason not to back up the data from your hard disk onto floppy disks or tapes. Backups are very important and will help alleviate much of the frustration you might feel when your hard disk crashes. You will be secure in the knowledge that your essential data is not lost forever.

The next few sections discuss some of the reasons people give for not doing backups and why they really should back up.

Don't have the time

This excuse is not a good one. If your data is worth anything at all, it is worth backing up. It takes only a few minutes to back up a large hard disk with some of the newer software. Find the time to do backups. Incorporate backups into your production schedule—at the end of each work day is best, but if this is not possible then at least once a week.

Too much trouble

Backups are less trouble than it takes to recover data that could be lost forever. It's true backups can require a bit of disk swapping, labeling, and storing. But with a little organizing, it can be done easily. If you keep all of the disks together, you don't have to label each one. Just stack them in order, put a rubber band around them, and use one label for the first one of the lot.

Yes, it is a bit of trouble to make backups and, of course, backups are easiest when you have an expensive tape-automated backup system. But if you don't have even a simple backup system, consider the trouble it would take to redo the files from a disk that has crashed. The trouble that it takes to make a backup is infinitesimal.

Don't have the necessary disks, software, or tools

Depending on the amount of data to be backed up, and the software used, a backup might require 50 to 100 360K floppy disks. And you will need a lot fewer if you use the high-density disks.

Again, it takes only a few minutes and a few disks to make a backup of only the data that has been changed or altered. In most cases, the same disks can be reused the next day to update the files. Several discount mail-order houses sell 360K floppy disks for as little as 19 cents apiece, 720K and 1.2Mb floppy disks for 39 cents each, and 1.44Mb floppy disks for 55 cents.

Failures and disasters only happen to other people

People who believe that disasters only happen to other people are those who have never experienced a disaster. There is nothing you can say to convince them and they just have to learn the hard way.

Other reasons why you should back up

The importance of backups cannot be stressed enough. In addition to the previous reasons for doing backups, there are a few other reasons that should be considered, which are discussed in the next few sections.

General failure

Outside of ordinary care, there is little one can do to prevent a general failure. It could be a component on the hard disk electronics or in the controller system. Or any one of a thousand other things. Even things such as a power failure during a read/write operation can cause data corruption.

Theft and burglary

Computers are easy to sell, so they are favorite targets for burglars. It would be bad enough to lose a computer, but many computers have hard disks that are filled with data that is even more valuable than the computer.

Speaking of theft, it might be a good idea to put your name and address on several of the files on your hard disk. It would also be a good idea to scratch identifying marks on the back and bottom of the case. You should also write down the serial numbers of your monitor and drives.

Another good idea is to store your backup files in an area away from your computer. This way there would be less chance of losing both computer and backups in a burglary or fire.

Archival

Another reason to back up is for archival purposes. No matter how large the hard disk, it will eventually fill up with data. Quite often, there will be files that are no longer used or they might only be used once in awhile.

Fragmentation

After a hard disk has been used for some time, files begin to *fragment*. The data is recorded on concentric tracks in separate sectors. If part of a file is erased or changed, some of the data might be in a sector on track 20 and another part on track 40. There might be open sectors on several tracks because portions of data have been erased. Hunting all over the disk can slow the disk down. If the disk is backed up completely, then erased, the files can be restored so that they will again be recorded in contiguous sectors. The utility programs mentioned above can unfragment a hard disk, by copying portions of the disk to memory and rearranging the data in contiguous files.

Data transfer

Often it is necessary to transfer a large amount of data from a hard disk that is not on a network. A good backup program will let you transfer from the hard disk easily and quickly. You can then make several copies to distribute to others.

This method could be used to distribute company policies and procedures, sales figures, and other information to several people in a large office or company. The data could also be easily shipped or mailed to branch offices, customers, or anywhere.

Methods of backup

Now that you understand why backups are important, you will need to learn about backup software and techniques, such as Norton Backup, Fastback, Back-It 4 LAN, XCOPY, and more. Look through computer magazines for backup programs not mentioned here.

Software

Two main types of software are used for backups: image and file-oriented. An *image backup* is an exact bit-for-bit copy of the hard disk copied as a continuous stream of data. This type of backup is inflexible and does not allow for a separate file backup or restoration.

The *file-oriented* backup identifies and indexes each file separately. A separate file or directory can be backed up and restored easily. Without the file-oriented backup, it can be very time-consuming to back up an entire 100Mb or more each day.

But with the file-oriented backup, once a full backup has been made, it is necessary only to make incremental backups of the files that have been changed.

DOS stores an archive attribute in each file directory entry. When a file is created, DOS turns the archive attribute flag on. If the file is backed up by using the DOS BACKUP command or any of the commercial backup programs, the archive attribute flag is turned off. If this file is later changed, DOS will turn the attribute back on. At the next backup, you can have the program search the files and look for the attribute flag. You can then back up only those that have been changed since the last backup. You can view or modify a file's archive attribute by using the DOS ATTRIB command.

If you only have a few megabytes of data that are changed each day, there are several very good software programs on the market that let you use a 5¼-inch or 3½-inch disk drive to back up your data. Again, you should have backups of all your master software, so you don't have to worry about backing up that software every day.

Backup.com   One of the least expensive methods of backup is to use the Backup.com and Restore.com that comes with MS-DOS. The price to pay is that it is slow, time-consuming, and rather difficult to use. But it will do the job if nothing else is available.

Norton Backup   Norton Backup, (213) 319-2000, is one of the faster backup programs on the market. It is also one of the easiest to use. It compresses the data so that fewer disks are needed.

Norton Desktop for Windows   Norton and Symantec have now merged. This software package has several very useful utilities: emergency unerase, manual or automatic backup, utilities for creating batch files, and managing directories and files under Windows.

Fastback Plus   Fastback Plus, (504) 291-7221, was one of the first backup software programs to be fast. It also compresses the data so that fewer floppy disks are needed. Fastback Plus is easy to learn and use.

Back-It 4 LAN   Back-It 4 LAN, from Gazelle Systems, (800) 233-0383, uses very high density data compression, as much as 3 to 1. It is also very fast and uses a sophisticated error-correction routine. Gazelle offers a 60-day money-back guarantee and toll-free technical support. The list price is $295 for 1 to 8 nodes.

PC Tools   PC Tools comes bundled with a very good backup program, which is also sold separately to anyone who doesn't want to buy the whole PC Tools bundle.

XCOPY   The XCOPY command is a part of MS-DOS versions higher than 3.2. Several switches can be used with XCOPY. (A *switch* is represented by a backslash (/)). For instance, XCOPY C:*.* A:/A will copy only those files that have their archive attribute set to on. It does not reset the attribute flag.

XCOPY C:*.* A:/M will copy the files, then reset the flag. Whenever a disk on the A: drive is full, you merely have to insert a new floppy and hit F3 to repeat the last command. You can continue to copy all files that have not been backed up.

XCOPY C:*.* A:/D:03-15-92 will copy only those files created after March 15, 1992. Several other very useful switches that I have not mentioned here, can also be used with XCOPY.

Several other very good backup software packages available. Check through computer magazines for their ads and for reviews.

Tape

Tape backups are easy, but they can be relatively expensive: $400 to over $1,000 for a drive unit, and $5 to $20 for tape cartridges. Most tape backup systems require the use of a controller that is similar to the disk controller. So they will use one of your precious slots. Unless they are used externally, they will also require the use of one of the disk-mounting areas. Because it is only used for backup, it will be idle most of the time.

Tape backup systems are fairly well-standardized today. One of the early problems with tapes was that there were few standards for tape size, cartridges, reels, or format. Quite often a tape that was recorded on one tape machine, even from the same vendor, would not restore on another. That is not much of a problem today. Most of today's tapes conform to the quarter-inch cartridge (QIC) standards. These standards cover several different formats and hardware interfaces. Several different tape capacities are available, from 50Mb up to more than 5 gigabytes (Gb).

The most common type drives use a quarter-inch cartridge (QIC) tape that is similar to that used in audio cassettes. But these tapes are manufactured to much stricter standards. There are also half-inch drive systems for high-end use, which are much more expensive than the quarter-inch systems and will cost as much as $3,000 to $10,000 or more.

One of the big problems with software backup is that you have to sit there and put in a new disk when one is full. One big plus for tape is that it can be set up so that it is usually done automatically. You don't have to worry about forgetting to back up or waste the time doing it. The backup is usually set up so that it is done at night or some hour that does not disturb the operation of the network.

Digital audio tape (DAT)

Several companies are offering *digital audio tape* (DAT) systems for backing up large computer hard disk systems. DAT systems offer storage capacities as high as 5Gb on a very small cartridge.

DAT systems use a helical scan-type recording that is similar to that used for video recording. There are DAT systems for both 4 millimeters and 8 millimeters.

Here are just four of the many companies who are offering DAT systems: Carlisle Memory Products, (800) 433-8273; Irwin Magnetic, (800) 421-1879; Tallgrass Technologies, (800) 736-6002; and Tecmar (800) 624- 8560.

Very high density disk drives

Two companies are now making very high density (VHD) 20Mb floppy disk drives. Insite Peripherals and Brier Technology have developed 3½-inch floppy disk drives that can store 20Mb on a 3½-inch floppy disk. The Bernoulli drive can put 90Mb on a 5¼-inch floppy disk. Stac Electronics's data compression can be used with these floppy systems to double their capacity.

A very high-density floppy drive can be better than a tape. The tape drives are only used for backup. But a high-density floppy disk drive has much more utility, possibly to the point where the hard disk is not needed.

Second hard disk

The easiest and the fastest of all methods of backup is to have a second hard disk. It is very easy to install because most controllers have the capability of controlling a second hard disk. You have to make sure that your second hard disk works with your first hard disk, but that should be easy to determine.

The second hard disk does not have to be large, 20Mb or 30Mb should be fine. With a second hard disk as a backup, you do not need a backup software package. A good backup software package might cost $200 or more, which is the about the same amount you would pay for a second hard disk.

An average hard disk will have an access speed of about 20 milliseconds (ms). Floppy disks have access speeds of about 300 ms. This difference can seem like an eternity compared to the speed of even the slowest hard disk. Depending on the number of files, how fragmented the data is on the disk, and the access speed, a second hard disk can back up 20Mb in a matter of seconds. To back up 20Mb using even the fastest software will require 15 to 20 minutes. It will also require that you do a lot of disk swapping in and out. Depending on the type of disks that you use for backup, and the type of software, it might require 50K to 60K of the 360K, about 17K of the 1.2Mb, or about 14K of the 1.44Mb disks. Some of the latest backup software makes extensive use of data compression, so fewer disks are needed.

Another problem with using software backup is that it is often difficult to find a particular file. Most backup software stores the data in a system that is not the same as DOS files. Usually there is no directory like that provided by DOS. Even the DOS BACKUP files show only a control number when you check the directory.

Hard cards

You can buy a hard disk on a card for $300 to $600, depending on capacity and company. The high-capacity disks are usually rather expensive. But compression software can also be used on these disks. It might be worthwhile to install a card in an empty slot and dedicate it to backup.

If your computer has no empty slots, you might even consider just plugging in the card once a week or so to make a backup, then removing the card until needed again. This would entail removing the cover from the machine each time. But I remove the cover to my computer so often that I only use one screw on it to provide grounding. I can remove and replace my cover in a very short time.

Fault tolerance

Remember the disadvantages of a tape machine. It uses one of your slots, you have to buy tape reels, and it is difficult to find a particular file. A fairly good tape machine will cost over $500. Then there is a certain amount of labor in making the tape backups. Even if you have a system that automatically makes a backup at the end of the day, you still must insert the tape, wait for it to backup, then label it, and store it.

Another disadvantage of a tape machine is possible tape failure. Suppose your hard disk happens to fail during the day or towards the end of the day. If you have not yet made a backup for that day, all of the data is gone.

A good way to prevent this type of disaster is with *disk mirroring*, where two identical hard disks are used. The same data is written to both disks and both disks are controlled by the same controller. It is not likely that both will fail, so you can be fairly sure that your data is safe.

It is possible that the controller might fail, so another method is *disk duplexing*. In this system a separate disk and controller is used for the second system. Both NetWare and LAN Manager support disk mirroring and disk duplexing.

If you have a network system server with a 200Mb hard disk, you can buy a second 200Mb hard disk for about $500, about what it would cost for a tape machine. If you install two identical mirror hard disks, you won't even have to worry about taking the time to back up. It will be done automatically. If 200Mb is not enough, you could install a Stac compression system, which will store 400Mb on each disk.

If you still have doubts, you can set up a RAID (*redundant array of inexpensive disks*) system. This system goes a step further than the disk mirroring system and uses inexpensive disks that store the same data.

WordStar

A lot of computing is word processing. I use WordStar. WordStar has a method that automatically saves the file I am using. Anytime I pause, it will wait till whatever time that I have set it for, then save the file to disk. This feature can prevent disasters.

Uninterruptible power supplies (UPSs)

In the event of a power failure due to an electrical storm, or some other act of God or man, any data or open files that you happen to be working on might be lost. Many areas of the country have brownouts periodically, in which the voltage drops to the point where a computer might fail. And the voltage in many parts of the country varies widely at different times of the day and of the year. Very high surges and spikes in the voltage can cause data corruption and damage.

To combat these problems, several companies have developed uninterruptible power supply (UPS) battery-operated systems that will take over when the normal power is disrupted. The UPS can supply power for a few minutes until the open files can be saved to disk.

Many of the systems have batteries that are similar to an automobile's 12-volt battery. The batteries are constantly being charged. If the power falls below a certain level such as in a brownout, or a full power failure, the UPS immediately takes over. The 12-volt dc (direct current) power from the battery is inverted to 120 volts ac (alternating current) and sent to the computers.

There are two types of UPS systems, online and standby. With the *online* system, the computer or network draws its power from the UPS at all times. If a power failure or dysfunction occurs, the computer never knows it until the battery is discharged. The on-line UPS systems are usually more expensive than the standby systems.

The *standby* system keeps a battery charged up, but the power is drawn from the normal wall plug unless there is a power failure. In that case the standby UPS takes over. In the early days, it took a few milliseconds for a standby UPS to switch over, but now they are very fast. In addition, most computer power supplies now have large capacitors that can hold the power for up to 20 milliseconds. For most applications, standby systems should work fine.

Of course, there is a limit as to how many computers a UPS system can handle. Some of the very large systems might be very expensive. The Emerson Company, (800) 222-5877, makes Accupower, a small half card with a rechargeable battery. It plugs into one of the slots in the computer. Computers use 5 volts dc and 12 volts dc. The small battery can supply these voltages for up to 10 minutes so that the system can be safely shut down. The Emerson Company also has several other UPS systems.

Here are a few other UPS manufacturers:

American Power Conversion	(800) 541-8896
Best Power Technology	(800) 356-5794
Clary Corporation	(818) 287-6111
Elgar Systems	(619) 458-0250
Para Systems	(800) 238-7272
Sola General Signal	(800) 879-7651
Tripp Lite	(312) 329-1777

LAN Manager and NetWare can be interfaced with some UPSs and when the power drops below a certain amount, the whole network is alerted to save any open files and log off.

A UPS can cost from a couple hundred dollars up to several thousand dollars. It might seem like an unnecessary expense, but consider the cost of the man-hours it would take to re-create and restore some of your data. It has been reported that there have been problems on some power systems as many as 1,500 times in one year. If you live in such an area, a UPS would probably pay for itself very shortly.

No matter what type of system or method is used, if your data is worth anything at all, you should be using something to back it up. You might be one of the lucky ones and never need it. But it is much better to be backed up than to be sorry.

Chapter 9

Monitors

Your monitor should be a good-quality monitor. Most of the time you spend working on your computer will be spent looking at it, so you should have the best possible one you can afford.

The joys of color

You can buy a monochrome monitor for as little as $65. This monitor might be sufficient for what you have to do, but work can be a lot more enjoyable if you have a good, high-resolution color monitor. Even if you do nothing but word processing, color makes the job a lot easier and more pleasant.

But like so many other things in life, color costs. The better the color and the higher the resolution, the higher the cost. Also, the larger the screen, or size of the monitor, the higher the cost.

There have been several improvements in the design and development of monitor electronics. New chipsets and VLSI integration have helped reduce the cost of manufacturing electronics. But not as much can be done to reduce the cost of manufacturing the main component, the *cathode ray tube* (CRT). A good color CRT requires a tremendous amount of labor-intensive, precision work. The larger the screen, the more costly it is to manufacture.

We, the public, are very fortunate in that so many manufacturers make many different types, sizes, and kinds of monitors. Of course, there is a lot of competition among the manufacturers, which helps keep the prices fairly reasonable.

Many options available

Many types of monitors and many options are available. You will have a wide choice as to price, resolution, color, size, and shape. A *video graphic array* (VGA) and Super VGA can cost from $200 and up. The average price for a good 14-inch VGA monitor is about $300. The brand-name models, such as NEC, will cost more.

Monitor basics

I am going to discuss a few of the monitor specifications, terms, and acronyms so that you can make a more informed decision as to which monitor to buy.

Basically a monitor is similar to a television set. The face of a television set or a monitor is the end of a CRT. They are vacuum tubes and have many of the same elements that made up the old vacuum tubes, which were used before the advent of the semiconductor age. The CRT has a filament that boils off a stream of electrons. The back of the CRT screen has a voltage potential of about 25,000 volts, which creates a very strong attraction for the electrons that are boiled off the cathode.

The electrons are "shot" from an electron gun toward the backside of the CRT screen where they slam into the *phosphor* (a substance that emits light when excited by radiation) and causes it to light up. Depending on the type of phosphor used, once the dot is lit up, it continues to glow for a period of time. The electron beam moves rapidly across the screen, but because the phosphor continues to glow for awhile, you see the images that are created.

When you watch a movie, you are seeing a series of still photos, flashed one after the other. Due to your persistence of vision, it appears to be continuous motion. It is this same persistence of vision phenomenon that allows us to see motion and images on our television and video screens.

In a magnetic field, a beam of electrons acts very much like a piece of iron. Just like iron, a stream of electrons can be attracted or repelled by the polarity of a magnet. In a CRT, a beam of electrons must pass between a system of electromagnets before it reaches the back side of the CRT face. In a basic system there would be an electromagnet on the left, the right, top, and at the bottom.

Voltage through the electromagnets can be varied so that the beam of electrons is repelled by one side and attracted by the other, or pulled to the top or forced to the bottom. With this electromagnetic system, a stream of electrons can be bent and directed to any spot on the screen. It is much like holding a hose and directing a high-pressure stream of water to an area. You could use the stream to write or draw lines or whatever.

Scan rates

When you look at the screen of a television set or a monitor, you see a full screen only because of the persistence of vision and the type of phosphor used on the back of the screen. Actually, the beam of electrons starts at the top left corner of the screen, then under the influence of the electromagnets, it is pulled across to the right-hand top corner. It lights up the pixels as it sweeps across. It is then returned to the left-hand side, dropped down one line, and swept across again. On a television set, this process is repeated so that 525 lines are written on the screen in about 1/30th of a second. These 525 lines would be one frame, so 30 frames are written to the screen in one second.

Vertical scan rate The time that it takes to fill a screen with lines from top to bottom is the *vertical scan rate*. Some of the newer multiscan, or multifrequency, monitors can have variable vertical scan rates from 40 times per second up to 100 per second to paint the screen from top to bottom.

Horizontal scan rate The horizontal scanning frequency of a standard television set is 15.75 KHz, which is also the frequency used by CGA systems. Higher resolutions require higher frequencies. The horizontal frequency for the EGA is about 22 KHz, the VGA is 31.5 KHz and up.

The multiscan or multisync monitors can accept various frequencies sent to it from the adapter card. They might accept horizontal signals from 15.5 KHz to 100 KHz. Some of the older software was written specifically for CGA, EGA, or VGA. The multiscan can run any of them.

Some of the low-cost monitors might accept only two or three fixed frequencies, such as the 15.75 KHz for CGA, the 22 KHz for EGA, and the 31.5 KHz for the VGA.

Depending on your needs and bank account, this type might be all you need. But the multiscanning is better if you can afford it.

Controlling the beam

The CRT has control grids, much like the old vacuum tubes, for controlling the signal. A small signal voltage applied to the grid can control a very large voltage. The control grid, along with the electromagnetic system, controls the electron stream somewhat as if it were a pencil. The control grid causes the electron stream to make a large voltage output copy of the small input signal. This amplified high voltage is then used to write a replica of the input signal on the screen. As the beam sweeps across the screen, if the input signal is tracing the outline of a figure, the control grid will turn the beam on to light up a dot of phosphor for the light areas. If the input signal is in a dark area, the beam is shut off so that a portion of the screen will be dark for that area of the image.

Monochrome

A *monochrome monitor* has a single electron beam gun and a single color phosphor. It writes directly on the phosphor and can provide very high resolution for text and graphics. It is even possible to get monochrome analog VGA that can display as many as 64 different shades. Large monochrome monitors are ideal for some desktop publishing systems (DTP) and even some computer-aided design (CAD) systems. But these large monochrome monitors can be almost as expensive as the equivalent size in color.

Color

Color TVs and color monitors are much more complicated than monochrome systems. During the manufacture of the color monitors, three different phosphors—red, green, and blue—are deposited on the back of the screen. Usually a very small dot of each color is placed in a triangular shape. They have three electron beam guns, one for each color. By lighting up the three colored phosphors selectively, all the colors of the rainbow can be generated.

The guns are called red, blue, and green (RGB), but the electrons they emit are all the same. They are called RGB because each gun is aimed so that it hits a red, green, or blue color on the back of the monitor screen. They are very accurately aimed so that they will converge or impinge only on their assigned color.

Resolution

If you look closely at a black-and-white photo in a newspaper, you can see that the photo is made up of small dots. There will be a lot of dots in the darker areas and fewer in the light areas. The text or image on a monitor or a television screen is also made up of dots very similar to the newspaper photo. You can see these dots easily with a magnifying glass. If you look closely, you can see spaces between the dots. These dots are much like the dots of a dot-matrix printer. The more dots and the closer together they are, the better the resolution.

A good high-resolution monitor will have solid, sharply defined characters and images. An ideal resolution would look very much like a high-quality photograph. But it will be some time before the resolution of a monitor reaches the resolution of film.

Pixels Resolution is also determined by the number of *picture elements* (pixels) that can be displayed. The following figures relate primarily to text, but the graphics resolution will be similar to the text. A VGA color monitor can display 640×480 pixels and can display 80 characters in one line with 25 lines from top to bottom. If you divide 640 by 80 you'll find that one character will be 8 pixels wide. There can be 25 lines of characters, so $480 \div 25 = 19$ pixels high. The entire screen will have $640 \times 480 = 307,200$ pixels. Super VGA has 800×600, which is $800 \div 80$ for 10 pixels wide and $600 \div 25$ for 24 pixels high. The XGA (extra graphic array) can display $1,024 \times 768$.

Most monitor adapters have text-character generators built into the board. When you press the A key, the adapter goes to its library and sends the signal for the A to the screen. Each character occupies a cell made up of a number of pixels, depending on the resolution of the screen and the adapter. In the case of the VGA, if all the dots within a cell were lit up, you would see a solid block of dots 8 pixels wide and 19 pixels high. When the A is placed in a cell, only the dots necessary to form an outline of an A light up. It is very similar to the dots formed by a dot-matrix printer when it prints a character.

A graphics adapter, along with the proper software, allows you to place lines, images, photos, normal and various text fonts, and almost anything one can imagine on the screen.

Interlaced vs. noninterlaced The VGA horizontal system will sweep the electron beam across the screen from top to bottom 480 times in 1/60th of a second to make one frame, or 60 frames in one second. For Super VGA it is 600 times, and for XGA it is 768 times in 1/60th of a second. As you can see, the higher the resolution, the more lines, the closer they are together and the faster they have to be painted on the screen. The higher resolution also causes the electron beam to light up more pixels on each line as it sweeps across.

The higher horizontal frequencies demand more precise and better-quality electronics, which, of course, costs more to manufacture. To avoid a higher price, IBM designed some of its VGA systems with an *interlaced horizontal* system. Instead of increasing the horizontal frequency, the systems merely painted every other line across the screen from top to bottom, then returned to the top and painted the lines that were skipped. Theoretically, this sounds like a great idea, but, practically, it doesn't work too well because it causes a flicker. It can be very irritating to some people who have to work with this type of monitor for very long.

This flicker might not be readily apparent, but some people have complained of eyestrain, headaches, and fatigue after prolonged use of an interlaced monitor. If you turn your head slightly sideways, you might see it in the corner of your eye along the edges of the screen. It might be more noticeable when doing intensive graphics. If the monitor is only used for short periods of time, the flicker might not be noticeable.

Some companies make models that use interlacing in some modes and noninterlacing in other modes. Most companies don't advertise the fact that their monitors use interlacing. The interlaced models are usually a bit lower in price than the noninterlaced. Many of them also use the IBM standard 8514 chipset. You might have to ask the vendor what system is used.

Other companies besides IBM make interlaced monitors. If you get a chance, compare the interlaced and noninterlaced. You might not be able to tell the difference. If saving money is a prime consideration, then you might want to consider the interlaced because it is usually a bit less expensive.

The adapter that you buy should match your monitor. Use an interlaced adapter with an interlaced monitor. An adapter that can send only interlaced signals might not work with a noninterlaced monitor. Some adapters are able to adjust and operate with both interlaced and noninterlaced monitors.

Dot pitch The distance between the dots is called the *dot pitch*. The dots per inch (dpi) determines the resolution. A high-resolution monitor might have a dot pitch of 0.31 millimeter (mm). (1.00 mm = 0.0394 inches, 0.31 mm = 0.0122 inches, or about the thickness of an average business card). A typical medium-resolution monitor might have a dot pitch of 0.39 mm. One with very high resolution might have a dot pitch of 0.26 mm or even less. The smaller the dot pitch, the more precise and more difficult they are to manufacture.

The size of the monitor makes a difference in dot pitch. A 0.31 mm would be good for a 20-inch monitor, but it would not be very good for a 12-inch one.

Some of the low-cost monitors have a dot pitch of 0.42 mm and some as high as 0.52 mm. The 0.52 mm might be suitable for playing some games but it would be difficult to do any productive computing on such a system.

Landscape vs. portrait

Monitors that are wider than they are tall have a *landscape* orientation. Monitors that are taller than they are wide have a *portrait* orientation. The elongated portrait type is used most often for desktop publishing and other special applications.

Adapter basics

It won't do you much good to buy a high-resolution monitor unless you buy a good adapter to drive it. You can't just plug a monitor into your computer and expect it to function. Just as a hard disk needs a controller, a monitor needs an adapter to interface with the computer. Also, like the hard disk manufacturers, many of the monitor manufacturers do not make adapter boards. Just as a hard disk can operate with several different types of controllers, most monitors can operate with several different types of adapters.

The monitor and adapter should be fairly well matched. It is possible to buy an adapter that has greater capabilities than the monitor. Or your monitor might be capable of greater resolution than the adapter can supply.

Analog vs. digital

Up until the introduction of the PS/2 with VGA, most displays used the digital system. But the digital systems have severe limitations.

Digital signals are of two states, either fully on or fully off. The signals for color and intensity require separate lines in the cables. As pointed out earlier, it takes six lines for the EGA to be able to display 16 colors out of a palette of 64.

The analog signals that drive the color guns are voltages that are continuously variable. It takes only three lines for the three primary colors. The intensity of the voltage for each color can then be varied almost infinitely. If a brighter red is needed, the voltage signal that lights up the red pixels can be increased. It is, therefore, easy to create as many as 256 colors out of a possible 262,144.

The digital systems are sometimes called TTL for *transistor-to-transistor logic*. Some monitors that can handle both digital and analog have a switch that says TTL for the digital mode.

Very high resolution graphics adapters

Many of the high-resolution adapters have up to one megabyte or more of video RAM (VRAM) memory on board. Some adapter boards are sold with only 512K of VRAM. They will probably have empty sockets for another 512K. You can buy VRAM and install it yourself. VRAM is about the same price as *DRAM*.

A single complex graphics image might require one megabyte of memory or more to store. By having the memory on the adapter board, it saves having to go through the bus to the conventional RAM. Some adapter boards even have separate plug-in daughterboards for extra memory. Many of them have their own coprocessor on board, such as the Texas Instruments 34010 or the Hitachi HD63483.

Depending on the resolution capabilities and the goodies that it has, a very high resolution adapter board can cost from $150 up to $3,400.

The high-resolution adapters are downward compatible. If you run a program that was designed for CGA, the monitor will display it in CGA format even though you have a very high-resolution monitor. But it will look a lot better than it would on a CGA monitor.

Screen size

The stated screen size of a monitor is measured diagonally—the same way as television screens. But there is usually a border on all four sides of the screen. The usable viewing area on my 13-inch NEC is about 9.75 inches wide and about 7.75 inches high. One reason is because the screen is markedly curved near the edges on all sides. This curve can cause distortion so the areas are masked off and not used.

This area is big enough for most of the things that I do. But for some types of CAD work or desktop publishing, it would be helpful to have a bigger screen. Prices go up almost at a logarithmic rate for sizes above 14 inches. A 14-inch screen might cost less than $500, a 16-inch about $1,200, a 19- or 20-inch, $2,500 or more.

Controls

You should check for the placement of controls to adjust the brightness, contrast, and vertical and horizontal lines. Some manufacturers place them on the back or some other difficult area to reach. It is much better if they are accessible from the front or side so that you can see the effects as you adjust them.

Glare

If a monitor reflects too much light, it can be like a mirror and be very distracting. Some manufacturers have coated the screen with a silicon formulation to cut down on the reflectance. Some have etched the screen for the same purpose. Some screens are tinted to help cut down on glare. If possible, you should try the monitor under various lighting conditions. If you have a glare problem, several supply companies and mail-order houses offer glare shields that cost from $20 to $100.

Cleaning the screens

Because there are about 25,000 volts of electricity hitting the back side of the monitor face, it creates a static attraction for dust. This dirt can distort and make the screen difficult to read.

Most manufacturers provide an instruction booklet that suggests how the screen should be cleaned. If you have a screen that has been coated with silicon to reduce glare, you should not use any harsh cleansers on it. In most cases, plain water and a soft paper towel will do fine.

Tilt-and-swivel base

Most monitors sit on top of the computer. If you are short or tall, have a low or high chair, or a nonstandard desk, the monitor might not be at eye level. A tilt-and-swivel base allows you to position the monitor to best suit you. Many monitors now come with this base. If yours does not have one, many specialty stores and mail-order companies sell them for $15 to $40.

Several supply and mail-order companies also offer an adjustable arm that clamps to the desk. Most have a small platform for the monitor to sit on. The arm can swing up and down and from side to side. It can free up a lot of desk space. It can cost from $50 to $150.

I can't possibly list all of the monitor and adapter vendors. You can find many ads in the computer magazines listed in the appendix.

A checklist

If at all possible, go to computer swap meet or to several different stores and compare various monitors. Comparing monitors might be a good idea even if you are going to buy through mail order. Here are some things that you might want to check:

- *Dot pitch.* Ask for a spec sheet. Check for dot pitch. It should be no less than 0.31 mm for good resolution; 0.28 mm or less is better.
- *Interlace.* Check for noninterlace if you expect to do a lot of graphics work.
- *Scan rate.* Check scan rate, both vertical and horizontal. The less expensive monitors have a fixed rate. Some have two or three fixed rates. The better ones use multiscanning.
- *Check bandwidth.* For a rough estimate, multiply the resolution times the vertical frequency. For instance, at a vertical frequency of 60 Hz it would be $800 \times 600 \times 60$ Hz = 28.8 MHz, or a minimum of 30 MHz. For a vertical frequency of 70 Hz, it would be $800 \times 600 \times 70$ = 33.6 MHz, or 35 MHz minimum.
- *Check controls.* The controls should be accessible from the front or side. Some manufacturers put them in the back of the monitor. It is very difficult to set up the screen if you can't look at it at the same time. But once the monitor is set up, you shouldn't have to touch it again.
- *Check brightness.* Turn the brightness up and check the center of the screen and the outer edges. The intensity should be the same in the center and edges. Check for glare in different light settings.
- *Check with applications.* Check the focus, brightness, and contrast with text and graphics. I have seen some monitors that displayed demonstration graphics programs beautifully, but were terrible when displaying text in various colors.
- *Check for adapter and drivers.* Buy the highest-resolution adapter that you can afford. Try to get an adapter with a minimum of 1Mb of VRAM or at least 512K of VRAM that is able to accept 512K more. You can add extra VRAM yourself.
- *Tilt-and-swivel base.* Even if you have to pay extra, get a monitor with a tilt-and-swivel base.
- *Software test.* Sonera Technologies has developed Display MATE, software that can make dozens of tests on a monitor. It can check for resolution, all types of distortion, speed, performance, and many other tests. If you expect to spend a lot of money on a monitor, it will pay you to order this software from Sonera Technologies, P.O. Box 565, Rumson, NJ 07760.

Chapter 10

Communications

Communications are one of the most important aspects of doing business. In some organizations, employees might spend half of their time on the telephone, in meetings, and writing reports and memos. When communications such as E-mail and fax machines are available to an employee, productivity increases.

LAN E-mail

Electronic mail (E-mail) is a great aid in communicating with employees, coworkers, or clients. Other forms of communication have problems that are partly solved by using E-mail. For example, if you have to leave your desk to attend a meeting, important phone calls might be missed and you usually find yourself playing a lot of telephone tag. Someone who is at a meeting or away from his desk returns your call, but then you are away from your desk.

Sending memos and reports by traditional delivery methods can also pose difficulties. They can get lost or sent to the wrong person. Or if a person gets a lot of mail, they might not be able to read and respond to all of it.

Setting up and organizing a meeting can be difficult because all kinds of conflicts crop up. An important player might not be able to show up at your meeting because of a previous commitment. Several E-mail programs or workgroup productivity programs can help alleviate these and other workgroup problems.

E-mail programs are installed on a server with a large hard disk. A section of the hard disk is dedicated as a "post office." Each user on the network then has a private post office box for incoming mail.

When a user logs onto the network, he or she might be notified that mail is waiting to be read. In this case, a small window usually pops up on the person's screen telling him or her about incoming mail. The user might be able to interrupt the task at hand and read the mail or wait until later to retrieve it from the mailbox. E-mail can only be retrieved or read by the addressee.

Users can send mail, memos, reports, drawings, and other data to anyone on the network. Many of the E-mail programs also have a "chat" feature, which allows two or more people to send messages back and forth in real time. This feature has the potential to save hundreds of dollars by helping to reduce the number of costly time-consuming meetings.

Besides E-mail, many programs have other goodies, such as a scheduler, personal calendar, calculator, a file manager that lets you arrange and notate your files, and software that allows a gateway connection to other E-mail systems such as MCI, AT&T, and MHS. Many of these features are RAM resident, so you can pop them up at any time and send or answer a message.

Your personal calendar can be used to write in dates and times of meetings and other occasions when you might not be available. A scheduler allows you to access and view the calendar of others on the network. This feature can be very helpful, especially to anyone who is trying to schedule a meeting.

Here are just a few of other productive communications programs. Call for brochures.

cc:Mail, Lotus	(415) 961-8800
Computer Mail Service	(800) 777-0535
Da Vinci Systems	(800) 328-4624
Higgins, Enable Software	(415) 865-9805
Gammalink	(408) 744-1430
Right Hand Man, Futurus	(800) 327-8296
WordPerfect Office	(801) 225-5000

Look for ads in LAN magazines for other E-mail programs.

Modems

Sometimes you will need to communicate with the world beyond your LAN. A *modem* is one way to do it. A modem is an electronic device that allows a computer to use an ordinary telephone line to communicate with other computers equipped with a modem. *Modem* is a contraction of the words *modulate and demodulate.*

Why the need for a modem

The voice signals sent over a telephone line are in the form of analog voltages. When you speak into the mouthpiece, a diaphragm moves back and forth due to the pressure of the sound waves. This diaphragm creates an analog alternating voltage that goes up and down to match the frequency and intensity of the sound waves. This voltage is sent out over the telephone lines. The earpiece on the other end of the telephone line is just like a miniature loudspeaker. The small speaker in the earpiece responds to the received signals and vibrates to re-create a fairly reasonable copy of the sound that was input at the other end of the line.

Computer data is usually in a digital voltage form. It might be five volts of direct current that is turned on and off to create the 1s and 0s. Because the telephone system is set up to transmit analog voltage, the modem is needed to modulate and change the digital voltage to analog alternating voltages for transmission. At the receiving end, a similar modem will demodulate the analog voltage back into a digital form.

It is easy to use a telephone to communicate with any one of several million persons anywhere in the world. A computer, with telecommunications capabilities, can just as easily communicate with several million other computers in the world. A computer with a modem can access over 10,000 bulletin boards in the U.S. With it, you can take advantage of E-mail, faxes, up-to-the-minute stock market quotations, and a large number of on-line services—such as home shopping, travel reservations, and many other services.

Most modems are on a board that plugs into one of the slots in a computer motherboard. The modems use one of the systems ports. There is usually a switch or jumper on the board for setting it to COM1 or COM2.

A simple modem test

It is often difficult to determine which COM port is being used by a device. You can use the AT command to determine if your modem is working. At the DOS prompt C:> type the following using uppercase letters: ECHO AT DT12345>COM1:. If the modem is set properly, you will hear a dial tone, then the modem will dial 12345. If two devices are set for COM1 there will be a conflict. The computer will try for a while, then give an error message and the familiar Abort, Retry, Ignore, Fail?. If nothing is attached to the port, you might get no message.

Communications software

In order to use a modem, it must be driven and controlled by software. You can choose from dozens of communication programs.

CrossTalk, (404) 998-3998, was one of the earliest modem programs, and now a CrossTalk for Windows version is available. It works with any Windows version, which makes it very easy to learn and use.

Procomm, (314) 474-8461, is one of several low-cost shareware programs. In many areas, it can outperform some of the high-cost commercial programs. The registration fee is $89.

Qmodem, (805) 395-0223, is another excellent shareware program for a registration fee of only $30. It is now a part of the Mustang Software Company. This company has developed a BBS software program that is very good. If you would like to set up your own bulletin board, give them a call.

You can get copies of shareware programs from bulletin boards or from any of the several companies who provide public-domain software.

Shareware is not free. You might try it out and use it, but the developers usually ask that you register the program and send in a nominal sum. For this low cost they will usually provide a manual and some support.

Hayes compatibility

One of the most popular early modems was made by Hayes Microcomputer Products. It has become the IBM of the modem world and have established a *de facto* standard. Almost all of the hundreds of modem manufacturers, except for some of the very inexpensive ones, emulate the Hayes standard.

Protocols

Protocols are procedures that have been established for exchanging data, along with the instructions that coordinate the process. Most protocols can sense when the data is corrupted or lost due to noise, static, or a bad connection. It will automatically resend the affected data until it is received correctly.

There are several protocols, but the most popular ones are Kermit (named for Kermit the Frog), Xmodem, and Ymodem. These protocols transmit a block of data along with an error-checking code, wait for the receiver to send back an acknowledgment, then send another block and wait to see if it got through okay. Noise and static is in the form of alternating voltage. A bit of static can easily corrupt a file that is being sent.

If a block does not get through, it is resent immediately. Protocols such as Zmodem and HyperProtocol send a whole file in a continuous stream of data with error-checking codes inserted at certain intervals. It then waits for confirmation of a successful transmission. If the transmission is unsuccessful, then the whole file must be resent.

The sending and receiving modems should both use the same protocol.

CCITT-recommended standards

The communications industry is very complex because there are many different manufacturers and software developers. Of course all of them want to differentiate their hardware or software by adding new features. So there have not been many real standards. You might have difficulties if you want to communicate with someone else who is not using the same features.

The Consultative Committee on International Telegraph and Telephone (CCITT) makes recommendations only. A company is free to use or ignore the protocols. But more and more companies are now adopting the recommendations.

All CCITT recommendations for small computers have a *V* or *X* prefix. The *V* series is for use with switched-telephone networks, which is almost all of them. The *X* series is for systems that do not use switched phone lines. Revisions or alternate recommendations have *bis* (second) or *ter* (third) added. Here are a few CCITT recommendations:

- *V.22*. A 1,200 baud standard.
- *V.22 bis*. A 2,400 baud standard.
- *V.32*. A 9,600 baud standard.
- *V.32 bis*. A 14,400 baud standard.
- *V.42*. An error-correcting protocol. It includes MNP-4 and LAP M error correction.
- *V.42 bis*. A standard for 4-to-1 data compression. Under ideal conditions, this standard could permit data transmission speed four times greater than the rated baud rate. With this compression a V.32 bis modem could transmit 57,600 bits per second (bps).
- *X.25*. A protocol for packet mode communications on data networks.
- *MNP*. Networking Protocol, a series of ten different protocols developed by the MicroCom company. Several of its protocols are very similar to the CCITT V series.
- *LAP M & LAP B*. Other protocols that are supported by AT&T and Hayes. They are similar to the CCITT V.42 error-correcting standard.

Baud rate

Telephone systems were originally designed for voice, so they have a very narrow bandwidth. The signals are subject to noise, static, and other electrical disturbances. These problems, and the state of technology at the time, limited the original modems to about five characters per second, or a rate of 50 baud.

The term *baud* comes from Emile Baudot (1845–1903), a French inventor. Originally, the baud rate was a measure of the dots and dashes in telegraphy. It is now defined as the actual rate of symbols transmitted per second. For the low baud rates, it is essentially the same as bits per second.

Remember that it takes eight bits to make a character. Just as there are periods and spaces to separate words, there must be one start bit and two stop bits to separate the on/off bits into characters. A transmission of 300 baud would mean that 300 on/off bits are sent in one second. Counting the start/stop bits, it takes 11 bits for each character. So 300 divided by 11 is about 27 characters per second (cps).

Some of the newer technologies might actually transmit symbols that represent more than one bit. For baud rates of 1,200 and higher, the cps and baud rate can be considerably different.

How to estimate connect time

You can figure the approximate length of time that it will take to transmit a file. Here's how:

1. Determine the cps by dividing the baud rate by 10. For instance, a 1,200 baud rate transmits 120 cps; a 2,400 baud rate transmits 240 cps.
2. Look at your directory and determine the number of bytes in the file.
3. Divide the number of bytes in the file by the cps.
4. Multiply the number of bytes in the file by 1.3 for the start/stop bits to get a final approximation.

For example, let's say you have a 2,400-baud modem. To figure the time for a 40K file, divide 40K by 240 cps and you get 167 cps. Multiply 167 cps times 1.3, which equals 217 cps or 3.6 minutes. With a 9,600-baud modem, the same 40K file could be sent in about 55 seconds. Using a V.32 bis modem at 14,400 baud and using V.42 bis 4-to-1 compression, a 40K file could be sent in about 9 seconds. Of course, an 80K file would double all these figures.

Viruses and Trojan horses

There have been reports of hidden viruses in some public-domain and even in some commercial software, like the recent Michelangelo virus, which was designed to go off on Michelangelo's birthday, March 6. Software infested by a virus might appear to work as it should for some time. But eventually, it might contaminate and destroy many of your files. The viruses often cause the files to grow in size and become larger.

Trojan horses usually do not contaminate other files. But they lie dormant for a certain length of time, or until a program has been run a certain number of times, then it destroys the file. Some commercial software is sold with a system that is somewhat similar to a Trojan horse. The buyer pays to use the program a certain number of times, then it will no longer operate.

If you download bulletin board software, it is probably best to run it from a floppy disk until you are sure that it is not contaminated. Several companies have developed software to detect viruses and prevent them from damaging your files.

People who create viruses deserve severe punishment, but unfortunately, several who have been caught have been released with little more than probation and a warning. This trend is starting to change.

Fortunately, viruses are not too common, but even if there is only one, it is still one too many.

Online services

Several large national bulletin boards run information and reference services, such as CompuServe, Dataquest, Dow Jones, and Dialog.

These companies have huge databases of information. A caller can search the databases and download information as easily as pulling the data off his own hard disk. The companies charge a fee for the connect time.

Prodigy, (800) 759-8000, is unlike other online services. Prodigy does not charge for connect time. It charges only a nominal monthly rate, and it has phone service to most large cities so that you don't even have to pay a toll charge. Prodigy has an impressive list of services, including home shopping, home banking, airline schedules and reservations, stock market quotations, and many others. One of the faults of Prodigy is that it is relatively slow. But because it is so inexpensive, I can live with it.

CompuServe, (800) 848-8990, Delphi, (800) 544-4005, and Genie, (800) 638-9636, are major online services that are now offering shopping services similar to Prodigy's.

Online E-mail

Many of the national bulletin boards offer E-mail (discussed earlier in this chapter) along with their other services. These services can be of great value to some individuals and businesses.

E-mail is becoming more popular every day, and there are now several hundred thousand subscribers. The cost for an average message is about one dollar. The cost for overnight mail from the U.S. Post Office, Federal Express, and UPS is $9 to $13.

Here are some of the companies who provide on-line E-mail:

AT&T Mail	(800) 367-7225
CompuServe	(800) 848-8990
DASnet	(408) 559-7434
MCI Mail	(800) 444-6245
Western Union	(800) 527-5184

Facsimile boards and machines

Facsimile (fax) machines have been around for quite a while. Newspapers and businesses have used them for years. They were the forerunners of the scanning machines.

The early machines were similar to the early acoustic modems. Both used foam rubber cups that fit over the telephone receiver-mouthpiece for coupling. They were very slow and subject to noise and interference. Fax machines and modems have come a long way since those early days.

A page of text or a photo is fed into the facsimile machine and scanned. As the scanning beam moves across the page, white and dark areas are digitized as 1s and 0s, then transmitted out over the telephone lines.

Modems and fax machines are quite similar and related in many respects. A modem sends and receives bits of data. A fax machine or board usually sends and receives scanned whole page letters, images, signatures, etc. A computer program can be sent over a modem, but not over a fax. A fax sends and receives the information as digitized data. At times, you might need either a fax machine or a modem. Both units would not be in use at the same time, so the same phone line can be used for both of them.

Millions of fax machines are in use today. Very few businesses cannot benefit from the use of a fax. A fax can be used to send documents, including handwriting, signatures, seals, letterheads, graphs, blueprints, photos, and other types of data around the world, across the country or across the room to another fax machine.

It costs from $8.50 to $13 to send an overnight letter. E-mail can send the same letter for $1. A fax machine can deliver it for about 40 cents and do it in less than three minutes. Depending on the type of business, and the amount of crucial mail that must be sent out, a fax system can pay for itself in a very short time.

Stand-alone fax units

Some fax machines are still stand-alone devices that attach to a telephone. They have been vastly improved in the last few years and most of them are as easy to use as a copy machine. In fact, most of them can be used as a copy machine.

Some overseas companies are making stand-alone units that are fairly inexpensive and cost as little as $400. You might not be happy with the low-cost ones. You will be better off if you can spend a bit more and get one that uses plain paper, and has a paper cutter, high resolution, a voice/data switch on the system, a document feeder, automatic dialer, automatic retry, delayed transmission, transmission confirmation, polling, built-in laser printer, and a large memory. You might not need, or be able to afford all of these features, but try to get a machine with as many as possible. Of course, the more features, the higher the cost.

Fax computer boards

Several companies have developed fax machines on circuit boards that can be plugged into computers. Many of the newer models have provisions for a modem on the same board, saving a precious slot in the computer.

Special software allows the computer to control the fax boards. Using the computer's word processor, letters and memos can be written and sent out over the telephone lines. Several letters or other information can be stored or retrieved from the computer hard disk and transmitted. The computer can even be programmed to send the letters out at night when the rates are lower.

The computer fax boards have one disadvantage. They cannot scan information unless a scanner is attached to the computer. Without a scanner, the information that can be sent is usually limited to what can be entered from a keyboard or disk. As pointed out, stand-alone units scan pages of information, including such things as handwriting, signatures, images, blueprints, and photos.

It is fairly easy to attach a scanner to your computer. You can choose from several different types and models of scanners that can be used with your network. Look through any computer magazine for ads.

The computer can receive and store any fax that is sent, serving as a log or record of all fax activity. The digitized data and images can be stored on a hard disk, then printed out on a printer.

The combination fax-modem boards can cost from $100 to $1,000, depending on the extras and goodies installed. The board can be installed in a server so that it is available to all users on the network.

ISDN

ISDN is an acronym for *Integrated Services Digital Network*. Eventually the whole world will have telephone systems that use this concept. It is a system that will be able to transmit voice, data, video, and graphics in digital form rather than the present analog form. When this change happens, we can scrap our modems and use only an interface. But don't hold your breath, and don't throw your modem away just yet!

Chapter 11

Printers

Hundreds of different printers are available today. They range in price from relatively inexpensive (dot-matrix printers) to very expensive (some laser printers), so you should be able to find one that fits your needs and your budget.

Choosing a printer

The type of printer you need depends primarily on how you plan to use the computer. A laser is best for some applications and a dot matrix is best for others. If at all possible, before you buy a printer, visit a computer store or a computer show and try it. Get several spec sheets of printers in your price range and compare them.

You should also look for reviews of printers in computer magazines. *PC Magazine* has done an annual printer review every year since 1984. It has excellent test labs and a well-informed review staff. Its reviews and tests are comprehensive, thorough, and unbiased.

Dot-matrix printers

Dot-matrix printers range in price from low to high. The low-priced ones are not very fast, the print quality can be poor, and the fonts and graphics capability limited. Some of the high-priced dot matrixes can print in near letter quality (NLQ) at a speed nearly equal to that of some lasers, and many of them can print different fonts and graphics.

Some things can be done with a dot matrix that can't be done with a laser. For instance, a dot matrix can have a wide carriage; most lasers are limited to $8\frac{1}{2} \times 11$ inches. The dot matrix can use continuous sheets or forms; the laser uses cut sheets, fed one at a time. A dot matrix can also print carbons and forms with multiple sheets.

Print-head pins

Most of the dot-matrix printers sold today have 24 pins in the print head, are fairly reasonable in price, and are sturdy and reliable. The 24-pin printer forms characters from two vertical rows of 12 pins in each row. Small electric *solenoids* (see glossary) are around each wire pin in the head. By pressing various pins as the head moves across the paper, any character can be formed and graphics can be printed.

Some of the less expensive printers have a vertical row of only 7 or 9 pins in the print head. As the head moves in finite increments across the paper, solenoids push individual pins forward to form characters.

Here is a representation of the pins in a 7-pin print head and how it would form the letter A:

```
1 o            o
2 o          o o
3 o          o   o
4 o          o     o
5 o          o o o o
6 o        o         o
7 o      o             o
```

The print head moves left to right. The numbers on the left represent the individual pins in the head before it starts moving across the paper. The first pin to be struck would be number 7, then number 6, then 5, 4, 3, 5 and 2, 1, 2, and 5, 3, 4, 5, 6, then 7.

A 24-pin head would be similar to the 7-pin representation above, except that it would have two vertical rows, side by side, of 12 pins in each row. The pins in one row would be slightly offset and lower than the pins in the other row. Because the pins are offset, they would overlap slightly and fill in the gaps normally found in a 7- or 9-wire system.

Dot-matrix speed

In draft mode, the speed of the dot-matrix printer can be from 200 characters per second (cps) to 600 cps or more. In near letter quality (NLQ) mode, it can be from 60 cps to 330 cps. At 60 cps, it would take a little over one minute to print a full page of 4,000 characters. At 330 cps, it would take less than 15 seconds, or about 4 pages per minute (ppm). Many of the low-cost lasers have a 4 ppm speed.

Some high-end dot-matrix line printers can print a whole line at once and are faster than most lasers. Some high-end dot-matrix printers might have two to four heads so that the line to be printed is divided up among the heads. The first head would print one-fourth of the line, while the next head was printing the next fourth and the other two were printing the rest of the line.

Dot-matrix color

Some dot-matrix printers use a ribbon with three different stripes of colors, usually red, green, and blue. By causing the head to strike the various colors, all of the colors of the rainbow can be blended and printed. Of course, to do this, you need special software. It is a bit slow, but if you need color to jazz up a presentation, or for accent now and then, color is great. The color option will usually cost about $100 more than the standard ribbon.

Print buffer

The computer can feed data to a printer much faster than it can print it. Printers might have a buffer that can hold from 1K to 50K or more. A single page of text only requires about 1K, so most medium-priced printers will have a 6K to 8K buffer. The data is loaded into the buffer by the computer and it is then fed to the printer as needed. With a large buffer, the computer can dump the data, then go about its business doing other things. But with a small buffer and a long file, the computer will have to sit there and continually load the data into the buffer.

Narrow carriage vs. wide carriage

At times, you need a wide-carriage printer, especially if you use some of the wide spreadsheet paper. I have often used my wide carriage to address large manila envelopes.

The wide-carriage models usually cost a bit more than the narrow ones, but they are worth the extra money.

Noise reduction

A dot-matrix printer can be very noisy. Enclosures can help reduce the noise, but they are a bit expensive. I sat mine on a two-inch sheet of rubber foam that had been used as packing material. The foam rubber reduces the noise considerably.

Low cost

Several companies are now producing low-cost laser printers and forcing manufacturers of dot-matrix printers to lower their prices. Many dot-matrix manufacturers are also adding features, such as more memory and more fonts, to attract buyers.

Many vendors are still pushing the 9-pin dot-matrix machines. A current issue of the *Computer Shopper* had the following ads: a 9-pin Panasonic KXP NX 1000 for $119; a 9-pin Panasonic KX-P1180 with several built-in features for $144; a wide-carriage 9-pin Panasonic KX-P1191 for $199; a narrow-carriage 24-pin Panasonic KX-P1124i for $269; and a wide-carriage 24-pin Panasonic KX-P1624 for $325.

Shop wisely. You'll find considerable savings. For example, I saw several other ads for these same printers with much higher prices. One ad listed the KX-P1124i for $295 and the KX-P1624 for $385.95.

For some heavy-duty office work, where a lot of multiple-sheet forms are printed, you would probably want a 9-pin, rather than 24-pin, dot-matrix printer.

Ink jets

Ink jets are similar to dot-matrix pins in one respect—they transfer ink to paper. They differ in that the dot matrix uses 9 to 24 pins to impact against a ribbon to create characters or graphics. The ink jets use from 30 to 60 small nozzles to spray ink onto paper to create characters or graphic images. Most of the inkjet machines print at a 300 dots per inch (dpi) resolution, the same as most lasers.

The HP DeskJet Plus is a small printer that has quality almost equal to that of a laser. It uses a matrix of small ink jets instead of pins. As the head moves across the paper the ink is sprayed from the jets to form the letters. It comes with Courier fonts, but it can use several more fonts that are available on plug-in cartridges. It has a speed of 1 to 2 pages per minute (ppm). It is small enough to sit on a desk top and is very quiet. It is currently advertised for $549.

The inkjet wells are good for about 300 pages of text. They must then be replaced or refilled, which is relatively inexpensive and easy to do.

Cannon also manufactures a couple of printers based on the inkjet technology, but the company calls it *bubblejet*. Cannon's BJ-10e is a small portable printer. It is advertised for $309. Its desktop model BJ-330e is advertised for $610.

The Diconix division of Kodak also makes a small portable inkjet printer. It is advertised for $341. These two portables are ideal for attaching to laptops.

Inkjet color

Hewlett-Packard has two models, the HP PaintJet for 8½-×-11-inch paper, and the HP PaintJet XL, which can handle paper as large as 11 × 17 inches. They can provide color by using ink cartridges with four different colored inks—black, cyan, yellow, and magenta. They offer a low-cost method of good-quality color. A few laser color printers rely on a thermal wax transfer method to create color, but they are four to five times more expensive than an inkjet printer.

The color inkjet printers are ideal for creating colored transparencies for presentations, for graphs, and for schematic plotting and drawings.

Canon's CJ10 is an inkjet copier, printer, and scanner, all in one.

Laser printers

Lasers have excellent print quality. They are a combination of copy machine, computer, and laser technology. On the down side, they have lots of moving mechanical parts and are rather expensive.

Laser printers use synchronized, multifaceted mirrors and sophisticated optics to write the characters or images onto a *photosensitive rotating drum*. The drum is similar to the ones used in copy machines. The laser beam is swept across the spinning drum and is turned on and off to represent white and dark areas. As the drum is spinning, it writes one line across the drum, then rapidly returns and writes another. It is quite similar to the electron beam that sweeps across the face of the monitor one line at a time.

The drum is sensitized by each point of light that hits it. The sensitized areas act like an electromagnet. The drum rotates through the carbon toner. The sensitized areas become covered with the toner. The paper is then pressed against the drum. The toner that was picked up by the drum leaves an imprint of the sensitized areas on the paper. The paper is then sent through a heating element where the toner is heated and fused to the paper.

Except for the writing to the drum, this process is the same thing that happens in a copy machine. Instead of using a laser to sensitize the drum, a copy machine takes a photo of the image to be copied. A photographic lens focuses the image onto the rotating drum.

Engine

An *engine* is the drum and its associated mechanical attachments. Canon, a Japanese company, is one of the foremost makers of engines. It manufactures them for its own laser printers and copy machines, and for dozens of other companies, such as Hewlett-Packard and Apple. Several other Japanese companies manufacture laser engines.

The Hewlett-Packard LaserJet was one of the first low-cost lasers. It was a fantastic success and has become the *de facto* standard. Most of the hundreds of laser printers now on the market emulate the LaserJet standard. HP is the IBM of the laser world. Even IBM's laser printer emulates the HP standard.

Low-cost laser printers

Competition has been a great benefit to consumers. It has driven prices down and forced many new improvements. Several new low-cost models have been introduced that print 4 to 6 pages per minute (ppm) instead of the 8 to 10 pages of the original models. They are smaller than the originals and can easily sit on a desktop. Most have 512K of memory with an option to add more. The discount price for some of these models is now down to less than $800. The original 8 to 10 page models have dropped from about $3,500 down to around $1,000. If you can afford to wait a few seconds, the 4 to 6 page models will do almost everything the 8 to 10 pagers will do. The prices will drop even more as the competition increases and the economies of scale in the manufacturing process become greater.

An ad in the *Computer Shopper* offers a Panasonic KX-P4420 laser for $699. It can print 8 ppm, comes with 22 fonts, 512K memory, and several other goodies. The Hewlett-Packard LaserJet III has about the same features as this printer. The LaserJet III is advertised for $1,498, in the same issue of the *Computer Shopper*. This price is more than twice the cost of the Panasonic KX-P4420. The HP LaserJet IIP, a 4-ppm printer, is advertised for $799.

For doing graphics, *PC Magazine* reported that the inexpensive 4-ppm units could print a page of graphics at about the same speed as the 8-ppm units. If you need a laser primarily for graphics, you can save quite a lot of money if you buy the 4-ppm units.

Memory

If you plan to do any graphics or desktop publishing, you will need to have at least one megabyte of memory in your printer. Of course, the more memory, the better. Not all lasers use the same configuration, so check before you buy. The HP LaserJet III has a provision for plugging in a special board with the memory chips. You have to buy a board with the memory that is designed for HP's connector and system. Memory is fairly inexpensive now. I recently bought a board for my LaserJet III from the Starion Corporation, (714) 573-0626. See Fig. 11-1. The board with 2Mb of memory cost $119. Several other companies offer laser memories. Look through computer magazines. Two other companies are ASP, (800)445-6190, and Elite, (800) 942-0018.

11-1 An HP LaserJet III memory board with 2Mb of memory.

Page-description languages (PDLs)

If you plan to do any complex desktop publishing you might need a page-description language (PDL) of some kind. Text characters and graphics images are entirely different. Monitor controller boards usually have all of the alphabetical and numerical characters stored in ROM. When you press the letter A from the keyboard, it dives into the ROM chip, drags out the A and displays it in a precise block of pixels wherever the cursor is positioned. These characters are called *bit-mapped characters*. If you wanted to display an A that is twice as large, you would have to have a complete font set of that type in the computer. With a good PDL, the printer can take one of the stored fonts and change it, or scale it, to any size you want. These are *scalable fonts*.

With a bit-mapped font, you have one typeface and one size. With scalable fonts, you might have one typeface with an infinite number of sizes. Most of the lasers printers will accept ROM cartridges that usually have as many as 35 or more fonts. You can print almost anything that you want with these fonts if your system can scale them.

Laser speed

Laser printers can print from 4 ppm to over 10 ppm depending on the model and what they are printing. Some very expensive high-end printers can print over 30 ppm. A dot-matrix printer is concerned with a single character at a time. A laser printer composes, then prints a whole page at a time. With a PDL, many different fonts, sizes of type, and graphics can be printed. But the laser must determine where every dot that makes up a character or image is to be placed on the paper before it is printed. This composition is done in memory before the page is printed. The more complex the page, the more memory it will require and the more time needed to compose the page. It might take several minutes to compose a complex graphic, but once composed, it will print out very quickly.

A PDL controls and tells the laser where to place the dots on the sheet. Adobe's PostScript is the best known PDL. Several companies have developed their own

PDLs. Of course, none of them are compatible with the others. This fact has caused a major problem for software developers, because they must try to include drivers for each one of these PDLs. Several companies are attempting to clone PostScript. But it is doubtful that they can achieve 100-percent compatibility. Unless you need to move your files from a machine that does not have PostScript to one that does, you might not need to be compatible. Hewlett-Packard includes its Printer Control Language 5 (PCL), a scalable font system, on its LaserJet IIIs.

PostScript printers

Printers sold with PostScript installed, such as the Apple LaserWriter, might cost as much as $1,500 more than one without PostScript. Hewlett-Packard is offering a PostScript option for its LaserJet IID (the IID and IIID print duplex on both sides of the paper) for a list price of $995. The PostScript option for the IIP and III printers is $695, but discount prices should be less. Pacific Data Products, (619) 552-0880, has a cartridge that has built-in bit-stream fonts that is comparable to Adobe's PostScript.

PostScript on disk   Several software companies have developed PostScript software emulation. One of the better ones is LaserGo's GoScript, (619) 450-4600. QMS, (800) 631-2692, offers UltraScript, and the Custom Applications Company, (508) 667-8585, has Freedom of the Press.

Resolution

Almost all of the lasers have a 300-×-300-dots-per-inch (dpi) resolution. This resolution is very good, but not nearly as good as the 1,200-×-1,200-dots-per-inch typeset used for standard publications. Several companies have developed systems to increase the number of dots to 600 × 600 dpi or more. LaserMaster, (612) 944-6099, has developed printer controllers that plug into a slot in the computer. It has several models that will increase resolution from 400 × 400 up to 1000 × 1000. At this time they are rather expensive. Eventually they will become more reasonable in price. At 300 × 300 dpi, it is possible to print 90,000 dots in one square inch. On an 8½-×-11-inch page of paper, if you deduct a one-inch margin from the top, the bottom and both sides, then you would have 58.5 square inches × 90,000 dots = 5,265,000 possible dots.

Paper size

Most laser printers are limited to 8½-×-11-inch paper (A size). The QMS PS-2200, (800) 631-2692, and the Unisys AP 9230, (215) 542-2240, can print 11-×-17-inch paper (B size), as well as the A size.

Maintenance

Most of the lasers use a toner cartridge that is good for 3,000 to 5,000 pages. The original cost of the cartridge is about $100. Several small companies are now refilling the spent cartridges for about $50 each. Of course there are other maintenance costs involved with laser printers.

Because these machines are very similar to copy machines, they have a lot of moving parts that can wear out and jam up. Most of the larger companies give a mean time between failures (MTBF) of 30,000 to 100,000 pages. But remember that these figures are only averages, not guarantees.

Paper

Many different types and weights of paper exist. Almost any paper will work in your laser. But if you use a cheap paper in your laser, it could leave lint inside the machine and cause problems in print quality.

Generally speaking, any bond paper or a good paper made for copiers will work fine. Colored paper made for copiers will also work fine. Some companies are marking copy papers for laser printers and charging more for it. Many of the laser printers are equipped with trays to print envelopes. Hewlett-Packard recommends envelopes with diagonal seams and gummed flaps. Make certain that the leading edge of the envelope has a sharp crease.

Address labels

The Avery Company, (818) 858-8387, has developed address labels that can withstand the heat of the fusing mechanism of the laser. Most office supply stores carry the labels. Avery also developed an excellent software program that can be used to print the labels. The program has a database in which addresses, phone numbers, and other information can be stored. Any of the addresses can be searched for, sorted, edited, or printed. The program can also read and import data and files from dBASE and WordPerfect, as well as import .pcx and .pcc graphics files. Avery has both laser and dot-matrix versions of the program. It is ideal for anyone who does a lot of mailing.

Other specialty supplies can also be used with your laser. The Integraphix Company, (800) 421-2515, carries several different items that you might find useful. Call them for a catalog.

Color printers

A few color printers are available, at a cost of $7,000 and up at this time. The prices should be less by the time you read this book. These printers are often referred to as laser color printers, but they don't actually use the laser technology. They use a variety of thermal transfer technologies using a wax or rolls of plastic polymer. The wax or plastic is brought into contact with the paper, then heat is applied. The melted wax or plastic material then adheres to the paper. Very precise points, up to 300 dots per inch, can be heated. By overlaying three or four colors, all of the colors of the rainbow can be created.

The cost of color prints ranges from about 5 cents a sheet for the Howtek Pixelmaster, which uses wax material similar to crayons, up to about 83 cents apiece for the large 11-×-17-inch sheets from the QMS ColorScript 30. A *PC Magazine* editor said that the magazine saves about $750,000 a year by using a color printer for corporate use rather than a photographic process. Another big plus is that the results from a color printer are available almost immediately and any errors or corrections can be made easily.

Most of the color printers have PostScript, or they emulate PostScript. The Tektronix Phaser CP can also use the Hewlett-Packard Graphics Language (HPGL) to emulate a plotter. These color printers can print out a page much faster than a plotter. Several other color printers will be on the market soon. With a lot of competition, the prices should come down.

Plotters

Plotters are devices that can draw almost any shape or design under the control of a computer. A plotter usually has from one to eight or more different colored pens. Several different types of pens for various applications exist, for example, writing on different types of paper, film, or transparencies.

Some pens are quite similar to ball point pens, others have a fiber point. The points are usually made to a very close tolerance and can be very small so that the thickness of the lines can be controlled. The line thicknesses can be very crucial in some precise design drawings. The plotter arm can be directed to choose any one of the various pens. This arm is attached to a sliding rail and can be moved from one side of the paper to the other. A solenoid can lower the pen at any predetermined spot on the paper.

While the motor is moving the arm horizontally from side to side, a second motor moves the paper vertically up and down beneath the arm. This motor can move the paper to any predetermined spot and the pen can be lowered to write on that spot. The motors are controlled by predefined x, y coordinates. They can move the pen and paper in very small increments so that almost any design can be traced out. Values could be assigned of perhaps 1 to 1,000 for the y, or vertical, elements and the same values for the x, or horizontal, elements. The computer could then direct the plotter to move the pen to any point or coordinate on the sheet.

Plotters are ideal for such things as printing circuit board designs, architectural drawings, making transparencies for overhead presentations, graphs, charts, and many CAD/CAM drawings. All of this work can be done in as many as eight or more colors. Several different-sized plotters are available. The desktop units are sometimes limited to only A- and B-sized plots and cost as little as $200 to $2,000. The large floor models can accept paper as wide as four or more feet long and cost from $4,000 to $10,000.

If you are doing very precise work, for instance designing a transparency that will be photographed and used to make a circuit board, you will want one of the more accurate and more expensive machines. Many good graphics programs are available that can use plotters.

Several companies manufacture plotters and the industry has no standards. Just like printers, each manufacturer has developed its own drivers, which is very frustrating for software developers that must try to include drivers in their programs for all of the various brands.

Hewlett-Packard (HP) has been one of the major plotter manufacturers and, as a result, many of the other manufacturers now emulate the HP drivers. Almost all of the software that requires plotters include a driver for HP. If you are in the market for a plotter, try to make sure that it can emulate the HP. Houston Instruments is also a major manufacturer of plotters. Its plotters are somewhat less expensive than the Hewlett-Packard.

One of the disadvantages of plotters is that they are rather slow. Now some software programs allow laser printers to act as plotters. Of course they are much faster than a plotter, but except for the colored printers, they are limited to black and white.

Plotter supplies

It is important that a good supply of plotter pens, special paper, film, and other supplies be kept on hand. Plotter supplies are not as widely available as printer supplies. A high-priced plotter might have to sit idle for some time if the supplies are not on hand. Most of the plotter vendors provide supplies for their equipment. One company that specializes in plotter pens, plotter media, accessories, and supplies is Plotpro, (800) 223-7568.

Installing a printer or plotter

Most IBM-compatible computers have four printer ports: two serial and two parallel. No matter whether it is a plotter, dot-matrix, daisy-wheel, or laser printer, it will require one of these ports. If you have a 286 or 386 computer, these ports might be built into the motherboard. (See the previous chapter and the discussion for installing modems). If you have built-in ports, you will still need a short cable from the motherboard to the outside and you will then need a longer cable to your printer. If you don't have built-in ports, you will have to buy interface boards.

Almost all laser and dot-matrix printers use the parallel ports. Some of them have both serial and parallel. Many of the daisy wheel printers and most of the plotters use serial ports. For the serial printers you will need a board with an RS232C connector. The parallel printers use a Centronics-type connector. When you buy your printer, buy a cable from the vendor that is configured for your printer and your computer.

Printer sharing

Ordinarily a printer will sit idle most of the time. (Some days I don't even turn on my printer.) For offices that have several computers, it would be a waste of money if each one had a separate printer that was used only occasionally. In a network, the printer cost is minimized because several computers can be connected easily to one printer or plotter. This configuration is called *printer sharing*.

Manual switches

If there are only two or three computers, and they are fairly close together, accessing a printer is not much of a problem. Manual A-B switch boxes, which cost $25 to $150, allow any one of two or three computers to be switched online to a printer. (They are called A-B because they usually have a pointer-control knob on the switch that points to position A or B). If a simple switch box is used, and the computers use the standard parallel ports, the cables from the computers to the printer should be no more than 10 feet long. Parallel signals will begin to degrade if the cable is much longer. A cable system that uses serial signals might be as long as 50 feet. It might not be a good idea to use some manual switches with laser printers. When the switches break one contact before connecting with the other contact, it could cause surges in the line that could damage electronic components.

Data switches

If an office or business is fairly complex, then several sophisticated electronic switching devices are available. They each have their own microprocessor that can allow the connection of several devices. Some of them can allow a large number of different types of computers to be attached to a single printer or plotter. Many of them have built-in buffers and amplifiers that can allow cable lengths up to 250 feet or more. The costs can range from $100 to $1,400 or more. Look in chapter 2 for more information about data switches.

Tanstaafl Manufacturing, (800) 776-5676, produces several different printer-sharing devices. See Fig. 11-2. Here are some other companies that provide print buffers, data switches, and printer-sharing devices:

Logical Connection Plus from Fifth Generation Systems	(800) 873-4384
MetroLAN from Datacom	(800) 243-2333
Solectek from Ralin	(800) 752-9512
Buffalo Products	(800) 345-2356
Cables To Go	(800) 225-9646
Dalco	(800) 445-5342
National Computer Accessories	(916) 441-1568
Computer Friends	(800) 829-9991
Technologic Systems	(513) 644-2230
Data Switches from Western Telematic	(800) 854-7226
Nu Data Company	(908) 842-5757

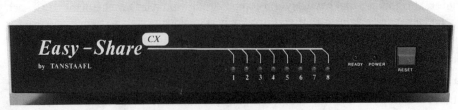

11-2   An electronic printer-sharing switch. (Tanstaafl)

Several other companies also offer these components. Again, look for ads in computer and LAN magazines.

Sneakernet: A low-priced printer-sharing option

One of the least expensive methods of sharing a printer is the old-fashioned "sneakernet." The data is generated on a computer that does not have a printer and copied to a floppy disk. The floppy disk is then carried to another computer with a printer. If you only have two or three computers, and you don't do much printing, this system works fine!

Printer server

If you have several computers on a network, a single computer could be used as a part-time printer server. This computer could be connected to both a laser and a dot-matrix printer. All of the print requests would be routed to this computer. It would queue the print jobs, then send them to the printer in the order received. If a lot of printing is to be done, then the computer might be dedicated as a print server only. A low-cost XT clone with a 20Mb hard disk would be fine as a dedicated print server. If you are using NetWare, LAN Manager, or almost any of the other network operating systems (NOS), they will have provisions for printing. But several other companies have developed software and hardware for network printing.

11-3 A printer adapter that connects directly to an Ethernet LAN. (Rose Electronics)

This software and hardware usually works with the NOS to make printing from the network faster or easier. One such device is MicroServ from Rose Electronics, (800) 333-9343. It is a small Ethernet adapter that connects directly to the parallel port of a printer. See Fig. 11-3. It runs under Novell NetWare on thin RG-58 cables or unshielded twisted pairs (UTP). Rose Electronics manufactures several other data-switch and printer-sharing devices. JetLAN from ASP Computer Products, (800) 445- 6190, is an Ethernet board that plugs into the Optional I/O socket of an HP LaserJet II or III. The printer is then available to any computer on the network. ASP also makes several other printer-sharing and data-switch devices.

Sources

Hundreds of companies manufacture printer and printer-related devices, so I can't possibly list them all. As always, take the time to look through computer and LAN magazines to compare prices and get the best buy.

Final thought

When Gutenberg invented movable type in 1450, it gave birth to printing. If Gutenberg were around today, I am sure that he would be quite pleased with the progress that has been made in the printing industry. We have come a long way in the last 543 years.

Chapter 12

Essential software

Software is an important part of your computer and LAN. In this chapter, you will learn about the software you must have to operate your LAN, and the software that makes it easy for you to use and maintain your LAN. Except for very unusual applications, you probably will never have to do any programming. More software is already written and immediately available than you can use in a lifetime.

Off-the-shelf & ready-to-use software

Some off-the-shelf programs can do almost anything you would ever want to do with a computer. Almost all of these programs work on networks, as well as single PCs. In most cases, you will need to buy a license to use the software on a network. The cost of the license is ordinarily based on the number of users on the network.

For most general applications, there are certain basic programs that you will need. Speaking of basic, BASIC (an acronym for Beginner's All-purpose Symbolic Instruction Code) is one that you might need. GW-BASIC from Microsoft is more or less the standard and is included with MS-DOS. Many applications still use BASIC. Even if you are not a programmer, it is simple enough that anyone can design a few special applications with it.

You will need several types of programs, such as a disk operating system (DOS), word processors, databases, spreadsheets, utilities, shells, communications, windows, graphics, and computer-aided design (CAD). Depending on how you intend to use your computer, thousands of other programs are available for special needs.

Software can be more expensive than hardware, but the prices vary from vendor to vendor. Few people pay the list price. I have seen software with a list price of $700 advertised by a discount house for as little as $350. Also remember that some excellent free public-domain programs can do almost everything that the high-cost commercial programs can do. Check your local bulletin board, user group, or ads for public-domain software in most computer magazines. Also, some excellent shareware programs that can be registered for a nominal sum.

I can't possibly list all of the thousands of software packages available. Again, subscribe to the magazines listed in chapter 13. Most of them have detailed reviews of software in every issue.

Operating systems

The *operating system* is a basic group of programs under the control of a data processing program, or an integrated collection of service routines, for supervising the sequencing and processing operations of a computer. The most common operating systems—MS-DOS, DR DOS 6.0, OS/2, and DESQview—are discussed in the next few sections.

MS-DOS

DOS is to a computer what gasoline is to an automobile: without DOS, the computer won't operate. DOS is an acronym for disk operating system. But it does much more than just operate the disks. In recognition of this, the newer OS/2 has dropped the "D".

If you are new to computers, DOS should be the first thing that you learn. DOS has over 50 commands, but chances are that you will never need to know more than 15 or 20.

When the operating system, config.sys, buffers, drivers, TSRs (terminate-and-stay-resident programs) and others are loaded into the 640K of available RAM, often not enough memory is left to load other programs. DR DOS 6.0 and MS-DOS 5.0 takes the operating system, TSRs, buffers, drivers and others, out of low memory and places them in memory above 640K. The older versions of DOS loaded everything into low memory.

Some commands in DOS, if not used properly, can be disastrous. Be very careful when using commands such as FORMAT, DEL, ERASE, COPY, and RECOVER. When invoked, RECOVER renames and turns all of the files into File0001.rec, File0002.rec... The disk will no longer be bootable and crucial files might be garbled. Many experts say that you should erase the RECOVER command from your disk files and leave it only on your original diskettes. It should only be used as a last resort. You should use Norton Utilities, Mace, PC Tools, or one of the other utilities to unerase or restore a damaged file.

COPY can cause problems if you copy a file onto a disk that has another file with the same name. The file with the same name on the disk will be copied over and gone forever. If you erase or delete a file, you can possibly recover it. But if it has been copied over or written over, it is history.

DR DOS 6.0

The DR in DR DOS stands for Digital Research, not doctor. The Digital Research Corporation was founded by Gary Kildahl, the developer of CP/M, the first operating system for personal computers.

DR DOS 6.0 is completely compatible with MS-DOS. It has several good features including FileLINK, which allows you to connect and transfer files over a serial cable, and ViewMAX to view, organize, and execute files and commands using only one or two keystrokes or a mouse. It has comprehensive online help, supports hard disk partitions up to 512Mb, has disk cache, a full-screen text editor, password protection, and many features not found in MS-DOS.

The ViewMAX shell feature lets DR DOS use icons to operate very much like Windows 3.0. You can use a mouse to quickly open files, copy, delete, and perform many of the other commands and functions.

ViewMAX also has a clock that can run in a window of the screen. Another feature is a calculator for on-screen calculations.

It is very easy to install on a hard disk by just copying it onto the disk. There is no need to reformat your disk. If you have a previous version of DOS on your disk, it will copy over and replace the older DOS.

Digital Research Corporation, (800) 443-4200, has now merged with Novell.

OS/2

OS/2 is designed specifically for high-end applications and large workstations. It is much the same as MS-DOS except that it has multiuser and has multitasking capabilities. OS/2 comes bundled with LAN Manager. IBM has extensively revised OS/2 2.0.

DESQview

DESQview is similar to Windows in some respects in that it runs on top of DOS. It allows multitasking and multiusers. You can have up to 50 programs running at the same time and have as many as 250 windows open. It runs all DOS software. It is simple to learn and use. Call Quarterdeck Office Systems at (213) 392-9851.

Word processors

Word processors are the most used of all software. Most of the word processor programs come with a spelling checker and some of them come with a thesaurus, which can be very handy. Usually they include several other utilities for such things as communications programs for your modem, outlines, desktop publishing, print merging, and many others.

WordStar

I started off with WordStar on my little CP/M Morrow with a "hefty" 64K of memory and two 140K single-sided disk drives. It took me some time to learn it. I have tried several other word processors since then and found that most of them would require almost as much time to learn as WordStar did originally. I don't have a lot of free time and WordStar does all I need. So I have not learned too many other processors.

There are probably more copies of WordStar in existence than any other word processor.

WordStar, (800) 227-5609, has an educational division that offers an excellent discount to schools, both for site licenses and for student purchases. The educational division is at (800) 543-8188.

WordPerfect

WordPerfect is one of the hottest-selling word processors, so it must be doing something right. One thing its manufacturer does right is give free, unlimited, toll-free support.

WordPerfect has the ability to select fonts by a proper name, do most desktop publishing functions, and columns, and has simplified printer installation, and many other useful functions and utilities. WordPerfect works with Windows. Contact WordPerfect at (801) 225-5000.

Microsoft Word for Windows

Microsoft Word for Windows was developed by the same people who produced MS-DOS. It lets you take advantage of all of the features and utilities of Windows and is among the best-sellers in the country. If you have previously learned a different word processor, Word for Windows includes a manual that lists the differences from most popular word processors, and it can help you quickly become accustomed to Word for Windows. Contact Microsoft at (206) 882-8080.

PC-Write

PC-Write is the least expensive of all word processors. It is a shareware program, and a $16 donation is requested if you use the program or copy it from an existing user. Full registration with a manual and technical support is $89. It is easy to learn and is an excellent personal word processor. Call Quicksoft at (800) 888-8088.

Many other good word processors are available so look for ads and reviews in computer magazines.

Grammar checkers

You might be the most intelligent person alive, but you might not be able to write a simple intelligible sentence. Several grammar-checking programs can work with most word processors. They can analyze your writing and suggest ways to improve it. Here are just a couple of them:

- Right Writer, Que, (800) 992-0244
- Grammatik, Reference Software, (800) 872-9933

Database programs

Database packages are very useful for business purposes. They allow you to manage large amounts of information. Most programs allow you to store information, search it, sort it, do calculations, make up reports, and do several other quite productive things.

At the present time, there are almost as many database programs as there are word processors. Few of them are compatible with others. There is a strong effort in the industry to establish some standards under the Structured Query Language (SQL) standard. Several of the larger companies have announced their support for this standard.

The average price for the better-known database packages is almost twice that of word processors.

dBASE IV

Ashton-Tate with its dBASE II was one of the first with a database program for the personal computer. dBASE is a very powerful program and has hundreds of features. It is a highly structured program and can be a bit difficult to learn. dBASE IV is much faster than dBASE III, has a built-in compiler, SQL, and an upgraded user interface along with several other enhancements. Ashton-Tate is now a division of Borland International, (408) 438-5300.

askSam

The funny looking name, askSam, is an acronym for *access knowledge via stored access method*. It is a free-form, text-oriented database management system, which is almost like a word processor. Data can be typed in randomly, then sorted, and accessed. Data can also be entered in a structured format for greater organization. It is not quite as powerful as dBASE IV, but is much easier to use and is much less expensive. askSam is ideal for personal use and for the majority of business needs. Seaside Software, (800) 327-5726, the manufacturer, also has an excellent discount program for students.

R:BASE 3.1

R:BASE, which has been around for a long time, has pull-down menus, mouse support, an English-like procedural language, and is fully relational for multitable tasks. It is one of the more powerful and more versatile of the present-day database programs.

Microrim, (206) 885-2000, which produces R:BASE, is so sure that you will like the program that it offers an unlimited, no-questions-asked, money-back, 90-day guarantee.

FoxPro

FoxPro is very easy to use. It has windows and can be controlled by a mouse or keyboard. Of course, using it with a mouse saves several keystrokes. It has several different windows, including a View Window as the master control panel to create databases, open files, browse, set options, and other functions. You don't have to be a programmer to type commands into the Command Window to operate FoxPro. The Browse Window lets you view, edit, append, or delete files. It also has Memo Fields; a built-in editor that allows you to create Macros; extensive context-sensitive help; and much more. Contact Fox Software at (419) 874-0162.

Paradox

Paradox is fairly easy to learn and use, is fast and powerful, and is designed for both beginners and expert users. It is a full-featured relational database that can be used on a single PC or on a network. The main menu has functions like View, Ask, Report, Create, Modify, Image, Forms, Tools, Scripts, and Help. Choosing one of these items will bring up options that are associated with that item. Function keys are used extensively.

The query-by-example feature is very helpful for beginners and experts alike. Paradox has a very powerful programming language, PAL. Experienced programmers can easily design special applications. Paradox is one of the Borland family of products. Contact Borland International at (408) 438-5300.

Spreadsheets

Spreadsheets are primarily number crunchers. They have a matrix of cells into which data can be entered. Data in a particular cell can be acted on by formulas and mathematical equations. If the data in the cell that is acted on affects other cells, recalculations are done on them. Several of the tax software programs use a simple form of spreadsheet where the income and all the deductions can be entered. If an additional deduction is discovered, it can be entered and all the calculations will be redone automatically.

In business, spreadsheets are essential for inventory, expenses, accounting, forecasting, making charts, and dozens of other vital uses. Some of the many spreadsheet programs available are discussed in the next few sections.

Lotus 1-2-3

Lotus was one of the first and most-popular spreadsheets because of its easy-to-use commands and ability to manipulate mathematical data in a convenient format.

Microsoft Excel

Excel is a very powerful spreadsheet program, with pull-down menus, windows, and dozens of features. It can even perform as a database. Call Microsoft at (206) 882-8080.

Quattro

The Quattro spreadsheet looks very much like Lotus 1-2-3, but it has better graphics capabilities for charts, calculates faster, has pull-down menus, can print sideways, and has several other features not found in Lotus 1-2-3. One of the better features is the suggested list price of $195, and only $148 from some discount houses. Call Borland International at (408) 438-8400.

SuperCalc5

SuperCalc, introduced in 1981, was one of the pioneer spreadsheets. It has never enjoyed the popularity of Lotus, though it has features not found in Lotus. It is compatible with Lotus 1-2-3 files and can link to dBASE and several other files. SuperCalc is an excellent spreadsheet. Computer Associates, (408) 432-1727, also has several excellent account packages costing from $595 to $695.

Many other spreadsheet programs are available. Check the ads and reviews in computer magazines.

Utilities

Utilities are essential tools that can unerase files, detect bad sectors on a hard disk, diagnose, unfragment, sort, and perform many other tasks. Norton Utilities was the first, and is still foremost, in the utility area.

Mace Utilities has several functions not found in Norton. Mace Gold is an integrated package of utilities that includes a power-out protection program (POP), a backup utility, and TextFix and dbFix for data retrieval. PC Tools has even more utilities than Norton or Mace.

Ontrack, the company that has sold several million copies of Disk Manager for hard disks, also has a utility program called DOSUTILS. It provides tools to display and modify any physical sector of a hard disk, scan for bad sectors, and diagnose and analyze the disk.

Steve Gibson's SpinRite and Prime Solution's Disk Technician are excellent hard-disk tools for low-level formatting, defragmenting, and detecting potential bad sectors on a hard disk.

Norton Utilities

Everybody should have Norton Utilities. Norton also has Norton Commander, a shell program, and Norton Backup, a very good hard-disk backup program. The Norton Company has recently merged with Symantec. Contact Norton at (213) 453-2361.

Mace Utilities

Mace Utilities was developed by Paul Mace. It was recently acquired by Fifth Generation Systems, (504) 291-7221, which developed Fastback, the leading backup program.

PC Tools

PC Tools an excellent program that just about does it all. It has data recovery utilities, hard-disk backup, a DOS shell, a disk manager, and more. PC Tools is available from Central Point Software, (503) 690-8090.

SpinRite II

SpinRite II can check the interleave and reset it for the optimum factor without destroying your data. It can also test a hard drive and detect any marginal areas. SpinRite can maximize hard-disk performance and prevent hard-disk problems before they happen.

Steve Gibson, the developer of SpinRite, writes a very interesting weekly column for *InfoWorld* magazine. Contact Gibson Research at (714) 830-2200.

Disk Technician

Disk Technician does essentially the same thing that SpinRite does, and a bit more. It has several automatic features and can now detect most viruses. For more information about Disk Technician, call Prime Solutions at (619) 274-5000.

CheckIt and CheckIt LAN

CheckIt LAN quickly checks and reports on your computer's configuration, the type of CPU it has, the amount of memory, the installed drives, and peripherals. It runs diagnostic tests of the installed items and can do performance benchmark tests.

CheckIt LAN can check a network configuration, the IRQ settings, perform PC diagnostic tests, scan the network for viruses, and it has several other very useful features. Call TouchStone Software at (800) 531-0450 or (714) 969-7746.

SideKick Plus

SideKick is in a class by itself. It was first released in 1984 and has been one of the most popular pop-up programs ever since. It has a calculator, notepad, calendar, and several other utilities. It's another Borland International, (408) 438-8400, product.

Directory and disk-management programs

Dozens of disk-management programs are available to help you keep track of your files and data on the hard disk—such as find, rename, view, sort, copy, and delete, and many other useful utilities. These programs can save an enormous amount of time and make your work a lot simpler.

XTreePro Gold

Executive Systems' XTree was one of the first and is still one of the best disk-management programs. It has recently been revised and it is now much faster and has several new features. Call Executive Systems, (800) 634-5545.

QDOS III

QDOS III is a disk-management program similar to XTree. It does not have quite as many features as XTree, but is less expensive. QDOS III is available from Gazelle Systems, (800) 233-0383.

Wonder Plus 3.08

Wonder, or 1DIR, was one of the early disk-management shells. For more information, call Bourbaki at (208) 342-5849.

Search utilities

I have about 3,000 files on my hard disk in several subdirectories, so you can imagine how difficult it is to keep track of all of them. I sometimes forget in which subdirectory I filed something. Search utilities find files for you.

Some programs can go through a directory and look for a file, or almost anything, and you don't even have to know the full name of the item. They will accept wild cards and identify their matches.

Magellan 2.0 is a very sophisticated program that can navigate and do global searches through files and across directories. It finds text and lets you view it in a window. It will let you compress files, do backup, compare, undelete, and several other excellent utilities. Magellan is available from Lotus, (800) 223-1662.

Other good search programs are available, including public-domain and shareware programs.

Computer-aided design (CAD)

Computer-aided design (CAD) techniques are used whenever conventional design methods prove excessively time-consuming. Considerable development has gone into computer methods and programs to solve complex network problems. A variety of CAD programs are available, including AutoCAD, DesignCAD 2D, and Design-CAD 3D.

AutoCAD

AutoCAD is a high-end, high-cost design program. It is quite complex, with an abundance of capabilities and functions. But it is also rather expensive at about $3,000. Some modules cost less. AutoCAD is the IBM of the CAD world and has more or less established the standard for the many clones that have followed. It is made by Autodesk, (415) 332-2344.

DesignCAD 2D & DesignCAD 3D

DesignCAD 2D and DesignCAD 3D will do just about everything that AutoCAD will do at about one-tenth the cost. DesignCAD 3D allows you to make three-dimensional drawings. Call American Small Business Computers, (918) 825-4844.

Several other companies offer CAD software. Check the computer magazines.

Miscellaneous

There are thousands of other programs for things such as accounting, statistics, finance, and many other applications. For example, Money Counts, It's Legal, WillMaker 4.0, The Random House Encyclopedia, ACT!, and Forms Express are just a few.

Money Counts

Money Counts is a very inexpensive program, priced at $40, that can be used at home or in a small business. With it you can set up a budget, keep track of all of your expenses, balance your checkbook, and several other functions. Call Parsons Technology, (800) 223-6925.

It's Legal

It's Legal helps you create wills, leases, promissory notes, and other legal documents. It's Legal is also from Parsons Technology.

WillMaker 4.0

WillMaker 4.0 is a low-cost program that can help you create a will. A will is an important document and everyone should have one no matter what age or how much you own. Many people put it off because they don't want to take the time, or they don't want to pay a lawyer a large fee. WillMaker 4.0, from Nolo Press, (415) 549-1976, is an easy and inexpensive way to put together a legal will.

The Random House Encyclopedia

The Random House Encyclopedia is the complete encyclopedia on disk and is designed to find any subject you need very quickly. It's available from Microlytics, (716) 248-9150.

ACT!

ACT! lets you keep track of business contacts, schedules, and business expenses; write reports; and perform about 30 other functions. ACT! is available from Contact Software, (800) 228-9228.

Forms Express

Most businesses have dozens of forms that must be filled out. Quite often, the information then has to be transferred to a computer. Forms Express lets you easily design and fill in almost any kind of form on a hard disk. If necessary, it can then be printed. Call Forms Express, (415) 382-6600.

Summary

I can't possibly mention all of the fantastic software that is available. Thousands and thousands of ready-made software programs allow you to do almost anything with your computer. Look through any computer magazine for reviews and ads. You should be able to find programs for almost any application.

Chapter 13

Mail order and magazines

Thousands of vendors and many more thousands of computer products are on the market. I have tried to list a few of these vendors when a product was mentioned in the book. But it is not possible to list them all. This chapter gives you a list of magazines and other resources that you can use to help you build your own LAN.

Local computer stores

If you live near a large city, you can visit computer stores in town. Local computer stores are good because you can get support that is conveniently located and you might even be able to work out a deal that lets you try the merchandise before you buy it.

Computer swap meets

Again, if you live near a large city, there will probably be a few swap meets every now and then. In the San Francisco Bay area and in the Los Angeles area, there is one almost every weekend. Going to a swap meet is usually better than going to a computer store. There will be lots of items that you can look at, price, and compare. Often several booths or vendors are all selling the same thing that you want to buy. You can take a pad and pencil, go to each vendor, get the best price, then make your best deal.

Sometimes you can even haggle a bit with the vendors. Some will try to meet the price of their competition. The best time to haggle is when it gets near closing time. Some of them would rather sell at a reduced price than pack the goods up and take them back to the store.

I sometimes go to the swap meets even if I don't need anything. There are usually lots of people and an atmosphere that is almost like a carnival.

Computer shows

One of the best ways to find out what is available is to attend a computer or LAN trade show. Several are held each year throughout the country. COMDEX (Computer Dealers Exhibition), produced by the Interface Corporation, has two shows each year. One is in the spring in the east and one is in the fall in Las Vegas. The fall show in Las Vegas is the biggest computer show in the country. It usually has about 1,500 exhibitors and about 125,000 visitors. A large part of these shows are devoted to LAN products. Interface Corporation also produces several other shows. You can reach Interface at 300 First Ave., Needham, MA 02194-2722, (617) 449-6600.

Several other shows are also devoted exclusively to networks. One is the ComNet shows, produced by the World Expo Corporation and the *Network World*

Magazine, P.O. Box 3091, Northbrook, IL 60065-9928. Another is Bruno Blenheim Networld shows, (800) 829-3976. One is usually held in Dallas and another in Boston.

When you go to a show, you usually see hundreds of products at one site. You can examine, touch, and feel the products and see actual demonstrations.

LANDA (Local Area Network Dealers Association) sponsors small shows occasionally. Its shows are often combined with a training and engineer certification program for LAN dealers and installers. LANDA has some excellent tapes and educational study materials that allow you to pass the certification tests. But you must be a member to get the materials at a decent price and to take the test. Membership fees are $1,500 for a business and $300 for an individual. Employees of the business can then get an associate membership for $50 a year. LANDA seems to be interested in the large VAR businesses. You can contact LANDA at 360 W. Butterfield Rd., #110, Elmhurst, IL 60126, (708) 279-2255.

Numerous small shows and seminars are held throughout the year in or near most large cities. Some of the seminars are offered free as a way to promote a certain product, others are rather expensive training and tutorial programs that might charge $300 to $900 for a one- or two-day seminar. I have never gone to one because I can't learn enough in such a short period of time to make it worthwhile.

Several other smaller shows are held in various parts of the country throughout the year. Some vendors are rather unhappy that so many shows are held each year. It can be very expensive to pay for the show floor space, the construction of a nice booth, moving the equipment in and out, employees, and other associated costs. But many vendors feel obligated to exhibit at these shows to get the exposure and the leads for sales.

If you have never attended one of these shows, you don't know what you are missing. By all means try to attend one.

Mail order

Shopping at a local store can sometimes be a real bother, especially in a place like Los Angeles. It usually means you have to give up a bit of time, risk your life on the highway, and fight the traffic to get to the store. Then comes the most difficult part of the whole process, finding a parking space within a mile of the store.

Or you can look through a magazine, find an ad for what you need, pick up your phone, order the components, and have them delivered to your door. Many of the mail-order companies have few distributors and do not have large showrooms, so the goods might cost 40 percent less than what you would pay at a local store.

Depending on where you live and from where you order the goods, you might not have to pay a sales tax when you order through the mail. In California, the state and local sales taxes are up to over seven percent. So it costs more than $7 for every $100 dollars you spend. But if you order goods from other states, you don't have to pay the sales tax unless the company has a store in California. Many of the states are trying to get the law changed so that they can collect the sales taxes no matter where you buy the goods. So far they have not been successful.

But what would life be without a few negatives. On the down side, you might have to wait three or four weeks before you get your goodies. Of course, you can usually pay extra and have them shipped by Federal Express or by UPS to get them overnight or within a couple of days.

Another negative is that you are buying the components sight unseen. You have only the word of the advertiser that they will be sent. But if you use a bit of common sense and follow a few basic rules, you shouldn't have to worry.

If it sounds too good to be true . . .

There was a case not long ago where very expensive items were advertised for a very low price. Only a post office box number was given as the place to send the money. A lot of people eagerly sent in money thinking it was a deal that was too good to be true. And of course it was. When some of the people complained, the U.S. Postal Service investigated, but the operators were long gone.

This incident made legitimate advertisers a bit unhappy because it made them all suspect. They worried that many people would no longer buy from them. It also worried the publishers of computer magazines, because if people didn't buy from the advertisers, they would stop advertising. Without advertising revenue, the magazines would go belly-up in no time. It also worried the U.S. Postal Service and the Federal Trade Commission. The publishers and the advertisers got together and formed the Microcomputer Marketing Council (MMC) of the Direct Marketing Association (DMA).

Ten rules for ordering by mail

The magazines now police the advertisers fairly closely. But just to be on the safe side, here are a few rules that you should follow when ordering through the mail:

Make sure the advertiser has a street address   Some ads give only a phone number. If you decide to buy from this vendor, call and verify that an actual person is on the other end with a street number. Some businesses list a telephone number, then set up an automated telephone system. The system answers the phone, takes the order, and asks for a charge card number. Later, a person verifies the charge card and fills the order. The vendor is saving a lot of money on labor and might be perfectly honest, but I still think it is wise to talk to an actual person when I spend my money.

Before you send any money, do a bit more investigation. If possible, look through past issues of the same magazine for previous ads. If the vendor has been advertising for several months, then it is probably legitimate.

Look through magazines for other vendors that sell that product and compare prices   The prices should be fairly close. If it appears to be a bargain that is too good to be true, you know the rest.

Buy from a vendor who is a member of the MMC, DMA, or other recognized association   About 10,000 vendors now belong to marketing associations. They have agreed to abide by the ethical guidelines and rules of the associations. Except for friendly persuasion and the threat of expulsion, the associations have little power over the members. But most of them realize what is at stake and put a great value on their membership. Most who advertise in the major computer magazines are members.

The U.S. Postal Service, the Federal Trade Commission, magazines, and the legitimate businesses that advertise have taken steps to try to stop the fraud and scams.

Do your homework   Know exactly what you want, state precisely the model, make, size, component, and any other pertinent information. Tell which ad you are ordering from, ask if the price is the same, if the item is in stock, and when you can expect delivery. If the item is not in stock, indicate whether you will accept a substitute or want your money refunded. Ask for an invoice or order number. Ask the person's name. Write down all of the information, the time, the date, the company's address and phone number, description of item, and promised delivery date. Save any and all correspondence.

Ask if the advertised item comes with all the necessary cables, parts, accessories, software, etc.   Ask what the warranties cover. Ask about the seller's return policies, refund policies, and with whom you should correspond if you have a problem.

Don't send cash   You will have no record of it. If possible, use a credit card. If you have a problem, you can possibly have the bank refuse to pay the amount. A personal check might cause a delay of three to four weeks while the vendor waits for it to clear. A money order or credit-card order should be filled and shipped immediately. Keep a copy of the money order.

If you have not received your order by the promised delivery date, notify the seller.

Try the item when you receive it   If you have a problem, notify the seller immediately by phone, and then in writing. Give all the details. Don't return the merchandise unless the dealer gives you authorization. Make sure to keep a copy of the shipping receipt or packing slip for evidence that it was returned.

If you believe the product is defective or you have a problem, reread your warranties and guarantees   Reread the manual and any documentation. It is very easy to make an error or misunderstand how an item operates if you are unfamiliar with it. Before you go to a lot of trouble, try to get some help from someone else. At least get someone to verify that you do have a problem. Many times a problem will disappear and the vendor will not be able to duplicate it.

Try to work out your problem with the vendor   If you cannot, then write to the consumer complaint agency in the seller's state. You should also write to the magazine in which the ad appeared, and to the Direct Marketing Association (DMA), 11 W. 42nd St., New York, NY 10036. Or call the DMA at (212) 768-7277.

Federal Trade Commission (FTC) rules

Here is a brief summary of the Federal Trade Commission (FTC) rules:

Rule 1   The seller must ship your order within 30 days unless the ad clearly states that it will take longer.

Rule 2   If it appears that the seller cannot ship when promised, it must notify you and give a new date. The seller must give you the opportunity to cancel the order and refund your money if you desire.

Rule 3   If the seller notifies you that your order cannot be filled on time, it must include a stamped self-addressed envelope or card so that you can respond to the notice. If you do not respond, the seller may assume that you agree to the delay. It still must ship within 30 days of the end of the original 30 days or cancel your order and refund your money.

Rule 4   Even if you consent to a delay, you still have the right to cancel at any time.

Rule 5   If you cancel an order that has been paid for by check or money order, the seller must refund the money. If you paid by credit card, your account must be credited within one billing cycle. Store credits or vouchers in place of a refund are not acceptable.

Rule 6   If the item you ordered is not available, the seller may not send you a substitute without your express consent.

You should try by all means to work out your problems with the vendor. But if the situation looks hopeless, contact the DMA (212) 768-7277, your local U.S. Postal Inspector, your local Better Business Bureau, and your State Consumer Affairs or Consumer Protection Agency. You might also call the Federal Trade Commission at (202) 768-3768 to complain if you can't resolve your problem.

Computer magazines

As I mentioned throughout the book, many magazines are available. One of the best ways to find what you need is by looking at advertising in magazines. Advertising is the lifeblood of magazines. So you'll find a lot of advertising and a lot of opportunity to compare prices and products.

FaxBack

For years many magazines have printed a number on each ad. They included a postcard with all of the ad numbers in the back of the magazine. If a reader wanted more information about a certain ad, he circled the ad number on the "bingo" card and sent it to the magazine. It sometimes took four or five weeks to get a response.

Computer Buying World is a new magazine that has instituted a unique FaxBack system. It numbers each of its ads, and if a person wants more information about a product advertised in the magazine, he or she can call (617) 246-5089. From a touchtone phone, you can press the number of the product ad, and more information is sent back to your fax machine immediately. I expect that some of the other magazines will soon follow this procedure.

The magazine business is highly competitive. Many enter the business, but many do not survive. Here is a current list of some of the magazines that you can subscribe to if you want to keep up:

Business Publishing
191 South Gary Ave.
Carol Stream, IL 60188-9900

Byte Magazine
P.O. Box 558
Hightstown, NJ 08520-9409

Compute!
P.O. Box 3244
Harlan, IA 51593-2424

Computer Buying World
P.O. Box 3020
Northbrook, IL 60065-9847

Computer Currents
5720 Hollis St.
Emeryville, CA 94608

Computer Monthly
P.O. Box 7062
Atlanta, GA 30357-0062

Computer Graphics World
P.O. Box 122
Tulsa, OK 74101-9966

Computer Shopper
P.O. Box 51020
Boulder, CO 80321-1020

Data Based Advisor
P.O. Box 3735
Escondido, CA 92025-9895

Desktop
P.O. Box 94175
Atlanta, GA 30341

Home Office Computing
P.O. Box 51344
Boulder, CO 80321-1344

LAN Magazine
Miller Freeman Publications
P.O. Box 50047
Boulder, CO 80321-0047

LAN Technology
P.O. Box 52315
Boulder, CO 80321-2315

MicroTimes Magazine
5951 Canning St.
Oakland, CA 94609

New Media
P.O. Box 1771
Riverton, NJ 08077-9771

PC Computing
P.O. Box 50253
Boulder, CO 80321-0253

PC Home Journal
544 Second St.
San Francisco, CA 94107
(800) 827-0364

PC World Magazine
P.O. Box 51833
Boulder, CO 80321-1833

PC Magazine
P.O. Box 51524
Boulder, CO 80321-1524

PC Today
P.O. Box 85380
Lincoln, NE 68501-9815

Personal Workstation
P.O. Box 51615
Boulder, CO 80321-1615

Publish!
P.O. Box 51966
Boulder, CO 80321-1966

Unix World
P.O. Box 1929
Marion, OH 43306

Windows Magazine
P.O. Box 58647
Boulder, CO 80321-8647

Free magazines to qualified subscribers

The magazines listed here as free are sent only to qualified subscribers. As I mentioned earlier, the subscription price of a magazine usually does not come anywhere near covering the costs of publication, mailing, distribution, and other costs. Most magazines depend almost entirely on advertisers for their existence.

The more subscribers that a magazine has, the more it can charge for its ads. Naturally it can attract a lot more subscribers if the magazine is free.

PC Week and *InfoWorld* are excellent magazines. They are so popular that the publishers have to limit the number of subscribers. They cannot possibly accommodate all the people who have applied, so they have set standards that have to be met in order to qualify. They do not publish the standards, so even if you answer all of the questions on the application, you still might not qualify.

To get a free subscription, you must write to the magazine for a qualifying application form. The form will ask several questions, such as how you are involved with computers, the company you work for, whether you have any influence in purchasing the computer products listed in the magazines, and several other questions that give the magazine a very good profile of its readers.

I filled out a qualifying form for a free magazine once and waited, but I never received the magazine. I met one of the editors at a computer show and complained. He said, "It's probably your own fault. You probably didn't lie enough on the form."

Those are his words. I would never tell you to lie. But it might help you qualify if you exaggerate just a bit here and there, especially when asked what your responsibilities are for the purchasing of computer equipment. I am pretty sure that the FBI will not be sent out to verify your answers.

The list of magazines below is not nearly complete. Hundreds of trade magazines are sent free to qualified subscribers. The Cahners Company alone publishes over 30 different trade magazines. Many of the trade magazines are highly technical and narrowly specialized.

PC Week
P.O. Box 5920
Cherry Hill, NJ 08034

InfoWorld
1060 Marsh Rd.
Menlo Park, CA 94025

Communication & Computer News
685 Canton St.
Norwood, MA 02062

Computer Design
Circulation Dept.
Box 3466
Tulsa, OK 74101-3466

Computer Systems News
600 Community Dr.
Manhasset, NY 11030

Communications Week
P.O. Box 2070
Manhasset, NY 11030

Computer Reseller News
P.O. Box 2040
Manhasset, NY 11030

Computer Products
P.O. Box 14000
Dover, NJ 07801-9990

Computer Technology Review
924 Westwood Blvd., Suite 650
Los Angeles, CA 90024-2910

California Business
Subscription Dept.
P.O. Box 70735
Pasadena, CA 91117-9947

Data Communications
P.O. Box 477
Hightstown, NJ 08520-9362

Designfax
P.O. Box 1151
Skokie, IL 60076-9917

EE Product News
P.O. Box 12982
Overland Park, KS 66212-9817

Electronics
P.O. Box 985008
Cleveland, OH 44198-5008
(216) 696-7000

Electronic Manufacturing
Lake Publishing
P.O. Box 159
Libertyville, IL 60048-9989

Electronic Publishing & Printing
650 S. Clark St.
Chicago, IL 60605-9960

Federal Computer Week
P.O. Box 602
Winchester, MA 01890-9948

Identification Journal
2640 N. Halsted St.
Chicago, IL 60614-9962

ID Systems
174 Concord St.

P.O. Box 874
Peterborough, NH 03458-0874

Automatic I.D. News
P.O. Box 6170
Duluth, MN 55806-9870

LAN Computing
P.O. Box 322
Horsham, PA 19044-0322

Lan Times
122 East, 1700 South
Provo, UT 84606

Lasers & Optronics
301 Gibraltar Dr.
P.O. Box 601
Morris Plains, NJ 07950-9827

Machine Design
Penton Publishing
P.O. Box 985015
Cleveland, OH 44198-5015

Modern Office Technology
Penton Publishing
1100 Superior Ave.
Cleveland, OH 44197

Manufacturing Systems
P.O. Box 3008
Wheaton, IL 60189-9972

Medical Equipment Designer
Huebcore Communications
29100 Aurora Rd., #200
Cleveland, OH 44139

Mini-Micro Systems
P.O. Box 5051
Denver, CO 80217-9872

Modern Office Technology
1100 Superior Ave.
Cleveland, OH 44197-8032

Network World
161 Worcester Rd.
Framingham, MA 01701-9172
(508) 820-7444

Networking Management
1421 S. Sheridan
P.O. Box 21728
Tulsa, OK 74121-9977

Office Systems 90
P.O. Box 3116
Woburn, MA 01888-9878

Office Systems Dealer 90
P.O. Box 2281
Woburn, MA 01888-9873

The Programmer's Shop
5 Pond Park Rd.
Hingham, MA 02043-9845

Quality
P.O. Box 3002
Wheaton, IL 60189-9929

Reseller Management
301 Gibraltar
Box 601
Morris Plains, NJ 07950-9811

Robotics World
6255 Barfield Rd.
Atlanta, GA 30328-9988

Software Magazine
P.O. Box 542
Winchester, MA 01980-0742

Scientific Computing & Automation
301 Gibraltar Dr.
Morris, Plains, NJ 07950-0608

Surface Mount Technology
Lake Publishing Corp.
P.O. Box 159
Libertyville, IL 600048-9989

Unix Review
Circulation Dept.
P.O. Box 7439
San Francisco, CA 94120-7439

Public-domain software

Here is a short list of companies that provide public domain, shareware, and low-cost software:

PC-Sig
1030D East Duane Ave.
Sunnyvale, CA 94086
(800) 245-6717

MicroCom Systems
3673 Enochs St.
Santa Clara, CA 95051
(408) 737-9000

Public Brand Software
Box 51315
Indianapolis, IN 46251
(800) 426-3475

Software Express/Direct
Box 2288
Merrifield, VA 22116
(800) 331-8192

Selective Software
903 Pacific Ave., Suite 301
Santa Cruz, CA 95060
(800) 423-3556

The Computer Room
P.O. Box 1596
Gordonsville, VA 22942
(703) 832-3341

Softwarehouse
3080 Olcott Dr., Suite 125A
Santa Clara, CA 95054
(408) 748-0461

PC Plus Consulting
14536 Roscoe Blvd., #201
Panorama City, CA 91402
(818) 891-7930

Micro Star
P.O. Box 4078
Leucadia, CA 92024-0996
(800) 443-6103

International Software Library
511 Encinitas Blvd., Suite 104
Encinitas, CA 92024
(800) 992-1992

National PD Library
1533 Avohill

Vista, CA 92083
(619) 941-0925

Computers International
P.O. Box 6085
Oceanside, CA 92056
(619) 630-0055

The above list is not complete. You might find several other companies advertised in some of the magazines listed earlier. Most of the companies listed above can provide a catalog listing of their software. Some are free and some of them charge a small fee. Write or call for details and latest prices.

Mail-order books

As you know, one of the best ways to learn about computers is through books. Many bookstores will ship computer and network books to you, or you can contact the publishers directly.

Windcrest/McGraw-Hill has a large selection of computer books. You can write or call for a catalog at Blue Ridge Summit, PA 17294-0850, (800) 822-8138. I recommend this publisher highly. The fact that it published the book that you are holding in your hands doesn't mean that I am biased. Well, maybe I am, just a bit.

Chapter 14

LAN management and troubleshooting

If you configured your network board properly, you should have no problem. And if the software was properly installed, everything should work like a charm. Your network should be giving you added productivity and saving you lots of money. Now you need to know how to manage and troubleshoot problems that might occur with your network.

LAN management

To keep your network up and running, you or your employee in charge of LAN management should keep a close watch over the network. You should be aware of any changes, alterations or additions to the network. You should have complete records and documentation of the server and each station. You should know what components are inside the server and each workstation and the configuration of each board.

If you have a large network system, there are some very complex and expensive LAN-management software programs and hardware tools. Some of the software can cost from $1,000 to $20,000. The hardware might be even more expensive. These tools can report on the quantity and quality of data passing through a particular point, keep track of who is using the network, the time that they spend on it, control the security of the network, act as a protocol analyzer, and report on dozens of other functions and network parameters.

If you have a system large enough to require these types of tools, you probably need some expert engineers to run your system. If you have a smaller system, all you need is a little common sense and an inexpensive copy of CheckIt LAN or any other programs. Call Syscon Resources at (800) 540-9498.

CheckIt LAN from TouchStone, (714) 969-7746, is an excellent LAN-management and LAN-diagnostic tool. It lets you troubleshoot LAN problems, perform diagnostic tests and a network virus scan, document LAN card configurations, perform configuration checking, survey the LAN workstations and servers, and put information in a database. It can do a software inventory of all the software in use on the network. It is a very important tool for the network LAN administrator.

The number one cause of problems

If your network is not up and running, there is always the possibility that something was not plugged in correctly or some minor error was made in the installation.

I have a friend who works for a large computer mail-order firm. His job is to check and repair all of the components that are returned from the customers. I asked him to tell me the biggest problem. His answer was "People just don't read and follow the instructions, or they make errors and don't bother to check their work."

By far the greatest problem in assembling a unit, adding something to a computer, or installing software, is not following the instructions. Quite often it is not necessarily the fault of the person trying to follow the instructions. I have worked in the electronics industry for more than 30 years. But sometimes I have great difficulty in deciphering and following the instructions in some manuals. Sometimes a very crucial instruction or piece of information might be inconspicuously buried on page 300 of a 450-page manual.

If you have just assembled a computer, or added something to it, recheck all the cables and any boards. Make sure the boards are configured properly and that they are properly seated. Read the instructions again, then turn on the power. If it works, put the cover on and button it up.

What to do if it is completely dead

Several software diagnostic programs are great in determining what the problem is with your computer. But if the computer is completely dead, the software won't do you any good. The first thing you should do is check the power. If you don't have a voltmeter, plug in a lamp in the same socket and see if it lights. Check your power cord. Check the switch on the computer. Check the fan in the power supply. Is it turning? Check the monitor, its power cord, its fuses, and its adapter.

If you have added a board or some accessory and your computer doesn't work, remove the item and try the computer again. If the computer works without the board, then you know that it must be the board.

If it is still dead, then you probably have some serious problems. You might need some high-level troubleshooting.

Levels of troubleshooting

There are many levels of troubleshooting. Advanced troubleshooting requires sophisticated equipment, such as oscilloscopes, digital meters, logic probes, signal generators, and lots of training. But most problems that you encounter should be rather minor, so you won't need all that equipment and training. Most problems can be solved with just a little common sense and the use of the five senses: sight, sound, touch, smell, and taste. Actually, you probably won't be using taste very often.

Electricity: the lifeblood of the computer

Troubleshooting will be a little easier if you know just a little about the electronics basics.

Computers are possible because of electricity. An *electric charge* is formed when there is an imbalance or an excess amount of electrons at one pole. The excess electrons will flow through whatever path they can find to get to ground or to the other pole. It is much like water flowing downhill to find its level.

Most electric or electronic paths have varying amounts of resistance so that work or heat is created when the electrons pass through them. For instance, if a flashlight is turned on, electrons will pass through the bulb, which has a resistive element. The heat generated by the electrons passing through the bulb will cause it to glow red hot and create light. If the light is left on for a period of time, all of the excess electrons from the positive anode of the battery will pass through the bulb to the negative pole of the battery. At this time, the amount of electrons at the negative and positive poles will be the same. There will be a perfect balance and the battery will be dead.

A computer is made up of circuits and boards that have resistors, capacitors, inductors, transistors, motors, and many other components. These components perform useful functions when electricity passes through them. The circuits are designed so that the paths of the electric currents are divided, controlled, and shunted to do the work that you want done.

Occasionally, too many electrons might find their way through a weakened component and burn it out, or for some reason the electrons might be shunted through a different path. This occurrence can cause an intermittent, partial, or complete failure.

The basic components of a computer

The early IBM PC had an 8088 CPU and four other basic support chips—the 8259 Interrupt Controller, the 8237 DMA Controller, the 8253/8254 Programmable Interval Timer, and the 8255 Programmable Input/Output Controller. These same chips are found in the 8086, 286, 386, and 486. But you will find two DMA and two Interrupt Controllers in the 286, 386, and 486. You might not be able to see these chips on the modern motherboards because they are usually contained in a very large scale integrated (VLSI) package.

The *central processing unit* (CPU) is the brains of the computer. It controls the basic operation by sending and receiving control signals and memory addresses. It sends and receives data along the bus to and from other parts of the system, and carries out computations, numeric comparisons, and many other functions in response to software programs.

The 8259 Programmable Interrupt Controllers respond to interrupt requests generated by system hardware components. These requests could be from such components as the keyboard, disk drive controller, and system timer.

The 8237 DMA Controllers are able to transfer data to and from the computer's memory without passing it through the CPU, allowing I/O from the disk drives without CPU involvement.

The Programmable Interval Timer 8253 or 8254 generates timing signals for various system tasks.

The Input/Output Controller 8255 provides an interface between the CPU and the I/O devices.

Of course, several other chips are interrelated to each of these main chips, and all of the main chips are interrelated. Because they are all so intimately related, a failure in any main chip, or a minor chip, can cause the whole circuit to fail. The actual defect can be very difficult to pinpoint.

Fewer bugs today

In the early days there were a lot of bugs and errors in IBM-compatible computers. Manufacturers didn't spend a lot of money on quality control and testing at the time. Most computer manufacturers have been making the parts long enough now that the designs have been firmed up and most bugs have been eliminated.

Document the problem

Chances are if a computer or network is going to break down, it will do it at the most inopportune time. This probability is one of the basic tenets of Murphy's immutable and inflexible law.

If it breaks down, try not to panic. Ranting, cussing, and crying might make you feel better, but it won't solve the problem. Instead, get out a pad and pencil and write down everything as it happens. It is very easy to forget. Write down all the particulars, how the cables were plugged in, the software that was running, and anything that might be pertinent. You might get error messages on your screen. Use the PrtSc (Print Screen) key to print out the messages.

If you can't solve the problem, you might have to call someone or your vendor for help. Having all the written information before you will help. Try to call from your computer, if possible, as it is acting up.

Power on self test (POST)

Every time a computer is turned on, or booted up, it does a power on self test (POST). It checks the RAM, the floppy drives, the hard disk drives, the monitor, the printer, the keyboard, and other peripherals that you have installed.

If it does not find a unit, or if the unit is not functioning correctly, it will beep and display an error code. The codes start with 100 and can go up to 2,500. Ordinarily the codes will not be displayed if there is no problem. If there is a problem, the last two digits of the code will be something other than 00s. Each BIOS manufacturer develops its own codes, so there are some slight differences, but most of them are similar to the following:

101	Mother board failure
109	Direct memory access test error
121	Unexpected hardware interrupt occurred
163	Time and date not set
199	User indicated configuration not correct
201	Memory test failure
301	Keyboard test failure or a stuck key
401	Monochrome display and/or adapter test failure
432	Parallel printer not turned on
501	Color graphics display and/or adapter test failure
601	Diskette drives and/or adapter test failure

701	Math coprocessor test error
901	Parallel printer adapter test failure
1101	Asynchronous communications adapter test failure
1301	Game control adapter test failure
1302	Joystick test failure
1401	Printer test failure
1701	Fixed disk drive and/or adapter test failure
2401	Enhanced graphics display and/or adapter test failure
2501	Enhanced graphics display and/or adapter test failure

DOS has several other error messages if you try to make the computer do something it can't do. But many of the messages are not very clear. The DOS manual might explain some of them, but it usually doesn't give too much detail. But don't despair, a lot of DOS books are available, and you should have some in your library.

Power supply

Most of the components in your computer are fairly low power and low voltage. The only high voltage in your system is in the power supply, and it is pretty well enclosed. So there is no danger of shock if you open your computer and put your hand inside it.

CAUTION: You should never connect or disconnect a board or cable while the power is on. Fragile semiconductors might be destroyed if you do so.

Most of the power supplies have short-circuit protection. If too much of a load is placed on them, they will drop out and shut down, similar to what happens when a circuit breaker is overloaded. Most of the power supplies are designed to operate only with a load. If you take one out of the system and turn it on without a load, it will not work. You can plug in a floppy drive to act as a load if you want to check the voltages out of the system.

Semiconductors have no moving parts. If the circuits were designed properly, the semiconductors should last indefinitely. Heat is an enemy of a semiconductor and can cause semiconductor failure. The fan in the power supply should provide adequate cooling. All of the openings on the back panel that correspond to the slots on the motherboard should have blank fillers. Even the holes on the bottom of the chassis should be covered with tape, to force the fan to draw air in from the front of the computer, pull it over the boards, and exhaust it through the opening in the power supply case. Nothing should be placed in front of or behind the computer that restricts air flow.

If you don't hear the fan when you turn on a computer, or if the fan isn't running, then the power supply could be defective.

Table 14-1 lists the power-supply connections and their functions. The eight-slotted connectors on the motherboard have 62 contacts—31 on the A side and 31 on the B side. The black ground wires connect to B1 of each of the eight slots. B3 and B29 have +5 VDC, B5 −5 VDC, B7 −12 VDC, and B9 +12 VDC. These voltages go to the listed pins on each of the eight plug-in slots.

Table 14-1.   Power supply connections.

Disk drive power supply connections

Pin	Color	Function
1	Yellow	+12 VDC
2	Black	Ground
3	Black	Ground
4	Red	+5 VDC

Motherboard power supply connections

P8 Pin	Color	Function
1	White	Power good
2	No connection	
3	Yellow	+12 VDC
4	Brown	−12 VDC
5	Black	Ground
6	Black	Ground

P9 Pin	Color	Function
1	Black	Ground
2	Black	Ground
3	Blue	−5 VDC
4	Red	+5 VDC
5	Red	+5 VDC
6	Red	+5 VDC

Instruments and tools

At high levels of troubleshooting, a person needs some rather sophisticated and expensive instruments to do a thorough analysis of a system. You need a good high-frequency oscilloscope, a digital analyzer, a logic probe, and several other expensive pieces of gear. You also need a test bench with a spare power supply, disk drives and a computer with some empty slots so that you can plug in suspect boards and test them.

You also need some of the basics discussed in chapter 5—a volt-ohmmeter, some clip leads, a pair of side cutter dikes, a pair of long-nosed pliers, various screwdrivers, nut drivers, a soldering iron, and solder.

You need plenty of light over the bench and a flashlight or a small light to light up the dark places in the computer case. And most importantly, you will need quite a lot of training and experience. But for many problems, just a little common sense will tell you what is wrong.

Common problems

For most of the common problems you won't need a lot of test gear. Often a problem can be solved by using sight, sound, smell, and touch.

Sight—If you look closely, you can see a cable that is not plugged in properly. Or a board that is not completely seated. Or a switch that is not set right. And many other obvious things.

Sound—You can use your ears for any unusual sounds. The only sound from your computer should be the noise of your drive motors and the fan in the power supply.

Smell—If you have ever smelled a burned resistor or a capacitor, you will never forget it. If you smell something very unusual, try to locate where it is coming from.

Touch—If you touch the components and some seem to be unusually hot, it could be the cause of your problem. Except for the insides of your power supply, there should not be any voltage above 12 volts in your computer. It should be safe to touch the components.

Electrostatic discharge (ESD)

Before you touch any of the components or handle them, you should ground yourself and discharge any static voltage that you might have built up. You can discharge yourself by touching an unpainted metal part of the case of a computer or other device that is plugged in.

It is possible for a person to build up a charge of 4,000 volts or more of electrostatic voltage. If you walk across some carpets and then touch a brass door knob, you can sometimes see a spark fly and often get a shock. Most electronic assembly lines have the workers wear a ground strap whenever they are working with any components that are sensitive to electrostatic discharge.

Recommended tools

Here are some tools that you should have around, even if you never have any computer problems. (This list is an expanded version of the list in chapter 5):

- *Screwdrivers*. You should have several sizes of screwdrivers and some of them should be magnetic for picking up and starting small screws. You can buy magnetic screwdrivers, or you can make one yourself. Just take a strong magnet and rub it on the blade of the screwdriver a few times. The magnets on cabinet doors will do. Or the voice coil magnet of a loudspeaker. Be very careful with any magnet around your floppy disks. It can erase them.
- *Small screwdriver with bent tip*. This type of screwdriver can be used to pry up integrated circuits (ICs). Some of the large ICs are very difficult to remove. One of the blank fillers for the slots on the back panel also makes a good prying tool.
- *Pliers*. You should have a couple of pairs of pliers. If this is not possible, you should have at least one pair of long-nosed pliers.
- *Side cutter dikes*. You will need a pair of side cutter dikes for clipping leads of components and cutting wire. You might buy a pair of cutters that also have wire strippers.
- *Soldering iron and solder*. You shouldn't have to do much soldering, but you never know when you might need to repair a cable or some other minor job.

- *Cable crimpers*. You will also need some cable crimpers if you build your own cables.
- *Volt-ohmmeter*. By all means buy a volt-ohmmeter. You'll find dozens of uses for a volt-ohmmeter. They can be used to check for the wiring continuity in your cables, phone lines, switches, etc. You can also use a volt-ohmmeter to check for the proper voltages in your computer. Only four voltages need to be checked: +12 volts, −12 volts, +5 volts, and −5 volts. You can buy a relatively inexpensive volt-ohmmeter at any electronics store, such as Radio Shack.
- *Several clip leads*. You should also have several clip leads. You can buy them at the local Radio Shack or electronics store.
- *Flashlight*. You need a flashlight for looking at the dark places inside the computer or at the cable connection behind a computer.

How to find the problem

Some problems are easier to determine than others. To determine the problem, you can do the following:

Swap it If a computer is down and you suspect a board, swap it with a spare board that is the same. If you don't have a spare, maybe you can borrow one from another computer.

Take the boards out If you suspect a board, but don't know which one, take the boards out to the barest minimum. Then add them back until the problem develops.

CAUTION: Always turn off the power when plugging in or unplugging a board or cable.

Wiggle the boards and cables Wiggle the boards and cables to see if it is an intermittent problem. Many times a board might not be seated properly. A wire or cable can be broken and still make contact until it is moved.

Check the ICs and connectors for bent pins If you have installed memory ICs and get errors, check to make sure that they are seated properly and all the pins are in the sockets. If you swap an IC, make a note of how it is oriented before removing it. There should be a small dot of white paint or a U-shaped indentation at the end that has pin 1. If you forgot to note the orientation, look at the other ICs. Most of the boards are laid out so that all of the ICs are oriented the same way. The chrome fillers that are used to cover the unused slots in the back of the case make very good tools for prying up ICs.

You might also try unplugging a cable or a board and plugging it back in. Sometimes the pins may be slightly corroded or not seated properly. Before unplugging a cable, you might put a stripe on the connector and cable with a marking pen or nail polish so that you can easily see how they should be plugged back in.

The copper contacts on a plug-in board can become corroded. You can clean them with an ordinary pencil eraser.

The problem could be in a DIP switch. You might try turning it on and off a few times.

CAUTION: Again, always write down the positions before touching the switches. Make a diagram of the wires, cables, and switch settings before you disturb them. It is easy to forget how they were plugged in or set before you moved them. You could end up making things worse. Make a pencil mark before turning a knob or variable coil or capacitor so that it can be returned to the same setting when you find out that it didn't help. Better yet, resist the temptation to reset these types of components. Most were set up using highly sophisticated instruments. They don't usually change enough to cause a problem.

Check motherboard switch settings   If you are having monitor problems, check the switch settings on the motherboard. There are several different kinds of motherboards. Some have DIP switches or shorting bars that must be set to configure the system for the type of monitor you are using, such as monochrome, CGA, EGA, or VGA.

Most monitors also have fuses. You might check them. Also check the cables for proper connections.

Printer problems   Printer problems, especially the serial type, are so many that I will not even attempt to list them here. Many printers today have both parallel and serial connectors. The IBM-compatible ISA systems default to the parallel system. If at all possible, use the parallel port. There are very few problems with parallel as compared to serial.

If you use the serial, you will probably have to use the DOS MODE command to change from the LPT port to the serial port. The commands might be something like this:

MODE COM1:9600,N,8,P then MODE LPT1:=COM1

In this command, the 9600 sets the baud rate, the N means no parity, the 8 means 8 bits, the P means send the output to the printer. The printer would have to be set to match these settings.

Every time the computer is booted up, it automatically defaults to the LPT port, so each time you want to use the serial port to print, you have to invoke the above commands. If you use the serial printer all the time, you can put the above commands in your Autoexec.bat file so that they will be loaded each time you boot up.

Most printers have a self test. It might run this test fine, but then completely ignore any efforts to get it to respond to the computer if the cables, parity, and baud rate are not properly set.

Reboot the computer   Sometimes the computer will hang up. You might have told it to do something that it could not do. You can usually do a warm reboot of the computer by pressing the Ctrl, Alt, and Del key simultaneously. Of course, this would wipe out any file in memory that you might have been working on. Occasionally the computer will not respond to a warm boot. You can pound on the keyboard all day long and it will ignore you. In that case, you will have to switch off the main power, let it sit for a few seconds, then power up again. Always wait for the hard disk to wind down and stop before turning the power on again.

Finding fault

When there is a problem on the network, you should look at the various components to determine where the fault lies. The next few sections will help you to make a determination.

Cables

If there is a problem on the network, check the cables first. Find out if anyone has moved a station or disturbed the cables in any way. One study found that about one-third of the problems on a LAN are due to cables. Make sure that the cables are constructed properly. Make sure that there is a bit of slack at each station. You should check the cable BNC connectors. Make sure that they are properly connected.

If you have a thin Ethernet system and some of the workstations are down, you can use a couple of ohmmeters and check each leg of the system. You can start at the end station, disconnect the BNC connectors from the adapter, and check the continuity of the cable segment. If you leave the cable connected to the adapter, you will get a false reading.

The thin Ethernet system might be compared to the city water system. A main water pipe goes by each house and a connection is made from the main to the house. If the main is ruptured at some point, the houses beyond that point will get no water. If a section of the cable is broken, then none of the stations beyond that point will be operable.

If the center conductor of the cable is grounded, or touches the braided shield, it will short out the signal throughout the network. All of the stations will be down if there is a short. An ohmmeter can be used to detect a short in a section of the cable. If there is a short in an adapter, it will be more difficult to detect.

Substitution and spare parts

If a single station becomes inoperable, it can be caused by a defective adapter or some component in the computer. One way to make a quick check is to use a portable or laptop computer with an adapter, such as the Xircom or Kodiak. The portable can be connected in place of the inoperable station, and, if it works, then you know that the fault is in the computer or adapter. If the portable does not work, then it is a cable problem.

If everything looks okay, then you might suspect the adapter. You can easily check it by plugging in an adapter that you know is good. You can buy a spare Ethernet adapter for less than $100. That might be a small price to pay to keep your network running. If you cannot afford to buy a spare board, you can shut down one of the operating workstations and use its adapter for testing.

It is a good idea to have spares of all the major components, or as many as you can afford, on hand. They are less expensive than the cost of high-level troubleshooting techniques. For example, it might be very difficult to determine the cause of a floppy disk drive failure, but it is very easy to plug in a spare disk drive to check it. A floppy disk drive costs about $50.

Another example is a keyboard, which can be ruined by a cup of spilled coffee. You can buy a spare for about $35.

Diagnostic and utility software

Most BIOS chips have many diagnostic routines and other utilities built-in. These routines allow you to set the time and date, tell the computer what type of hard disk and floppy disk drives are installed, the amount of memory, the wait states, and several other functions. The AMI and DTK BIOS chips have a very comprehensive set of built-in diagnostics. They can allow hard and floppy disk formatting, check speed of rotation of disk drives, do performance testing of hard drives, and several other tests.

I mentioned some utility software programs in chapter 12. Many of them have a few diagnostics among the utilities.

- Norton Utilities, (213) 453-2361, also includes several diagnostic and test programs such as Disk Doctor, Disk Test, Format Recover, Directory Sort, System Information, and many others.
- Mace Utilities, (504) 291-7221, does about everything that Norton does and a few other things. It has recover, defragment, diagnose, remedy, and several other very useful programs primarily for the hard disk.
- PC Tools, (503) 690-8090, is from Central Point Software and has several utilities much like the Norton and Mace Utilities. It has a utility that can recover data from a disk that has been erased or reformatted, DOS utilities, hard disk backup, and several utilities such as those found in SideKick.
- SpinRite from Gibson Research, (714) 830-2200, and Disk Technician from Prime Solutions, (619) 274-5000, are utilities that allow you to diagnose, analyze, and optimize your hard disk.
- CheckIt from TouchStone Software, (714) 969-7746, checks and reports on your computer configuration by letting "you look inside your PC without taking off the cover." It reports on the type of processor, amount of memory, video adapter, hard and floppy disk drives, clock/calendar, ports, keyboard, and mouse, if present. CheckIt also tests the motherboard, hard and floppy disk drives, RAM, ports, keyboard, mouse, joystick, and others. It can also run a few benchmark speed tests.

TouchStone also has CheckIt Floppy Drive Testing System. If any one of your floppy disk drives gets out of alignment, you might not be able to read disks from other computers. Or drives in other computers might not be able to read disks made from a defective drive.

CheckIt measures how well the floppy drive is aligned, the rotation speed, the ability to read the very important track 0, and several other tests. The system includes precise test disks in both 3½-inch and 5¼-inch formats. It is inexpensive, but a valuable tool.

The POST-Probe, (818) 547-0125, is a plug-in board that can check and analyze computer problems. Advanced Software, (800) 835-2467, also has a diagnostic board.

Is it worth it to repair it?

If you find a problem on a board, a disk drive, or some component, you might try to find out what it would cost before having it repaired. You can buy a floppy disk drive for about $50 or a network adapter board for about $100. A repair shop would charge $50 to $100 an hour to repair them. It is often less expensive to scrap a defective part and buy a new one.

Software problems

I have had far more trouble with software than I have had with hardware. Quite often it is my fault for not taking the time to completely read the manuals and instructions. For instance, I tried to install Charisma. It is a large program and works under Windows. I kept getting errors and it would not load. I finally read the manual and found that it requires at least 500K of memory to install. I have several drivers, TSRs, and other things in my Config.sys file that eat up a lot of RAM. I had to boot up with a floppy disk that had a very simple Config.sys file and left me over 500K of RAM. I had no trouble after that.

MS-DOS 5.0, DR DOS 6.0, DESQview, and several other programs can load drivers, TSRs, and other things into memory above 640K. It can leave as much as 630K of free RAM. Windows 3.0 comes with a Himem.sys that is necessary for accessing extended memory. This file is loaded with the Config.sys file. If Himem-.sys is loaded, it will conflict with the DR DOS high-memory files. You can run one or the other, but if both are loaded, the computer will not boot up.

Thousands and thousands of other software problems will probably happen to you. Many vendors have support programs for their products. If something goes wrong, you can call them. A few of them offer toll-free numbers, but with most of them you have to pay for the call. Some companies charge for their support. Some have installed 900 telephone numbers and charge you for the amount of time on the phone. It can cost a lot of money to maintain a support staff.

If you have a software problem, document, or write down, everything that happens. Before you call, try to duplicate the problem, or make it happen again. Carefully read the manual. When you call, it is best to be in front of your computer, with it turned on, and with the problem on the screen if possible.

Also before you call, have the serial number of your program handy. One of the first things they will probably ask is for your name and serial number. If you have bought and registered the program, it will be in their computer.

There are still compatibility problems in areas of updates and new releases of software. I had lots of problems trying to get the latest WordStar release to work with files I had created with an early version. It was mostly my fault again because I didn't take the time to read the manual. Like so many other updates and revisions, they make them bigger and better, but out of necessity, they often change the way things were done earlier.

Most software programs are reasonably bugfree. But millions of things can go wrong if the exact instructions and procedures are not followed. In many cases, the exact instructions and procedures are not very explicit.

User groups

There is no way to list all of the thousands of problems that can occur with software or hardware. Computers are dumb and very unforgiving. It is very easy to plug a cable in backwards, or forget to set a switch. Sometimes it can be a combination of both software and hardware. Often there is only one way to do something right, but ten thousand ways to do it wrong. Sometimes it is difficult to determine if it is a hardware problem caused by software or vice versa. There is no way that every problem can be addressed.

One of the best ways to find answers is to ask someone who has had the same problem. One of the best places to find those people is at a user group. If at all possible, join one and become friendly with all of the members. They can be one of your best sources of troubleshooting. Most of them have had similar problems and are glad to help. A list of user groups is provided in the appendix.

Appendix

Network user groups

Join a network user group, as well as a computer user group, if at all possible. You will no doubt have problems and one of the best ways to find answers is to talk to someone who has had a similar experience. Most people in a user group are glad to help you find the answers. There will probably be times when you also can help others, and when someone benefits from your experiences, it can give you a great feeling.

Computer Shopper and some of the other computer magazines often publish addresses of user groups. This appendix is a list of network user groups that appeared in a recent issue of *LAN Times* magazine.

Novell user groups
North American region

United States

Alabama
Birmingham
Cindy Johnston, (202) 599-8436

Livingstone
Don Fears, (205) 652-6741

Mobile
Kathy Robeinson, (205) 471-7279

Alaska
Anchorage
Lydia Lourbacos, (907) 261-4357

Juneau
Dennis Harris, (907) 586-2384

Arizona
Flagstaff
John Crane, (602) 526-2129

Phoenix
Karl Ozols, (602) 352-5000

Tucson
John Garcia, (602) 740-5610

Arkansas
Little Rock
Ron Stanfield, (501) 682-7326

Jonesboro
Kevin Watkins, (501) 972-0626

California
Bakersfield
Tony Hoffman, (805) 321-6145

East Bay, (Oakland)
George Gold, (415) 444-4899

Eureka
Elaine Page, (707) 443-8338

Fresno
Karen Billingsley, (209) 487-5791 ext. 245

Los Angeles
Michael Wegerbauer, (213) 206-2807

Macintosh, (SIG)-SF
Kathleen Prevost, (415) 855-7275

Modesto/Merced
Carol Blevins, (209) 577-5151

Mt. Shasta
Will Duncan, (916) 842-8284

North Bay (Novato)
Diane Doig, (415) 889-2855

Orange County
Frank Goodyear, (714) 651-1140

Palmdale/Lancaster
Barri Sibbald, (805) 272-4550

Palm Springs
Nicholas Behrman, (619) 323-7125

Sacramento
John Moyle, (916) 823-5206

Salinas
Jim Clark, (408) 757-8877

San Bernardino
Mike Fowler, (714) 889-0526

San Diego
Paul Christiansen, (619) 565-1153

San Francisco
Thomas Thibault, (415) 944-9500

San Mateo
Dennis Mays, (415) 347-9970

Santa Barbara
John Lewis, (805) 568-2685

Santa Cruz
Charlie Gibson, (408) 426-3313

South Bay (San Jose)
Bill Strouse, (408) 453-3321

Stockton
Rick Utley, (209) 239-2637

Colorado
Colorado Springs
Chris Green, (719) 598-5327

Denver
Christi Hatfield, (303) 971-5687

Connecticut
Hartford
Robert Carpenter, (203) 547-6860

Norwalk
Glenn Keet, (203) 761-8600

Delaware
Wilmington
Chris O'Brien, (215) 251-2123

Florida
Altamonte Springs
Vern Dubendorf, (407) 774-9713

Ft. Meyers
Bill Lauzon, (813) 337-1505

Jacksonville
David Eison, (904) 391-1465

Miami
Stuart Needel, (305) 920-6622 ext. 10

Orlando
Court Clara, (407) 823-2000

Pensacola
Terry Hoffman, (904) 478-6279

Tallahassee
Elaine Dennison, (904) 487-8667

Tampa
Douglas E. Crum, (813) 443-6738

West Palm Beach
Paul Leder, (407) 686-6300

Georgia
Atlanta
Kelley Osburn, (404) 941-1900

Savannah
Matt Heath, (912) 966-4434

Guam
David Hicks 011 (671) 477-6212

Hawaii
Honolulu
Scott McMillan, (808) 956-5183

Idaho
Boise
Dan L. Sessions, (208) 383-6100

Illinois
Chicago
John O'Laughlin, (708) 575-5273

Macomb
James Farmer, (309) 833-4380

Springfield
Graham Murdock, (217) 793-8440

Indiana
Bloomington
Tom Zeller, (812) 855-6214

Evansville
Brian Ricci, (812) 476-6662

Fort Wayne
Tom Watt, (219)484-8631

Indianapolis
Tom Smith, (317) 232-3356

Lafayette
Timothy M.Lange, (317) 494-1787

Iowa
Cedar Rapids
Jim Albright, (319) 398-8211

Davenport
Jeff Slayton, (319) 326-9817

Des Moines
Mike Davidson, (515) 284-2277

Iowa City
Guy D.Falsetti, (319) 335-6140

Waterloo
Bill Atkins, (319) 235-7131

Kansas
Kansas City
See Kansas City, MO

Manhattan
Larry Havenstein, (913) 532-6270

Wichita
Tim Downs, (316) 265-1201

Kentucky
Lexington
Dale Ladnier, (606) 277-6834

Louisville
Tom Guenthner, (502) 582-5262

Louisiana
Monroe
Scott Hayward, (318) 362-8778

New Orleans
Bill Haskell, (504) 593-7508

Shreveport
Marion Marks, (318) 797-7900

Maine
Augusta
Peggy Landry, (207) 289-1070

Portland
R.L.Bergeron, (207) 775-0547

Maryland
Baltimore
John Babich, (301) 252-7113

Massachusetts
Boston
Glen Fund, (603) 885-6242

Cambridge
Jesus Zeus Estrada, (617) 253-0774

Hyannis
Diana Smith, (508) 775-7819

Michigan
Ann Arbor
Bill Connett, (313) 764-4417

Detroit
Dave Barnett, (313) 540-7933

Grand Rapids
Mark Yeater, (616) 454-8074

Kalamazoo
John Parmelee, (616) 674-8001

Lansing
Bryan Renaud, (517) 373-2710

Minnesota
St. Paul
Don Williams, (612) 829-2323

Mississippi
Jackson
Orbra Porter, (601) 825-3131

Missouri
Columbia
David Witten, (314) 449-2180

Kansas City
Jim Herrigan, (913) 772-3334

Nebraska
Omaha
Robin Hawkins, (402) 398-2313

Grand Island
Gary Smith, (308) 381-5404 ext.35

Nevada
Las Vegas
Lee Augsberger, (702) 383-2306

Reno
Mike Whaley, (702) 785-6106

New Hampshire
Manchester
Lori Liberty, (603) 882-1111

New Jersey
Newark
Bill Spencer, (201) 307-9000

New Mexico
Albuquerque
Susan Byrke, (505) 842-0001

Las Cruces
James Jackson, (505) 522-7688

Santa Fe
Stewart B.Kane, (505) 473-6586

New York
Albany
Edward S. Diez, (518) 463-5000

Buffalo
Kevin Sullivan, (716) 845-5010

Hopkinton
Steve Spence, (315) 328-4491

Ithaca
Brian Oursler, (607) 255-5080

Long Island
John Petrucci, (516) 544-9100

New York City
Paul Epstein, (212) 482-6021

Poughkeepsie
Charlie Hoehing, (914) 565-1600
ext.53

Rochester
Dick McNamara, (716) 428-5926

Syracuse
Joseph Ottaviano, (315) 454-4473

Windsor
Sylvia Ryan, (607) 770-3563

North Carolina
Asheville
Bob Orr, (704) 227-7341

Chapel Hill
Ruth Marinshaw, (919) 966-6785

Charlotte
Mike Milton, (704) 588-7000 Ext. 200

Greensboro
Chuck Curry, (919) 334-5350

Wilmington
Peggy Baddour, (919) 343-0161

North Dakota
Fargo
Bruce Carlson, (218) 236-4786

Ohio
Canton
Rose M.Love, (216) 264-2527

Cincinnati
Mark Keirle, (513) 321-2736

Cleveland
Jerry Hare, (216) 749-0238

Dayton
J.P. Nauseef, (513) 255-8201

Kent
Dave Futey, (216) 672-2970

Lancaster/Columbus
Leo Hernandez, (614) 653-7144

Mansfield
Joanna Phillips, (419) 433-4013

Oklahoma
Oklahoma City
Pam Burton, (405) 528-1500 ext.225

Tulsa
Mike Johnson, (918) 493-2337

Oregon
Bend/Madras
Eric Skidmore, (503) 475-2234

Eugene
Jim Demmers, (503) 341-1876

Medford
Shari Feltner, (503) 773-6633

Portland
Ed Sawicki, (503) 635-6370

Salem
Jon Brammeier, (503) 588-6351

Pennsylvania
Harrisburg
Mike Cohen, (717) 986-5615

Philadelphia
Janette Burruano, (215) 293-0600

Philadelphia Metro
Fred Munizza, (215) 246-6000

Pittsburgh
George Altenbaugh, (412) 234-2674

Reading/Easton
Mike Bohl, (215) 258-1888

Scottdale
Jay Copenhaver, (412) 887-9700

Scranton
Dave Giaimo, (717) 383-4155

Rhode Island
Kingston
Allan Wild, (401) 792-2611

South Carolina
Charleston
Greg Peralta, (803) 571-7420

Columbia
Eddie King, (803) 777-7145

Greenville
Mike Dill, (803) 281-6847

South Dakota
Sioux Falls
Phil Haskett, (605) 688-6136

Tennessee
Chattanooga
Jim Large, (615) 238-7111 ext.2630

Knoxville
Harry Herman, (615) 544-9530

Memphis
Mike Kimble, (901) 372-8008

Nashville
Jeff Carden, (615) 259-3932

Texas
Amarillo
Al Haines, (806) 352-1309

Austin
Aaron Cleaver, (512) 250-5333

Brownsville
Dick Wade, (512) 318-2300 ext.757

Clearlake
Bebe Kelly-Sorato, (713) 483-5136

Corpus Christi
Bill Burke, (512) 854-8644

Dallas
Bill Faulkner, (817) 624-5633

Houston
Adam Reuf, (713) 590-7788

Lubbock
Tom Payton, (806) 793-1958

San Angelo
John Johnson, (915) 465-4391

San Antonio
Bruce King, (512) 228-2271

Tyler
Randy Brown, (214) 882-5511
ext.2586

Waco
Elizabeth Davis, (817) 799-3611
ext.3274

Wadsworth
Lynn Carmichael, (512) 972-3611
ext.6046

Utah
Brigham City
Art Mitchell, (801) 863-4192

Logan, (SEG)
Steve Nielson, (801) 750-3166

Provo
Drew Briggs, (801) 429-7898

Salt Lake City
David Hoisve, (801) 581-6025

Vermont
Burlington
Loren Tindall, (802) 879-2552

Virginia
Richmond
Rich Hanson, (804) 965-1622

Virginia Beach
Donald L. Small, (804) 490-1294

Washington
Kennewick
Paul Huber, (509) 736-0720

Olympia
Pete Leonard, (206) 753-5424

Port Townsend
Randall Daley, (206) 385-9370

Seattle
Kim McCoy, (206) 775-7050

Spokane
Randy Kembel, (509) 623-1512

Washington, D.C.
Stephanie Kelly, (703) 522-0820

West Virginia
Charleston
Mark Eckert, (304) 348-2294

Clarksburg
Tom Moran, (304) 293-4821 ext.202

Wisconsin
Appleton
John Ensley, (414) 731-0268

Ashland
Dan Row, (715) 682-1262

Green Bay
Kathy Sternitsky, (414) 433-1137

LaCrosse
Steve Chapman, (608) 785-0530

Madison
Steve Sopcak, (608) 831-9222

Milwaukee
Arv Klemz, (414) 784-3420

Wausau
Jeff Syring, (715) 359-5080

Wyoming
Cheyenne
Roger Keslar, (307) 637-6267

Canada

Alberta
Calgary
Sharon Fisk, (403) 269-0622

Edmonton
Brad Tennant, (403) 469-2525

British Columbia
Nanaimo
David Barker, (604) 753-8251

Vancouver
Peter Lincoln, (604) 263-7438

Manitoba
Winnipeg
Perry Freiling, (204) 986-3626

New Brunswick
Peter Doten, (506) 357-8465 ext.271

Newfoundland
Raymond Ducet, (709) 576-5454

Nova Scotia
Don Trotter, (902) 424-8878

Ontario
Copper Cliff/Sudbury
Dan Merrick, (705) 682-5654

Ottawa
Bill Madore, (613) 744-2616

Toronto
Claudia Ortali, (416) 982-6757

Quebec
Quebec City
Andre Belan, (418) 644-8697

Saskatchewan
Regina
Big Little, (306) 777-7261

Saskatoon
Carol Martel, (306) 244-8900

Yukon
Whitehorse
Gordon Moffatt, (403) 668-5504

Yellow Knife
Gordon Moffatt, (403) 668-5504

Latin American region

Argentina
Buenos Aires
Mariano Natale, +54-1-312-7829

Chile
Santiago
Carlos Danes, +56-2-274-3508

Mexico
Mexico City
Gustavo Pavon,
+6-21-50-91,5-34-00-34, ext. 5506

Puerto Rico
Puerto Nevo
Archer LeBron, (809) 723-0909
ext.245

Uruguay
Montevideo
Mario Tucci, +598-296-2922

Venezuela
Caracas
Herman Gomez, +58 2 913285

Australian region

Australia
Canberra
Fulvio Bagliani, +06-2-707-141

Sydney
Roger Pegler, +61-2-256-7000

Melbourne
Charles Bergess, +61-3-606-3333

Perth
David Heath, +61-9-322-0141

New Zealand
Auckland
Neil Forster,
+0011-64-9-366-8420

Christchurch
F. Derham McAven,
+00011-64-3-798-150

Wellington
Andy Robertson,
+0011-64-4-746-195

European region

Denmark

Copenhagen
Thomas Nielsen, +45-43282119

Finland
Helsinki
Thomas Baltsheffsky,
+358-0-709-5203

Germany
Frankfurt
Markus Wartha, +49-821-571041

Hungary
Budapest
Csaba Hazay (secretary),
+36-(1)-185-3111

Ireland
Dublin
John Turner, +353-1-727177

Netherlands
Utrecht
Ernst Fuld, +31-(3448)-2015

Switzerland
Zurich
Alexander Rubensaal,
+41-(1)-730-6000

United Kingdom
Glasgow (Scotland)
Kevin McGuire,
+44-(355)-239166

London
Tim Lazenby, +44-(480)891001

West Yorkshire
Ian Button, +44-422-357257

Yugoslavia
Llujbljana
Filip Remskar, +38-(61)-312524

Asian region

Hong Kong
Lingo Lau, +4987331

Other regions

Botswana
Russell M.Gittleson, +267-(31)-4888

India
Bombay
P.K. Agal, +636 4722/636 4724

Calcutta
Deepak Mehta, +(33)-298141,297812

Israel
Tel Aviv
Trevor Matz, +03-293112/3

Pakistan
Karachi
Arif Siddiqui, +485803

Saudi Arabia
Sharjah
Pradeep Soneja, +971-(6)-547265

South Africa
Johannesburg
Karl Campbell, +27-11-393-1222

3COM user groups
North American region

United States

Alabama
Huntsville
Bill Hicks, (205) 730-2677

Arizona
Phoenix
John Wilcox, (602) 274-7253

California
Fair Oaks
Noel Morgan, (916) 965-3112

Petaluma
Greg Bulette, (707) 769-1553

San Diego
Matt Scholz, (619) 297-3218

Simi Valley
Richard Cole, (805) 527-2326

Stanford
Sandra Senti, (415) 723-1683

Torrance
Andrew Crawford, (213) 363-5815

Colorado
Colorado Springs
Bruce Pearman, (719) 599-4700

Florida
Miami
Victor Delgadillo, (305) 624-4200

Temple Terrace
Jerry Murray, (813) 978-7981

Georgia
Atlanta
Craig Miller, (404) 671-2049

Hawaii
Honolulu
Burt Lum, (808) 546-4919

Illinois
Chicago
Erica Zeimer, (708) 391-1016

Urbana
Scott Novak, (217) 333-0563

Indiana
Indianapolis
Daniel Schultz, (317) 571-5834

Kentucky
Lexington
Gary Cunningham, (606) 253-6692
Mary Atcher, (606) 253-4381

Maryland
Baltimore
Joe Breslin, (301) 955-3735

Bethesda
Judy Fabrikant, (301) 402-2661

Greenbelt
Debbie Sharpe, (301) 286-8519

Michigan
Grand Rapids
Carl VanderZee, (616) 942-9800

Southfield
Jon Lytle, (313) 354-9018

Minnesota
St. Paul
John Noll, (616)733-2965

Missouri
Kansas City
Tim Gerdts, (816) 926-7266

Nebraska
Omaha
Michael Sibilia, (402) 341-0500

New York
Chappaqua
Henry Elam, (914) 238-9219

East Rochester
Fred Skrotzki, (716) 385-6740

North Carolina
Fort Bragg
Helen Pikay, (919) 396-3131

Research
Bill Birckhead, (919) 549-0611

Ohio
Cincinnati
Steve Senft, (513) 566-4901

Columbus
Bruce Adamczak, (614) 261-2738

Oregon
Portland
Fred Van Drimmelen, (503) 230-6124

Pennsylvania
Horsham
Linda Caroll, (215) 956-8593

Texas
Austin
Bud Hesch, (512) 891-3091

Dallas
Dick Tribble, (214) 820-2989

Houston
Willy Pan, (713) 233-2356
Richard Westerman, (713) 623-6506

Virginia
Fairfax
Rolf Lang, (703) 503-9430

Washington
Olympia
Art Brown, (206) 753-2525

Richland
Charles Moses, (509) 546-8155

Washington D.C.
David M. Smith, (202) 357-5904
Christopher Burry, (202) 224-2043

Wisconsin
Janesville
Russ Miller, (608) 755-4166

Canada

Ontario
Ottawa
Arthur Berger, (613) 951-5592

Quebec
Montreal
Ted Ryan, (514) 630-4777

Australian region

Australia
Berala
David Miller, 61 2 925-1555

New Zealand
Rotoura
Yvonne Langridge, 64 4 767889

European region

England
London
Steve Howes, 743 321515

Finland
Espoo
Kari Ervasti, 358 0 52721

France
Cedex
Elizabeth Jantzen, 33 1 69 86 68 00

Germany
München
Jean-Pierre Lucaire, 49 089-4708196

Remscheid
Eckhard Klockhaus, 49 2191-51741

Italy
Milano
Primo Conacina, 39 2 254-9741

Sweden
Kista
Gabriellla Civalero-Stolpe, 46 8 703 4870

Commonwealth of Independent States (formerly USSR)
St. Petersburg
Vladimir Kislenko, 81 2 312-6973

Asian region

Japan
Tokyo
Hayao Washizaki, 81 03 356 6351

Korea
Seoul
Peter S.H. Park, 82 02 332-0141

Malaysia
Kualua Lampur, Jalan Raja
Lim Foong Lin, 60 03 238-3894

Singapore
Anthony Lim, 278 2211

Taiwan.R.O.C.
Taipei
H.C. Wang, 886 2 3630855

Banyan user groups

North American region

United States

Alaska
Anchorage
Mike Barsalou, (907) 338-0285

Arizona
Phoenix
Desert Banyan Users Group, (DBUG)
Jo Ann Harrington, (602) 262-5758
Compuserve ID:76326,1431

California
Los Angeles
Dave Beran, (213) 538-7625
Compuserve ID:76306,1115

Colorado
Denver
J. Scott Fabling, (303) 680-0551

Delaware
Wilmington
Delaware Banyan User Group
(DEBUG)
Robert Czeinzinger, (302) 739-4766

Florida
Melbourne (FBUG)
Randal Owens, (407) 727-6039
John Silling, (305) 776-3912

Illinois
Chicago
Jim Leterer, (312) 263-1451

Massachusetts
Boston (Mass BUG)
Bill Sheehan, (617) 727-4859
Compuserve ID:47017,1730

Michigan
Great Lakes Area
Wayne Starr, (313) 487-3141

Missouri
Kansas City
Terry Oehrke, (816) 941-1926

New Jersey
Tri-State Area
Roy Cohn
Compuserve ID:76346,773

New Mexico
Santa Fe
Gabe Montoya, (505) 988-6505

New York
New York City
Bob Fratangelo, (212) 578-7082

North Carolina
Raleigh/Durham Area
Deborah Hughes, (919) 467-1101

Ohio
Columbus
Ohio Banyan Users Group, (OBUG)
James Cunningham, (614) 223-3606
Cheryl Seeds, (614) 461-2767

Oklahoma
Oklahoma City
Banyan Users of Central Oklahoma
(BUCO)
Jimmy Mock, (406) 478-5353

Pennsylvania
Harrisburg
Central PA BUG
Curtis Vreeland, (717) 293-3858

Lancaster
Mary Beth Barron, (717) 293-3858

Pennsylvania State University
Bill Hillner, (814) 865-1940

Philadelphia
Maureen Zug, (215) 963-6981

Pittsburgh
Pittsburgh Chapter of ABUI (PCABUI)
Mike Ehrenberger, (412) 369-2587

Texas
Dallas
Earl H. Browing,
(214) 361-5578,ext.277

Houston
Houston Users of Banyan (HUB)
Robert Laird, (713) 627-4323
Compuserve ID:70070,460

San Antonio
Banyan Users of South Texas (BUST)
Brent Daugherty, (512) 344-1515

Washington, D.C.
Federal Banyan User Group
(FEDBUG)
Elizabeth Nesbit, (202) 205-3355

Canada
Assoc. of Banyan Users of Canada
(ABUC)
David Dores, (403) 885-4200,
(403)885-4434

Australian region

Australia
Assoc. of Banyan Users of Australia
(ABUA)
Don Muir, 03 344 6840

European region

Denmark
Allan Ejlerskov, 45 2 94 73 77

England
Assoc. of Banyan Users U.K. Ltd.
(ABU UK)
Graham Marriott, 0268 522822, 0268
295272

Germany
Banyan Anwender Gruppe Deutschland
e.V. (BAG)
Rainer Pfenning, 0211 204001-3, 49
211 204006

Netherlands
A.T. Lamers, 31 30 45-07-88

Norway
Dag Heim, 47-2-371075

Sweden
Christer Eksvard, 08 362970

Asian region
(Australia, Hong Kong, Korea, Japan,
Singapore, Taiwan)
Curtis Gayle, Far East Acct. Mngr.
Aegis International Corp.
1775 Broadway, New York, NY 10019

Hong Kong
North Point
Datacraft, Hong Kong 652 5 807 2574

Japan
Bryce Jendrickson, 81-3-3475-2135,
81-3-3479-1138

Other regions

Saudi Arabia
Joseph B. Decard, 6918787, 6918525

Corporate Banyan user groups
World Bank
Rohan Wijeratne, (202) 473-2717

Network user group-AT&T (NUGATT)

United States

Illinois
Peoria, (309) 677-3450

LANtastic user groups

United States

Alabama
Birmingham
Rick Curl, (800) 326-4332

California
Bakersville
Paul Trent, (805) 834-7411

Georgia
Atlanta
Leon Stafford, (404) 578-0805

Massachusetts
Boston
David Patterson, (508) 836-2654

Washington, D.C.
National User Group
Jeffery Ludin or Mike King, (703) 478-2888

Microsoft user groups

United States

Los Angeles
Jeff Cohen, (213) 568-2620

Mid-Atlantic
Mark Jasen, (202) 895-2034

North Texas
Richard Highduke, (214) 716-2642

Glossary

ac Abbreviation for alternating current.

access time The amount of time it takes the computer to find and read data from a disk or from memory. The average access time for a hard disk is based on the time it takes the head to seek and find the specified track, the time for the head to lock on to it, and the time for the disk to spin around until the desired sector is beneath the head.

active partition The partition on a hard disk that contains the boot and operating system. A single hard disk can be partitioned into several logical disks, such as drive C:, drive D:, and drive E:. This division can be done at the initial formatting of the disk. Only one partition, usually drive C:, can contain the active partition.

adapter boards or cards Plug-in boards needed to drive monitors. Monitor boards might be monochrome graphic adapters (MGA), color graphic adapters (CGA), enhanced graphic adapters (EGA), or video graphics adapters (VGA).

algorithm A step-by-step procedure, scheme, formula, or method used to solve a problem or accomplish a task. For example, a subroutine in a software program.

alphanumeric Data that has both numerals and letters.

analyst A person who determines the computer needs to accomplish a given task. The job of an analyst is similar to that of a consultant. Note that there are no standard qualification requirements for either of these jobs, so anyone can call themselves an analyst or a consultant. They should be, but might not be, experts in their field.

ANSI American National Standards Institute, the principal standards development organization in the United States. It is a member of the International Standards Organization (ISO). It is a voluntary organization that is supported by trade organizations, professional societies, and industry.

application software Any software program—such as a database, word processor, or spreadsheet—that manipulates and processes data.

architecture The fundamental structure of the hardware and software of a system. Network architecture defines the functions, data formats, protocols, and procedures used on a LAN.

ARCnet Attached Resource Computer Network, an early network system developed by Datapoint Corporation. It is a 2.5 mbps system that uses a modified token-passing protocol.

ASCII American Standard Code for Information Interchange, the standard for digital information made up of 256 codes. Originally, there were only 128 codes for all of the letters, symbols, and operations of a keyboard. Then IBM added graphical symbols such as happy faces, playing cards, musical notes, and others, for a total of 256 codes.

asynchronous transmission Used extensively for transmission by modems and networks. Each character that is transmitted is enclosed and identified by one or more start bits and stop bits. It is similar to putting spaces between words to identify them as a single word.

AT systems   Advanced Technology, the name IBM gave to its 286 system in 1984. AT systems now include the 286, 386, and 486 systems.

AUI   Attachment universal interface port, a connector on adapter boards for a transceiver such as that used on thick Ethernet systems. Many adapters have AUI and BNC connectors, which allow more flexibility.

backbone   A high-speed link that might join several LAN bridges.

BALUN   Balance/unbalance, a small impedance-matching transformer that can be inserted in a network that has two different systems. For instance, a BALUN would be needed to match the impedance of a shielded coaxial cable to that of an unshielded twisted pair.

.bak files   Anytime that you edit or change a file in some word processors, they will save the original file as a backup and append the extension .bak to it.

bandwidth   The range of frequencies that a system can handle. Bandwidth is usually expressed in hertz (Hz) between lowest and highest frequencies.

baseband   Usually uses coaxial cable to transmit digital signals. This system was first used by Ethernet.

baud   A unit of transmission speed equal to the number of discrete signal events per second. For low frequency transmissions, it might be the same as bits per second (bps), but for higher frequencies that use data compression and other technologies, it might not reflect a true bps.

bindery   A database maintained by Novell NetWare that contains information about all of the resources, users, and other elements on a Novell NetWare LAN.

BIOS   Basic input/output system, which is responsible for handling the input/output operations on a computer.

BNC connector   A connector used on coaxial cables, such as those found on Ethernet systems. The *B* is for bayonet. The connector twists on with a simple half turn similar to the way a bayonet is fixed to a rifle.

boot or bootstrap   When a computer is turned on, all the memory and other internal operators have to be set or configured. A small amount of the program to do this is stored in ROM. Using this information the computer pulls itself up by its "bootstraps." A *warm boot* is sometimes necessary to get the computer out of an endless loop, or if it is hung up for some reason. A warm boot can be done by pressing Ctrl, Alt, and Del keys simultaneously.

bps   Bits per second.

bridge   A connection between two networks. Usually requires both a hardware device and controlling software.

broadband   A system that has a wide bandwidth and high transmission speeds. Such systems can carry several signals simultaneously. An example is the CATV cable that can transmit several channels on a single wire.

brouter   A combination bridge and router. It can route and bridge one or more protocols.

buffer   The process of temporarily storing data, usually in RAM, until it can be processed.

bug/debug   The early computers were made with high-voltage vacuum tubes. It took rooms full of hot tubes to do the job that a credit card calculator can do today. One of the large systems went down one day. After several hours of troubleshooting, the technicians found a large bug that had crawled into the high-voltage wiring. It had been electrocuted, but had shorted out the whole system. Since that time, any type of trouble in a piece of software or hardware is called a bug. To *debug* it, of course, is to try to find all of the errors or defects.

bus   The physical path for data between devices and circuits, a data highway. The term bus is also used to designate a linear-shaped LAN.

cache   Some systems might have an area of very fast RAM to store data that was last used. Many software programs use the same data over and over. It takes time to access and load the data, especially if it is from a disk. If the data is stored in fast RAM, it is accessed very fast.

campus   Any area where there might be several buildings tied to a LAN (not necessarily a college or university area.)

capacitor   An electronic component consisting of two metal plates separated by a nonconductor. A capacitor consists of two conductors, A and B, each having an extended surface exposed to that of the other and separated by a dielectric, which is designed so the electric charge on conductor A is equal in value, but opposite in polarity, to conductor B.

CATV   Refers to cable TV networks or networks that use the same technology.

CCITT   Consultative Committee on International Telegraph and Telephone, established by the United Nations to formulate standards for worldwide communications technology. Devices that conform to the CCITT recommended standards and protocols can communicate with all similar devices. The CCITT committee constantly review and revise standards to reflect changing technologies.

centralized file server   A LAN with a single server.

centralized processing   A system, such as a mainframe or minicomputer system, that does all of the processing for the terminals and stations. *See* distributed processing.

chatter and jitter   Noise on UTP.

CISC   Complex Instruction Set Computer. The ordinary CISC CPUs such as the 386 execute many instructions that slow it down. *See* RISC.

cladding   A layer of glass that surrounds the fibers in fiberoptic cables.

client   On networks that have servers, the workstation is the client of the server. The server furnishes data to the client which then processes it.

clock   Everything that a computer does depends on precise timing. A computer has very accurate oscillators that generate timing signals, which is called the clock. The oscillator circuits are usually called *clock circuits*.

CMIP   Common Management Information Protocol, a protocol developed by the ISO for formatting and transmitting information between data collection programs and reporting devices. It can be used with TCP/IP networks.

compression   A technique that can reduce the number of bits in a file. Compression requires eight bits to form a character. (Someday a compression system might be devised that would use a single bit for a single alphanumeric character.) Each space between words is considered to be a character. A compression system might use two unique bits to represent spaces. A good compression system can store two to three times as much data in the same amount of space that a standard program would require.

concentrator   A device for connecting several network devices into a single transmission device, also called a *wiring hub*.

coprocessor   Usually an 8087, 80287, or 80387 that works with some software in conjunction with the CPU to increase the speed of some operations.

CPU   Central processing unit, the main chip in a computer that is the brain. Some PC systems are named for the type of CPU it has such as the 286, 386, or 486.

CRC   Cyclic Redundancy Check, an error-checking system used in communications. The numeric value of the bits in a packet is added and this value is transmitted with the packet. If the receiving end adds up the bits and the value is different, then an error has occurred. The packet is then usually retransmitted.

crosstalk   Happens if a signal from one channel spills over into another channel.

CSMA/CD   Carrier sense multiple access with collision detection. If two stations try to transmit at the same time, the data on the single line will become mixed and garbled. The carrier sense listens for other transmissions, and if a collision occurs, the transmission is ended, then retried later.

CSU   Channel service unit, an interface device that provides functions such as electrical isolation, performance monitoring, and loopbacks.

database   A collection of related records, such as a list of customers.

daughterboard   Provides additional work capacity for other plug-in boards.

dc   Abbreviation for direct current.

DCE   Data communications equipment, usually refers to modems.

DDS   Digital Data Service, a wide bandwidth, privately leased line that transmits in digital form rather than the standard telephone analog.

device driver   Special software that is needed for a particular piece of hardware, such as a SCSI hard drive or tape, a mouse, an adapter card, and others. The driver is usually made a part of the Config.sys and is loaded into memory every time the system is booted up.

disk mirroring   The use of two hard disks attached to one controller so that both disks are written with the same data. If one disk should fail, data will still be available on the other one. *See* RAID.

dedicated file server   A file server that provides data to work stations but does no computing.

dielectric   1. The insulating material separating the two plates of a capacitor. Provides a medium capable of recovering all or part of the energy required to establish an electric field. The field, or voltage stress, is accompanied by displacement or charging currents. 2. A nonconducting material through which induction of magnetic lines of force may pass. It is a medium in which an electrical field can be maintained.

disk caching   A system that stores the most-used data from the disk in RAM. This data can be accessed much faster than going to the disk to read it out.

disk duplexing   In disk mirroring, two hard disks are attached to a single controller. The same data is written to both disks simultaneously. In disk duplexing, the two disks use separate controllers.

distributed processing   A system where data is downloaded from a server and processed at a local station. *See* centralized processing.

DMA   Direct memory access, a method of moving data from a disk or storage device directly to RAM.

drop cable   A cable that connects the main bus to a workstation.

DSU   Data, or digital, service unit, an interface device that converts low-rate digital signals into the type to be transmitted over the network.

DTE   Data terminal equipment, usually refers to computers or terminals.

EISA   Extended Industry Standard Architecture, developed as an alternative to IBM's MCA. EISA recommends a 32-bit bus standard for PCs. This system can also use the 8- and 16-bit hardware. *See* ISA.

electronic mail (E-mail)   A system to send and receive messages between computers. The system, however, must have the necessary hardware and software.

Ethernet   A system made up of hardware, software, and its associated protocols, first developed by Xerox. Originally the system used only coaxial cable, but many systems now run on untwisted pairs. The Ethernet system is used on about 70 percent of all systems, the most widely used of all systems.

FAT   File allocation table, the system used by DOS to keep track of the files on a disk, like a table of contents in a book.

fault tolerant   Methods to ensure that the computer or network system is resistant to software errors or hardware failures. Such systems might include several redundant systems, frequent backups, uninterruptible power supplies (UPS), disk mirroring or RAID, and redundant cabling. Even all these measures might not prevent some types of failures, such as human error.

FDDI   Fiber Data Distributed Interface, a standard designed for use with fiberoptic cables to operate at 100 mbps.

fiberoptics   Cables made up of flexible glass fibers. The digital information is converted to on and off light pulses and transmitted. When a message reaches its addressed station, it is then converted back to digital data.

file locking   The process whereby only one person on a network can alter or change a particular file. Others on the network may download and read the file, but will not be able to make any changes until the first person is finished. *See* record locking.

file server   A station dedicated to providing files and data to client workstations.

FTP   File Transfer Protocol, describes how a host computer can allow other computers to transfer files in either direction.

gateway   A hardware and software system that allows two different networks such as one made up of DOS and one made up of Macintosh machines to communicate with each other. The gateway provides the necessary protocol conversion.

giga   A prefix meaning billion. A gigabyte is 1,073,741,824 bytes.

GOSIP   Acronym for Government Open Systems Interface Protocol.

GUI   Graphical user interface, a program such as Windows that uses icons and a mouse.

handshaking   Exchange of control codes or specific characters to control data flow.

hidden files   Some files might not show up in a normal directory display. They are usually files that are protected so that they cannot be erased or changed by mistake. Programs like XTree will show them and allow you to change their attributes.

Hz   Hertz, units of frequency equal to cycles per second. MHz would indicate millions of cycles per second.

hub   The center, gateway, or connection of a network. In a star topology, a hub can be the center and contain several ports. A hub can also be a gateway between two different networks or provide connections for Ethernet, token ring, FDDI, and other systems. Some hubs are intelligent and house the network software and direct communications on the LAN.

IEEE   Institute of Electrical and Electronic Engineers, reviews and determines rules and standards for many of the network and communications protocols.

IEEE 802.3   The standard for Ethernet.

IEEE 802.5   The standard for token ring.

interrupt   A signal that suspends a program temporarily and transfers control to the interrupting device. Interrupts may have certain priorities that take precedence over other operations.

IPX   Internet Packet Exchange, a Novell NetWare protocol. IPX moves data between server or workstations with programs running on different nodes, such as NetBIOS.

impedance   All wires offer some resistance or opposition to the passage of electrons. If it is a high frequency transmission, there might be an inductive and capacitive reactance to the flow of electrons. The combination of the resistance and the reactance is called impedance. The impedance will vary depending on the construction of the cable and the frequency.

ISA   Industry Standard Architecture, the PC system that one time was called IBM compatible.

ISDN   Integrated Services Digital Network, a CCITT-recommended model for universal telephone and communication services. It will eventually be used throughout the world and enable us to transmit high-speed digital information over ordinary telephone lines.

interactive processing   Systems that process an item, then wait for a response from the user. For example, many tutorials and teaching systems might ask a question, then wait for a response.

ISO/OSI International Standards Organization Open Systems Interface, all hardware and software that conform to the ISO/OSI protocol recommendations are similar. You should be able to buy systems from different vendors, plug them together, and they should work.

LU 6.2 A protocol developed by IBM to operate on their System Network Architecture (SNA) to allow peer-to-peer communications.

mainframe computer A very large computer sometimes called "big iron."

MAU Multistation access unit, a wiring concentrator used on token ring networks to connect several stations. MAU also stands for medium attachment unit, the transceivers used with thick Ethernet.

mbps Megabits per second.

MCA Micro Channel Architecture, the system that IBM uses on its PS/2 systems. The MCA plug in boards and other hardware is incompatible with their original IBM PCs.

MHS Message Handling Service, a family of software products that delivers messages through store-and-forward networks and PCs. Messages can be routed to and through PCs, LANs, and WANs.

minicomputer An expensive and powerful computer, a bit smaller and less powerful than a mainframe.

mirrored drives A fault-tolerant system in which the data is saved to two different drives. If one fails, the data will still be available on the second drive.

modem MOdulator and DEModulator, an electronic device that modulates or converts digital signals to analog voltages so that they can be sent over telephone lines. At the other end of the line, the modem demodulates the analog signals back into digital information that is usable by the computer.

motherboard The main board in a computer into which the circuits are plugged.

MTBF Mean time before failure, an average figure that indicates the time product should operate before failing.

multitasking Software that will allow a single computer to perform several tasks at the same time, such as running a spreadsheet and database program at the same time and interchanging information between them. The protected memory of 386 and 486 systems can allow this to be done but it is not always used on a network system.

multiuser A network system. A multiuser system allows several people at different computers to simultaneously share the same software.

NDIS Network Device Interface Specification, proposed by Microsoft. This specification would allow adapter device drivers to interface with other protocols.

NetBIOS A software interface developed by IBM for use on its Token-Ring and other systems.

NIC Network Interface Card, usually a board that is plugged into a computer to interface with a network system. Is also called an *adapter board*.

NFS Network File System, a protocol developed by Sun Microsystems that allows a computer on a network to use the files and peripherals of another. This protocol has been adopted, modified, and used by several other vendors.

NIU Network interface unit, a device with one or more RS232 ports that allow access to the LAN.

NMP Network Management Protocol, a protocol developed by AT&T designed to exchange information with and control devices and peripherals on a network.

node A workstation, a terminal, or other device in a network.

OEM Original equipment manufacturer.

oscilloscope A test instrument that uses a cathode-ray tube to display graphic representations of pulses and waveforms.

OSI Open Systems Interconnection, systems that conform to the protocols and standards established by the International Standards Organization (ISO). Any device manufactured to these standards will operate with other ISO/OSI devices.

OSF Open Software Foundation, a set of specifications for Unix systems.

OS/2 Operating System/2, jointly developed by Microsoft and IBM. It is a multitasking operating system that goes beyond the 640K barrier of DOS and is a much more powerful system than DOS. Most of the commands are similar to those of DOS.

packet switching A system for transmitting data. Each message is handled as a complete unit with the address of the recipient and sender.

PABX/PBX Private Automated Branch Exchange/Private Branch Exchange. A telephone-type switching network for voice or data. Is usually expensive to set up.

PAD Packet assembler/disassembler, a device used on networks that use packet switching.

PC Personal computer, and usually refers to an IBM-compatible desktop computer.

peer-to-peer The linking of two or more similar computers.

peripheral Any device attached to the computer such as printers, disk drives, keyboard, modems etc.

platform A standard for a particular piece of hardware, software, or computer, such as the IBM PC or Macintosh.

platform independent The capability to connect different computers, such as IBM and Macintosh, on a network.

proprietary A proprietary system is one that works on a single vendor's hardware or software.

protocol A formal set of rules or procedures governing the communications between devices. The protocols are commonly agreed upon by industry committees, such as the IEEE or the CCITT.

protocol analyzer A device that attaches to the LAN and monitors the activity. Usually a protocol analyzer can analyze a packet, file transfer, E-mail, printer activity, and other LAN traffic, and is an essential tool for larger networks.

public volume Usually an area of a hard disk server that can be read by anyone on the network, but cannot be erased or edited. Users may be assigned an area of the disk where they may change or edit any of the data on it.

quad 1. A packaged integrated circuit containing four identical stages. 2. Containing four identical or nearly identical electrodes, terminals, or leads (as outputs).

RAID Redundant Array of Inexpensive Disks, a fault-tolerant system where several hard disks are used. If one should happen to fail, the data will be on another one. This system is similar to disk mirroring where two disks are both used for the same file.

RAM Random access memory, a computer's primary working memory. Whenever a program or piece of software is being run, it is loaded into RAM where all of the manipulations take place. While in RAM, the data can be altered or erased. RAM is volatile and all data in RAM can be lost if the power is turned off or the data is not saved to disk before loading another program.

record locking Several users may edit the same file simultaneously, but no two users may edit the same record at the same time.

repeater Signals might become weak due to the impedance of a cable and the length between stations. A repeater can amplify the signal and bring it back up to its original strength.

RF Radio frequency.

RISC Reduced instruction set computer, a CPU in which the number of instructions is reduced to a minimum. *See also* CISC. The RISC computers are much faster than the CISC.

RJ11/RJ45 The RJ is for registered jack. The RJ11 are the common connectors used on almost all telephones. The RJ45 is similar to the voice grade RJ11, but it has more contacts.

ROM Read-only memory, memory that is burned into a chip. It can be read, or it can perform certain functions, but it cannot ordinarily be erased or changed. *See* RAM.

router The hardware and software necessary to link two similar networks together.

SAA Systems Application Architecture, a set of standards developed by IBM for communication among various types of IBM computers. SAA influenced the development of Windows, OS/2, and Presentation Manager.

SDLC Synchronous Data Link Control, a system developed by IBM for use with their Systems Network Architecture (SNA). A message can contain any collection or sequence of bits that will not be mistaken for a control character.

semaphore A flag that is set to prevent two users from editing a file simultaneously.

server A server answers requests and provides service to the clients or workstations on the LAN. It is a combination of hardware and software. A server may be an ordinary PC, one of the workstations, or a dedicated system, such as a 386 or 486, with a large hard drive.

servo A system in which electrical signals are used to produce mechanical movement in a remote device, wherein the rate and direction of motion are represented by specific signal characteristics.

site licensing The permission to use a software package at a particular location.

SCSI Small Computer System Interface, a SCSI board is typically used for applications requiring intensive real-time disk I/O activity with a minimum of bus loading.

SNA Systems Network Architecture, a system developed by IBM.

SNMP Simple Network Management Protocol, a protocol used on many major networks.

solenoid A current-carrying iron-core coil of wire typically used as a controllable magnet for opening or closing mechanical contacts or valves.

SQL Structured Query Language, pronounced "sequel." A database management system developed by IBM, is a method for client servers to access the resources of corporate databases.

star A topology that has a central device or hub that handles network requests. The star topology, which gets its name from its shape, is used mostly with ARCnet and Ethernet UTPs.

STP Shielded twisted pair of wires.

suite As used in the computer industry, it is usually a group of related software packages.

system fault tolerance The duplication of hard drives and other systems so that there will be a complete copy of all data in the event of a failure.

T1 and fractional T1 T1 describes a system that transmits at 1.544 mbps. It consists of a four-wire circuit that provides 24 separate 64 kbps channels. A fractional T1 is a service that provides less than the 24 channels, or a fraction of the amount that could be used.

10BaseT An IEEE standard for 10 mbps unshielded twisted pair (UTP) networks. The 10 means 10 mbps; base refers to baseband transmission.

T2 Digital transmission at 6.312 mbps, equivalent to 4 T1 signals.

T3 Digital transmission at 44.736 mbps, equivalent to 28 T1 signals.

TCP/IP Transmission Control Protocol/Internet Protocol, a set of protocols first developed by the Department of Defense (DOD). These protocols have been widely adopted by manufacturers and have become a de facto standard.

tera A prefix meaning trillion. A terabyte is 1,000 gigabytes or one million megabytes or more specifically, 1,099,511,627,776 bytes.

token A electronic data packet used to transmit information on a token ring LAN.

Token-Ring A topology developed by IBM that has several computers all attached in a ring. A token ring system uses a token to prevent collisions and only the PC with the token can transmit data.

topology The map or layout of a LAN. The physical topology describes how the cables are laid out; the logical topology describes how the messages flow.

TSR Terminate and stay resident, programs like SideKick, that are available at all times and will pop up at the touch of a key. They are very convenient, but they usually use a lot of your precious 640K of RAM.

turnkey system Usually an off-the-shelf preassembled system that can be plugged in and used immediately.

twisted pair   Two wires that are twisted together, which can be shielded or unshielded. The twisting minimizes and counteracts inductance.

UMB   Upper memory block, refers to the memory above 640K. DOS 5.0, DR DOS 6.0, DESQview, and other programs can move some TSRs and device drivers into upper memory to free the lower memory.

UPS   Uninterruptible power supply, a backup power supply that will take over in the event of a power failure. An absolute necessity in areas where there are frequent lightning storms and power outages.

user groups   Usually a club that uses computers or LANs. Often the club will be devoted to a particular type of computer or LAN but in most clubs, anyone is welcome to join. Some of the groups charge a small fee.

UTP   Unshielded twisted pair wires.

V.32   CCITT recommendation for 9600-baud modems.

V.42   CCITT recommendation for data compression.

volt-ohmmeter (VOM)   A portable instrument for measuring voltage and resistance.

Winchester disks   Another name for hard drives.

Windows   A graphical user interface (GUI) software program from Microsoft that allows the use of a mouse to point and click.

workstation   A network node where operators input and output data. The configuration of a workstation varies considerably from system to system.

X.25   An international protocol recommended by the CCITT that defines how communications should take place over bridges, routers, telephone lines, satellites, and other systems. It defines packet switching, circuit switching, message switching, and store and forward switching.

X.400   The CCITT recommended-standard for international E-mail systems.

Index